Opposing *the* Second Corps *at Antietam*

Opposing *the* Second Corps *at Antietam*

The Fight for the Confederate Left and Center on America's Bloodiest Day

MARION V. ARMSTRONG JR.

The University of Alabama Press
Tuscaloosa

The University of Alabama Press
Tuscaloosa, Alabama 35487-0380
uapress.ua.edu

Hardcover edition published 2016.
Paperback edition published 2024.
eBook edition published 2016.

Inquiries about reproducing material from this work should be addressed to the
University of Alabama Press.

Typeface: Caslon

Cover image: The rebels covered by a ledge of rock repulsing the troops on the right in
the woods beyond the Dunker Church, battle of Antietam. Sketch by Alfred R. Waud
(1828–1891); courtesy of the Library of Congress, Prints and Photographs Division
Cover design: Sandy Turner Jr.

Paperback ISBN: 978-0-8173-6169-3

A previous edition of this book has been cataloged by the Library of Congress.
ISBN: 978-0-8173-1904-5 (cloth)
E-ISBN: 978-0-8173-8957-4

Contents

Maps

Preface

In 2008, The University of Alabama Press published my book *Unfurl Those Colors!: McClellan, Sumner, and the Second Army Corps in the Antietam Campaign*. The book was a study in command, operations, and tactics at the army corps level. Its focus was the decisions made by Major General George B. McClellan, the commander of the Army of the Potomac, and how those decisions were communicated to and carried out by Major General Edwin V. Sumner, commander of the Second Army Corps, and his division and brigade commanders. The work also considered the perspectives of the junior officers and enlisted soldiers of the Second Corps as they carried out the orders sent down to them from the command level.

Given this subject matter and approach, the book necessarily addressed the campaign only from the perspective of its subjects, and did not reveal what their opposite numbers were doing. All that the reader knew of the Confederate side of the action was what the subjects themselves knew at any particular time during the campaign and battle. As one reviewer of the book commented, the Confederates were nothing more than "dim figures" in the distance. But this was how it needed to be because decisions, orders, and actions are always undertaken with an imperfect knowledge of what the enemy is doing. I wanted the reader to see the campaign and the battle through the eyes of the commanders and soldiers who were making the decisions and doing the fighting.

This work, *Opposing the Second Corps at Antietam: The Fight for the Confederate Left and Center on America's Bloodiest Day*, is intended as a companion volume to *Unfurl Those Colors* that considers the Confederate side of the fight against the Second Army Corps during the Battle of Antietam on 17 September 1862. As such, it addresses the battle for the Confederate left and center, primarily the battle from the Confederate prospective for the West Woods and the Sunken Road. As with *Unfurl Those Colors*, *Opposing the Second Corps at Antietam* is set in the context of the army commander's decisions—in this case, those of General Robert E. Lee—in his effort to fight, as suggested by Joseph L. Harsh in *Taken at the Flood: Robert E. Lee and Confederate Strategy in the Maryland Campaign of 1862*, not so much a defensive battle but a battle to retain the initiative in the larger campaign.

In writing this work, I was aided exponentially by the recent publication of Ezra A. Carman's *The Maryland Campaign of September 1862*, edited by Thomas G. Clemens. This unique edition of the Carman manuscript, in which Clemens identifies the sources used by Carman, gave me access to the voluminous correspondence of Carman with other veterans during the 1890s and early 1900s. As commander of the 13th New Jersey Regiment, Carman was a veteran of the battle and later a member of the Antietam Battlefield Board charged with setting up and marking the battlefield for future generations. Using the letters that the veterans wrote to Carman as pieces of a puzzle, I have been able to combine them into a comprehensive account of the Confederate side of the battle and to support that account with the words of the veterans themselves. I believe that the result is the most detailed narrative of the Confederate battle for the West Woods and the Sunken Road yet published.

No historian works alone, and I am deeply indebted to many others who have studied the Battle of Antietam in depth and have been willing to share their knowledge and unique perspectives with me. Tom Clemens was always willing to share with me his deep knowledge of the battle, as well as documents that he gathered from various archives around the country. Ted Alexander, Paul Chiles, and many other members of the Antietam National Battlefield park staff provided assistance during my many visits to the battlefield. The Antietam battlefield guides often shared their knowledge of the battle with me and took me to parts of the field that I had not before seen. And I am especially grateful to the members of the Save Historic Antietam Foundation (SHAF) who have done so much to preserve and restore the battlefield so that we today can see it as it was in 1862.

Opposing *the* Second Corps *at Antietam*

1

Maintaining the Initiative

I

JUST AS UNDERSTANDING THE OPERA-
tions of the Second Army Corps at Antietam requires an understanding of
Major General George B. McClellan's plan of battle, so also understanding the
Confederate opposition to the Second Corps in the West Woods and at the
Sunken Road requires an understanding of General Robert E. Lee's plan of
battle at Antietam. McClellan and the Army of the Potomac were fighting an
offensive battle with the objective of defeating Lee's Army of Northern Virginia or, at least, of forcing it back across the Potomac River from Maryland into
Virginia. Accordingly, McClellan developed a plan of maneuver in which all of
the corps of his army had a definite role. Lee, however, was fighting a defensive
battle and consequently his plan was less definitive with regard to maneuver and
was more oriented toward reacting to Federal movements. Lee's objective was
to regain the initiative in order to sustain his campaign north of the Potomac.

Lee chose the field on which the Battle of Antietam would be fought. He
first saw it early on the morning of 15 September as the elements of the Army
of Northern Virginia that had fought at South Mountain the previous day were
withdrawing from that field toward a Potomac crossing near Shepherdstown,
Virginia, called Boteler's Ford. At that time Lee intended to cross into Virginia,
where he could safely reunite with the elements of his army that had been detached for the purpose of capturing the Federal garrison at Harpers Ferry before moving the entire army into Pennsylvania, the objective of the campaign.
Because the Harpers Ferry operation, under the direction of Major General
Thomas J. (Stonewall) Jackson, had taken longer than anticipated, and because
McClellan's pursuit of Lee's army into Maryland had been hastier than expected, Lee had had to turn back the lead elements of the army from Hagers-

town to defend the South Mountain passes. The battle there on the 14th slowed the advance the Army of the Potomac, but by the end of the day the Federals gained the summit and the Confederate position was no longer tenable. Lee was forced to order a withdrawal toward Virginia and to abandon his original campaign plan.

After passing through Keedysville, Lee, who was riding in an ambulance because he had severely injured both hands in a fall more than two weeks earlier, stopped in a high meadow east of Antietam Creek to survey the terrain. Gazing west across the creek toward Sharpsburg, he noted the strength of a ridge running from north to south over which the road to the Potomac passed. This ridge was the height of land between Antietam Creek and the Potomac little more than a mile farther to the west. As Lee was making his observations, a courier arrived with a dispatch from Jackson announcing the capitulation of the Harpers Ferry garrison. Instantly Lee determined that rather than withdrawing to Virginia, he would occupy the high ground near Sharpsburg and reassemble his army on Maryland soil. It was a risky decision. Although the ground was well suited to the defense, he was being pursued by a Federal army of much greater strength. If forced from this defensive position his army would be pinned against the Potomac and likely destroyed. But if he was not pressed by the enemy and he could reassemble his army, the turnpike north from Sharpsburg to Hagerstown—thirteen miles distant—offered the opportunity for reseizing the initiative and restarting the campaign.[1]

II

When the Army of Northern Virginia began crossing the Potomac into Maryland on 4 September 1862, Robert E. Lee had been its commander for only ninety-five days. He had taken command on 2 June when that army numbered only sixty thousand men and was backed into the trenches in front of Richmond, threatened from the east by the Federal Army of the Potomac, which numbered more than one hundred thousand men. During that month, a second Federal army of almost fifty thousand, the Army of Virginia under Major General John Pope, was formed in central Virginia, and began threatening Richmond from the north. In two spectacular campaigns of initiative and maneuver, however, the Seven Days Campaign from 25 June to 1 July and the Second Manassas Campaign in August, Lee managed first to drive McClellan's army away from Richmond and then to defeat Pope's army on the plains of Manassas, forcing it back to the defenses of Washington and the recall of McClellan's army from the Peninsula.

As spectacular and successful as these campaigns were in clearing Virginia of major Federal formations, they did not appreciably change the military equation in Virginia. Safe inside Washington's fortifications, the Federal armies, though "much weakened and demoralized" as Lee wrote to Confederate President Jefferson Davis on 3 September, could easily be reinforced and rebuilt. The Federals could then reseize the initiative with several months of excellent campaigning weather remaining in 1862. To keep the initiative on the Confederate side, Lee told Davis that the "present seems to be the most propitious time since the commencement of the war for the Confederate Army to enter Maryland." Lee went on argue, "We cannot afford to be idle, and though weaker than our opponents in men and military equipments, must endeavor to harass if we cannot destroy them."[2]

As argued by Joseph Harsh in *Taken at the Flood*, Lee's objective in entering Maryland in September 1862 was nothing less than winning the war. Harsh concluded that Lee recognized "that Confederate victory must necessarily result from the frustration rather than the destruction of the enemy." Moreover, by September 1862 a nascent antiwar movement was growing in the Northern states. Congressional elections scheduled for November would offer Northern voters the opportunity to speak out concerning the war. To take advantage of antiwar feeling and possibly influence the elections, Lee suggested that the Confederate government propose to the U.S. government the formal recognition of Southern independence. "Such a proposition coming from us at this time . . . would show conclusively to the world that our sole object is the establishment of our independence and the attainment of an honorable peace." Rejection of the offer, Lee predicted, would demonstrate that "the continuance of the war does not rest upon us" but on the party in power in the United States. "The proposal of peace would enable the people of the United States to determine at their coming elections whether they will support those in favor of a prolongation of the war, or those who wish to bring it to a termination." Making this proposal work, though, would mean demonstrating that the war would be a prolonged one, which could best be done by continued Southern military success, particularly if that continued success was on Northern soil. If Lee could lure the Army of the Potomac out of the Washington defenses before it had fully recovered from the reverses of the summer and draw it into battle in western Maryland or central Pennsylvania well away from its sources of supply, he would have an excellent chance of achieving just such a success.[3]

Accordingly, Lee planned a campaign in Maryland that would allow him to retain the strategic initiative and ultimately determine the time and place of the campaign's concluding battle. But when Federal forces did not vacate Harpers Ferry as expected and McClellan moved more precipitously than anticipated, Lee lost the initiative and concluded that he had no choice but to abandon the campaign and return to Virginia. But now on the morning of the 15th with Harpers Ferry about to surrender, Lee was looking at terrain that might permit him to regain the initiative, continue the campaign, and realize the objectives for which the campaign was undertaken.

Laying almost literally at Lee's feet as he surveyed the landscape was Antietam Creek, a modest stream running on a north-south axis. Beyond it, at distances that varied between two and a half and four miles, was the Potomac, also following a meandering north-south course. In between was a ridge of high ground—the height of land—that at its highest point was 210 feet above the streams, raising in sometimes dramatic undulations characteristic of rolling farm country. Indeed, the entire area was in cultivation with randomly arranged fields of corn, pastures for livestock, fields plowed in anticipation of winter or spring planting, and carefully gleaned woodlots that provided fuel for cooking and heating. It was strong defensive terrain that would allow Lee to arrange the portion of the army withdrawing from South Mountain in such a way as to create the impression, if not the reality, of an imposing defense. Behind that exterior, unseen by the enemy because of the intervening ridge, he could assemble the rest of his army as it arrived from Harpers Ferry.

In addition to the terrain itself, there was another geographical feature that made this the ideal location for reassembling the army: the road network. Western Maryland was crisscrossed by excellent roads and turnpikes that afforded ease of movement and maneuver for large bodies of infantry and cavalry and their supporting artillery and wagon trains. One of those turnpikes, the Boonsboro-Sharpsburg- Shepherdstown Pike, was being used at that moment to withdraw Lee's army rapidly from South Mountain. This road ran from Boonsboro and the National Road at the western foot of South Mountain southwest to Sharpsburg, a village nestled about a mile west of Antietam Creek in a trough behind the height of land, and then continued on another four miles across the

Potomac to Shepherdstown, Virginia. The bridge that in better times had carried this turnpike across the river had fallen victim to the war, so crossing the river meant using Boteler's Ford a mile downstream. The road that most attracted Lee's attention, though, was the Hagerstown Turnpike running north from Sharpsburg to Hagerstown, a distance of about thirteen miles. This first-class turnpike would permit Lee's reassembled army to make a rapid march to Hagerstown from whence he could continue into Pennsylvania drawing the Federal army after him.

But the terrain also made problematic taking position and reassembling the army at Sharpsburg. To begin with, the army would be in a sack formed by the confluence of Antietam Creek and the Potomac two miles south of Sharpsburg. From this sack Lee's forces would have only two exits. The first was to the north following the height of land along the Hagerstown Pike. An easterly bend of the Potomac two miles north of Sharpsburg narrowed this opening to just a little more than two miles. An enemy force gaining possession of the Hagerstown Pike east of the bend could effectively close this exit. The second was Boteler's Ford southwest of Sharpsburg. If the enemy attacked in force and drove the army back on this inadequate escape route, the Confederates might be crushed against the river. Next, the area was too large to be effectively defended by the force available to Lee even if the whole army were present. It is true that his flanks could be anchored on the Potomac to the north and Antietam Creek to the south, but the distance to be defended between these two points would seriously overextend the army. Last, Lee could not effectively cover at one time the three main avenues of approach available to the enemy—the three strong stone bridges crossing the Antietam in the vicinity of Sharpsburg. The Middle Bridge that carried the Boonsboro Pike and the Rohrbach Bridge a mile south could be defended because high ground overlooked both. But to cover the Upper Bridge, which was a mile and a half north of the Middle Bridge and well east of the height of land, would stretch the army too thin. This left Lee with no option other than to leave that avenue of approach open.

III

Deciding to risk taking position at Sharpsburg for the purpose of reassembling his army, Lee began posting the three divisions that were withdrawing from South Mountain on the high ground west of the creek to cover the avenues of approach at the Middle and Rohrbach bridges. The first division to arrive was Major General Daniel Harvey Hill's. Hill had with him three of his five brigades, which, shortly after they crossed the Middle Bridge and began ascending the height of land, turned north and took position along an old zigzag farm lane facing east. Hill's remaining two brigades, which had gone through Sharpsburg during the night toward Boteler's Ford, were recalled and placed in position on the extreme left of this line. The brigade of Colonel Alfred H. Colquitt took position facing north in a sunken farm lane that was the westerly extension of the lane Hill's other three brigades were posted along, and the brigade of Brigadier General Roswell S. Ripley took position as a reserve even farther to the west near where the sunken lane met the Hagerstown Turnpike on the farm of Henry Piper. Next to arrive were two divisions under the command of Major General James Longstreet: first came the division of Brigadier General David R. Jones and then that of Brigadier General John B. Hood. These divisions, consisting of eight brigades, were used to extend the line south of the Boonsboro Pike along the height of land as far as the Rohrbach Bridge.[4]

With all of the available troops posted, Lee's line on the afternoon of the 15th was about two miles in length, on strong ground, supported by more than one hundred guns, and with a brigade of cavalry covering either flank. It was a formidable array that would be clearly visible to the lead elements of the Army of the Potomac arriving east of the creek. Lee's purpose in establishing the line as he did was probably to discourage a hasty attack by the Federal army. The appearance of a strong defense would force McClellan to deploy his own army, reconnoiter the ground, and prepare a deliberate plan of attack. All this would take time, time that Lee could use to assemble the rest of his army behind the height of land and possibly even enough time, given McClellan's reputation for caution, that he could reseize the initiative of the campaign by moving north before McClellan was ready to attack.

If this was Lee's plan, it worked. When the lead elements of the Army of the Potomac began arriving at about 2:00 P.M. on the 15th, Major General Joseph Hooker, leading the Federal van, estimated the strength of the line to be about 30,000—twice what it actually was—and too strong to attack in front. McClellan, who arrived at about 5:00 P.M., concurred. He had earlier issued orders "that if the enemy were overtaken on the march, they should be attacked at once," but now seeing the strength of Lee's line and with only two divisions immediately available, McClellan decided that it was too late in the day to make a hasty attack and directed the bivouacking of his army for the night on the east side of the creek. Several Federal batteries, however, were established on the high ground above the creek and commenced a duel of long-range guns that lasted until sunset.[5]

Lee was no doubt pleased that he avoided an engagement on the 15th. Late in the afternoon, he made a final adjustment to his line by strengthening his left, anticipating a general movement in that direction. He ordered Hood with his two brigades, commanded by Colonels William T. Wofford and Evander M. Law, from their positions south of the Hagerstown Pike to a position somewhat north of Ripley's brigade near a small church and wood on the Hagerstown Pike, sites history would soon recognize as the Dunker Church and West Woods. During the night, Lee also ordered Colonel Stephen D. Lee to take four of the six batteries of his artillery battalion, which had been supporting the center, north to the vicinity of the Dunker Church; there, Lee reported that they took "a sheltered position on the Sharpsburg and Hagerstown Pike, in front of [the] church."[6]

On the morning of the 16th, a dense fog covered the valley of the Antietam, buying Lee even more time since it would make an early attack by the enemy impossible; it would even prevent planning one because reconnaissance would necessarily be delayed until the fog had burned off. At about 8:00 A.M., Jackson arrived from Harpers Ferry and found Lee with Longstreet on Cemetery Hill on the eastern edge of Sharpsburg where the Boonsboro Pike crossed the height of land. Jackson brought the welcome news that three of his divisions, those of Brigadier Generals John R. Jones (Jackson's own), Alexander R. Lawton (Ewell's), and John G. Walker, were crossing the Potomac at Boteler's Ford and would be in Sharpsburg by early afternoon.[7]

With the fog burning off and little indication that the enemy was about to launch an attack, Lee told Jackson to halt these divisions west of the town and allow them some rest after their strenuous night march, rest they would certainly need if Lee were to restart his campaign of maneuver by marching north. Earlier in the day Lee had taken another step in preparation for just such a move by sending the cavalry division commander, Major General James E. B. (Jeb) Stuart, with three regiments of cavalry on a reconnaissance of the area north of Sharpsburg between the Hagerstown Pike and the Potomac.[8]

For the most part, late morning and early afternoon of the 16th remained quiet, the only exception being an occasional exchange of long-range artillery fire. At about 3:00 P.M. Lee again called Jackson and Longstreet to an informal council of war, this time at the Jacob Grove house in the center of town. The generals pored over several large maps of the area, possibly discussing the details of a move by the army north toward Hagerstown and Pennsylvania. As they did a courier arrived with the news that a large Federal force had crossed the Antietam in the vicinity of the Upper Bridge and was advancing west toward the height of land and the Hagerstown Pike. At almost the same time a report of another large enemy force approaching the Rohrbach Bridge was received and Federal artillery resumed firing opposite Lee's center. In an instant, any possibility of regaining the initiative of the campaign was gone, and it became apparent that Lee would now have to make an immediate withdrawal to Virginia or stand and fight at Sharpsburg.[9]

Unable to discern at first which Federal movement was the greatest threat, Lee ordered Jackson to take charge of the left and sent J. R. Jones's division with him. Longstreet would take charge of the right of the army, and Lawton's division was ordered to the vicinity of the Rohrbach Bridge. Walker's division, which had been the last to cross the river, would remain as the army reserve in its central location west of town. After only a short period of time, however, Lee concluded that the Federal force approaching his left constituted the greater danger, and he sent orders to Lawton to change direction and march north to join Jackson.[10]

Although Lee could not know it at the time, the Federal column that had crossed at the Upper Bridge was Hooker's First Army Corps, a force of approximately thirteen thousand men, ten infantry brigades supported by nine batteries of artillery. Hooker, who on arrival at Antietam Creek on the 15th noted that the Confederate position opposite the Middle Bridge was too strong to attack, also saw the possibility of crossing the Antietam to the north. He dispatched an engineer officer, Major David C. Houston, "up the river to find practicable fords, by the means of which my troops might be thrown across the Antietam River to attack the enemy." McClellan, although he thought it too late to initiate such a move on the 15th, did order Hooker to bivouac his corps in the vicinity of the Upper Bridge for the night of the 15th to 16th. Once the fog burned off on the morning of the 16th, McClellan was able to make a reconnaissance and by midday formulated his plan of attack. "The design," he wrote in his official report in October 1862, "was to make the main attack upon the enemy's left—at least to create a diversion in favor of the main attack, with the hope of something more by assailing the enemy's right—and, as soon as one or both of the flank movements were successful, to attack their center with any reserve I might then have on hand."[11]

Hooker's move across the creek on the afternoon of the 16th was in preparation for executing McClellan's plan, and his corps started at about 2 P.M. According to McClellan in his final report of the battle, Hooker's objective was "to attack and, if possible, turn the enemy's left." But Hooker saw it differently. Having gotten such a late start, he saw his objective as "being to gain the high ground or divide between the Potomac and Antietam Rivers, and then incline to the left, following the elevation toward the left of the rebel army." Hooker also questioned whether his corps alone was strong enough to attack the whole rebel army. Late in the afternoon, when McClellan crossed the stream to check on Hooker's progress, Hooker told him "that if reinforcements were not forwarded promptly, or if another attack was not made on the enemy's right, the rebels would eat me up."[12]

Hood, still encamped in the vicinity of the Dunker Church from the evening before, was made aware that a Federal column had crossed the creek and was marching toward him. Immediately, he positioned both of his brigades to meet the oncoming Federals. Wofford's marched some eight hundred yards north from the Dunker Church and went into line facing north along the southern edge of a large cornfield belonging to David R. Miller, whose farmstead was north of the cornfield straddling the Hagerstown Pike. Wofford's line stretched from the Hagerstown Pike into a woodlot east of the cornfield—now known as the East Woods. Connecting with the right of Wofford's line in the woods was Law's brigade, which initially faced east along a small country lane called the Smoketown Road that ran north to south through the center of the woodlot. At about 5:00 P.M., Hooker's lead brigade, under the command of Brigadier General Truman Seymour, entered the woods from the north and following Smoketown Road engaged the portion of Hood's division that was in the woods. The skirmishing lasted until dark, which was at about 6:30 P.M.[13]

At about the time that the skirmishing began in the East Woods, Jackson arrived in the vicinity of the Dunker Church with J. R. Jones's division. He immediately had Jones send two small brigades—Jones's own and the brigade formerly commanded by Brigadier General Charles S. Winder that were combined under the command of Colonel Andrew J. Grigsby—across an intervening pasture and into the northern extent of the West Woods to extend Wofford's line west of the pike. The remaining two brigades—Brigadier General William E. Starke's and a brigade formerly commander by Brigadier General William B. Taliaferro—combined under the command of Starke to form a second line some three hundred yards to the rear. About an hour later Lawton's division finally arrived, and Jackson took two of his brigades, those under Brigadier Generals Jubal A. Early and Harry T. Hays, and placed them in the West Woods on the right of Jones's division facing west with Early in front and Hays in rear. Lawton's remaining two brigades under Colonels Marcellus Douglass and James A. Walker went into bivouac as a reserve in the vicinity of the Dunker Church. To support this line, S. D. Lee established the batteries of his artillery battalion on the plateau across the turnpike from the Dunker Church. Later in the evening, Robert E. Lee himself acted to further strengthen his left by ordering D. H. Hill to move Ripley's brigade from its position of the afternoon of the 15th on the Piper farm to a position on Hood's right facing east at the Samuel Mumma farm.[14]

At about 8:00 P.M., General Hood appeared in person at Lee's headquarters located in a fine oak grove along the Shepherdstown road at the western edge of Sharpsburg. He told Lee that the officers and men of his command had "been without food for three days, except a half ration of beef for one day, and green corn." He asked Lee if his division could be replaced on the front line long enough for him to bring up the division supply wagons and issue rations. Lee told Hood that he should take his request to Jackson, and Hood rode off toward the Dunker Church to find that officer. After searching in the dark for some time, Hood finally found Jackson asleep "by the root of a tree." Jackson told Hood that he would send the remaining two brigades of Lawton's division to take Hood's place if Hood would promise that he "would come to the support of these forces the moment [he] was called upon." Consequently, Hood moved his division to the south end of the West Woods behind the Dunker Church, and Douglass's and Walker's brigades moved up to take their place. Douglass formed his brigade in line in a pasture about two hundred yards south of Miller's cornfield, and Walker extended the line east across Smoketown Road and along the lane leading to the Mumma farm. Grigsby and Jones also drew their brigades back to conform to the new line established by Douglass and Walker.[15]

After Hood's departure Lee worked in his headquarters tent into the early-morning hours of the 17th. He had many details to attend to, yet with the Federal side having gained the initiative, there was little more that he could do. While the command structure was in many cases indefinite, the army at

Sharpsburg was in position to deal with whatever McClellan intended for the following day. Jackson commanded on the left and had with him the divisions of J. R. Jones and Lawton. Hood's division was also on the left, although until this point in the campaign Hood had taken orders from Longstreet. Nevertheless, Hood had promised Jackson he would come when needed. On the right, east of Sharpsburg and south of the Boonsboro Pike, Longstreet supervised D. R. Jones's division and the independent brigade of Brigadier General Nathan G. Evans. In the center connecting Jackson's and Longstreet's informal "commands" was D. H. Hill's division, which had joined the army only at the beginning of the campaign and had not been subject to the orders of either Jackson or Longstreet. Walker's small two brigade division, which had been under Jackson in the Harpers Ferry operation, remained just west of Sharpsburg as the reserve.[16]

Lee's major remaining concern was the three divisions of the army that were not yet at Sharpsburg—the divisions of Major Generals Lafayette McLaws, Richard H. Anderson, and Ambrose Powell Hill. McLaws's and Anderson's divisions had operated independently under McLaws's command on the Maryland side of the Potomac during the Harpers Ferry operation, while A. P. Hill had been with Jackson. McLaws and Anderson had the greatest distance to travel after the surrender of Harpers Ferry because they had to come from Pleasant Valley east of Maryland Heights, cross the Potomac into Harpers Ferry and then make the march up the Virginia side of the Potomac to Shepherdstown to recross the river into Maryland. The journey was a difficult one. McLaws complained that even though he reached the pontoon bridge across the Potomac at Harpers Ferry on the afternoon of the 15th, the crossing "was very much impeded by the paroled prisoners passing over the bridge." The crossing kept his troops up all night. The next morning the streets of Harpers Ferry "were crowded with prisoners and wagons," which prevented him from stopping to draw rations for the large numbers of his command that had no provisions, so he had continued on to Halltown five miles west of Harpers Ferry before stopping to rest at about 11:00 A.M. In the afternoon he received orders "to hasten the troops to Sharpsburg," and the march was resumed at 3:00 P.M. Reaching to within two miles of Shepherdstown by 9:00 P.M.—a march of another six miles—he again stopped to rest his much fatigued divisions with "many of the regiments still without provisions." But again orders arrived "to hasten forward," so at midnight McLaws was on the march to Boteler's Ford.[17]

Jackson left A. P. Hill's division at Harpers Ferry to supervise the collection of captured supplies and equipment and to see to the paroling of prisoners. This task should have been long since completed, but there was as yet no news about Hill's approaching division. As with McLaws and Anderson, couriers were dispatched with orders for Hill to come to Sharpsburg at once. At this point, little else could be done.

IV

It rained some during the night of 16 September 1862 and into the 17th. Not a hard rain, but a drizzle that barely wet the ground. By early morning it was over, yet the sky remained overcast and the air was heavy with humidity. It was also a warm night, the overnight low temperature reaching only sixty-five degrees.[18]

At about 3:00 A.M. Walker's division, on orders from Lee given at the time or possibly the previous afternoon, moved from its position on the Shepherdstown Pike west of Sharpsburg to a position on the extreme right flank of the army overlooking and guarding Snavely's Ford across Antietam Creek. The release of Walker's division as the army reserve may have been brought about by word that the divisions of McLaws and Anderson were finally fording the Potomac and thus would reach Sharpsburg before dawn.[19]

Once he had gotten his division started across the ford, McLaws left it and rode to Sharpsburg to report to Lee. Unable to find headquarters in the dark, McLaws was returning to his division when he encountered Longstreet, who told him where Lee could be found. But Longstreet also directed McLaws to order "Anderson's division direct down the road to the hill beyond Sharpsburg, where he would receive orders." McLaws started again for headquarters but first met Jackson, who ordered him to bring his division forthwith to the extreme left of the army line. Finally reaching army headquarters, McLaws found Lee, who was much relieved to see him. Lee countermanded Jackson's order and directed McLaws "to halt my division near his [Lee's] headquarters," replacing Walker as the army reserve. McLaws returned to his division and positioned it according to Lee's orders, delivered Longstreet's orders to Anderson, and, then, exhausted, fell fast asleep in the tall grass by the side of the road.[20]

At first light, approximately 5:00 A.M., the expected battle opened with an exchange of fire between Confederate batteries (located on Nicodemus Heights and along the east side of the West Woods, along with S. D. Lee's batteries on the plateau across from the Dunker Church) and Federal batteries in the vicinity of the Alfred Poffenberger farm and the long-range 20-pounder Parrott rifles east of Antietam Creek. Fighting also erupted in the East Woods, as Seymour's brigade resumed its efforts from the evening before to clear the woods of Confederate skirmishers. Within thirty minutes, however, Hooker was pushing his entire corps forward with the objective of gaining "the high ground nearly three-quarters of a mile in advance of me, and which commanded the position taken by the enemy on his retreat from South Mountain." Hooker had the division of Brigadier General James B. Ricketts on the left of the corps advance, which brought it into the eastern half of an open quadrangle formed by the East, North, and West Woods (hereafter referred to as the quadrangle or cornfield quadrangle because of the large thirty-acre cornfield of D. R. Miller in its center). On the right was the division of Brigadier General Abner Doubleday guiding along the Hagerstown Turnpike and crossing the D. R. Miller farmstead. The division of Brigadier General George Gordon Meade moved forward behind Ricketts and Doubleday as a reserve. Each of the lead divisions was in a column of brigades formation, the brigade of Brigadier General Abram Duryée leading Ricketts's division, while the brigade of Brigadier General John Gibbon led Doubleday's. Positioned from the evening before to meet the attack were the divisions of J. R. Jones and Lawton supported by Ripley's brigade of D. H. Hill's division at the Mumma farm and Hood's two brigades behind the Dunker Church. In all, Jackson had eleven brigades available to oppose the advance of Hooker's ten (Map 1.1: Situation 0600).[21]

As the fighting for the quadrangle developed, Jackson reported that "the carnage on both sides was terrific." Jones was wounded and passed command of his division to Starke, who was killed almost instantly, leaving what was left of the division to Grigsby. Lawton was also wounded, and Jackson had to send for Early to take command of what remained of that division. According to Jackson, "More than half of the brigades of Lawton and Hays were either killed or wounded, and more than a third of Trimble's, and all the regimental commanders in those brigades, except two, were killed or wounded. Thinned in their ranks and exhausted of their ammunition, Jackson's division and the brigades of Lawton, Hays, and Trimble retired to the rear," taking shelter in the south end of the West Woods and beyond.[22]

To stop the continuing Federal advance, Lawton called on Hood to bring his two brigades forward. Rations for the division had only just arrived—the troops got nothing more than flour—when it was called into action. Never-

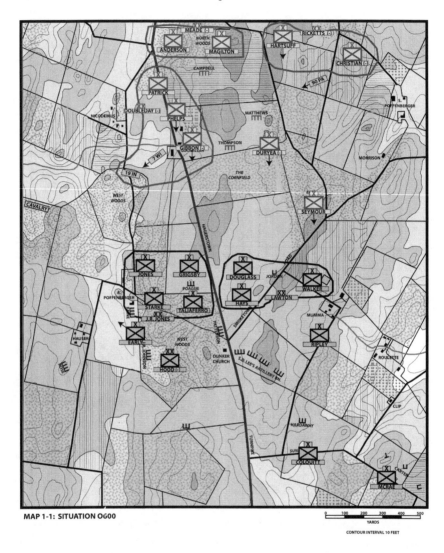

MAP 1-1: SITUATION 0600

0   100   200   300   400   500
YARDS

CONTOUR INTERVAL 10 FEET

theless, the troops responded, and Hood led his two brigades out of the West Woods and formed them into line of battle across the lower end of the quadrangle just north of the junction of Smoketown Road and the turnpike, with Law's brigade on the right and Wofford's on the left. The division drove north through the quadrangle all the way to the northern end of Miller's cornfield, clearing the East Woods in the process.[23]

The situation on the Federal side was now nearly as desperate as it had been

for the Confederates only minutes before. All of Ricketts's division and Seymour's brigade of Meade's division were out of action. The elements of Gibbon's and Phelps's brigades that had advanced nearly to the Dunker Church
were driven precipitously to their line of supporting batteries beyond the northern edge of the cornfield and to the west of the cornfield along the turnpike.
Meade, seeing "the enemy were driving our men from the cornfield," sent the
brigades of Lieutenant Colonel Robert Anderson and Colonel Albert L. Mag-
ilton forward to form a "line of battle along the fence bordering the corn-field,
for the purpose covering the withdrawal of our people and resisting the farther advance of the enemy."[24]

The position of the enemy, Hood's division, was not good. In the withdrawal,
two of Gibbon's regiments, the 7th Wisconsin and 19th Indiana, fell back west
of the turnpike and took shelter behind a rock ledge that gave them a field of
fire toward the cornfield and the flank of Wofford's advancing brigade. Two
regiments of Brigadier General Marsena R. Patrick's brigade, the 21st and 35th
New York, moved up to support them. In addition, just to their left were the
six 12-pounder Napoleons of Captain Joseph B. Campbell's Battery B, 4th U.S.
Artillery, ideally positioned along the turnpike to blast the advancing Confederates with double canister at close range. The effect of this concentrated infantry and artillery fire from front and flank was appalling. Wofford's brigade
virtually disintegrated; one of its regiments, the 1st Texas, suffered 82.3 percent
casualties. On the eastern side of the cornfield Law's brigade was faring no better, taking heavy fire from the front and from the East Woods on the left. Law
reported, "It was evident that this state of affairs could not long continue. No
support was at hand. To remain stationary or advance without it would have
caused a useless butchery, and I adopted the only alternative—that of falling back to the wood from which I first advanced." The support that Law was
looking for was actually nearby in the form of Ripley's brigade only five hundred yards to the south on the Mumma farm. Hood was also expecting Ripley
to come up in support and complained that this brigade, "continuing to hold
their ground, caused the enemy to pour in a heavy fire upon the rear and right
flank of Colonel Law's brigade, rendering it necessary to move the division to
the left and rear into the woods near the Saint Mumma [Dunker] church,"
the position from which the division had advanced less than an hour before.[25]

As Hood withdrew, Ripley finally did move into the cornfield quadrangle
after receiving orders to do so, though he did not say who gave the orders.

Reaching the cornfield, however, Ripley not only met continuing resistance from the remaining First Corps regiments positioned north and west of the cornfield, but also from a new advance of fresh Federal troops from the Twelfth Army Corps under the command of Major General Joseph K. F. Mansfield. McClellan had ordered this corps across the creek the evening before to support Hooker in his advanced position. The plan was for this corps "to take such position as may be designated for it by General Hooker." But, despite having asked for this support, Hooker provided no guides, and the corps drifted to the northwest, where it finally bivouacked on the George Line farm, one mile to the rear of Hooker's position, at about 2:00 A.M. Hearing the sound of the guns at first light, Mansfield got his corps into motion, "marching in column of companies, closed in mass." One of the Twelfth Corps division commanders, Brigadier General Alpheus E. Williams, recalled in his report of the battle that as the corps moved forward, "information was brought that [Hooker's] reserves were all engaged and that he was hard pressed by the enemy." Consequently, the "columns were hastened up and deployed in line of battle with all the rapidity that circumstances would permit."[26]

Williams's division led the Twelfth Corps column. As he approached the front his plan was to send his lead brigade, that of Brigadier General Samuel W. Crawford, to the right of the cornfield quadrangle, extending it as far as the Hagerstown Turnpike; his second brigade, that of Brigadier General George H. Gordon, would deploy on the left just to the west of the East Woods. Such, however, would not be the case. Crawford made initial contact with the enemy as he approached the north end of the East Woods and began deploying his regiments there. In the hasty deployment, his brigade became badly divided by the woods. Still, he was able to clear the northern extension of the woods and advance some of his regiments into the cornfield, driving back Ripley's brigade. But they, in turn, were driven back by the arrival of two more of Hill's brigades, Colquitt's, which advanced from its position in the Sunken Road, and Brigadier General Samuel Garland's, which because of the death of Garland at South Mountain on the 14th, was under the command of Colonel Duncan K. McRae. Colquitt's brigade pushed past Ripley's and advanced as far as the northern border of the cornfield, while McRae moved his regiments through the East Woods to come up behind two of Hood's regiments, the 4th Alabama and 5th Texas, and the 21st Georgia of Lawton's division, which had not withdrawn. From his position at the cornfield fence Colquitt reported the "enemy was near and in full view. In a moment or two his ranks began to break before our fire, and the line soon disappeared under the crest of the hill upon which it had been established. It was soon replaced by another, and the fire opened with renewed vigor."[27]

The new line of Federal troops moving against Colquitt was from Gordon's brigade. With three of his five regiments, the 2nd Massachusetts, 3rd Wisconsin, and 27th Indiana, and one of Crawford's detached regiments, the 124th Pennsylvania, Gordon formed a line across the northern end of the quadrangle and drove into the cornfield. He reported that "before the impetuous charge and the withering fire of our line, the enemy halted, wavered, fled in confusion, and sought shelter in the woods opposite from whence he had emerged [West Woods]." What Gordon did not mention, perhaps because he did not know, was that he had help from two brigades of the Twelfth Corps's Second Division under the command of Brigadier General George S. Greene.[28]

As Greene's column approached the front, one of his three brigades, the one under Colonel William B. Goodrich, was detached and sent to support the extreme right of the First Corps west of the North Woods and the turnpike. The remaining two brigades, under Lieutenant Colonel Hector Tyndale and Colonel Henry J. Stainrook, continued on toward the East Woods, with Tyndale on the right and Stainrook on the left. Tyndale's brigade entered the northern end of the woods and found Colquitt's right flank exposed in the open quadrangle. Stainrook's brigade swung wide to the east of the woods and came in on the flank of the remaining two regiments of Hood's division, the 21st Georgia, and McRae's brigade in the center of the woods. The result was instant panic. Hill explained that McRae's brigade "had been much demoralized" by a flanking fire at South Mountain, such that the realization of that happening again "spread like an electric shock along the ranks, bringing up vivid recollections of the flank fire at South Mountain. In a moment they broke and fell to the rear." Hill went on in his report to admit that "three of my brigades had been broken and much demoralized." Confederate flight from the cornfield quadrangle was now general and desperate to the extent that Hill ordered S. D. Lee to remove his batteries from the plateau across from the Dunker Church and reestablish them on a ridge some six hundred yards to the southwest, south of the West Woods and west of the turnpike.[29]

As Confederate forces withdrew from the East Woods and the quadrangle, Gordon's regiments and the 124th Pennsylvania drove to the south border of the cornfield, while Greene's brigades continued through the East Woods and into the open area south of the woods and the burning Mumma farm. There below the ridge the two brigades came to a halt because their supply of ammunition was running low. Three batteries sent by Hooker soon arrived to support Greene in this forward position and set the stage for continuing the assault. The first was the First Corps battery of Captain J. Albert Monroe, Battery D, 1st Rhode Island Light Artillery. Monroe put his guns in position ahead of Tyndale's brigade, west of the crown of the ridge and directly across the turnpike from the Dunker Church. The second was another First Corps battery commanded by Lieutenant Frederick M. Edgell, 1st Battery, New Hampshire Light Artillery, which took position on the crown of the ridge behind Greene near the junction of Smoketown Road and the Mumma farm lane. The last was the Second Corps battery of Captain John A. Tompkins, Battery A, 1st Rhode Island Light Artillery, which took position below the ridge ahead of Stainrook's brigade. Greene's detached brigade, Goodrich's, had also been successful in driving back the enemy west of the North Woods and the turnpike. Supported by Patrick's brigade of the First Corps, Goodrich was pushing into the northern extent of the West Woods.

At this point the left of the Army of Northern Virginia was in grave peril. The original defensive line, which had been anchored in the West Woods and stretched across the height of land to the Mumma farm, was gone. Of the eleven brigades that had composed or supported that line, only two remained, Early's, which had not yet been engaged, and an ad hoc brigade of two to three hundred men from Jones's division rallied by Colonel Grigsby. Both were now in the north end of the West Woods resisting the advance of Goodrich and Patrick. South of the quadrangle, only four hundred yards ahead of Greene's left, Hill was desperately attempting to form a new defensive line in the sunken farm lane that ran east from the Hagerstown Turnpike. For that line Hill had only the last two of his five brigades, those of Brigadier Generals Robert E. Rodes and George B. Anderson. These two brigades had been brought up from the center to support Hill's other three brigades in counterattacking on the left, but the counterattack had collapsed before they arrived and Hill positioned them in the Sunken Road using it as an expedient line of defense, Rodes's brigade on the left and G. B. Anderson's on the right.[30]

Lee, who up to this point had been watching the progress of the battle from Cemetery Hill just north of the Boonsboro Pike, was well aware of the desperate situation on his left. By 8:00 A.M. he had received three messages indicating the imminent collapse of the left and calling for reinforcements. The first message was brought by D. H. Hill in person, who reported Jackson's need for reinforcements and requested permission to take his division to the left to support Jackson. Lee acquiesced in this request and also decided to send Colonel George T. Anderson's brigade of D. R. Jones's division, which was nearby. The second message was brought by Major J. W. Ratchford, Hill's adjutant general. This message requested "help to meet the enemy's reinforcements." In this case, Lee decided against sending anymore reinforcements to the left. It was not until Captain Sandie Pendleton, Jackson's adjutant general, arrived with warnings of a complete collapse on the left that Lee finally decided to commit more troops to the battle for the left. He sent one of his own staff officers, Major Walter Taylor, to order McLaws to take his division to the left immediately, and he sent his military secretary, Colonel Armistead Long, to bring Walker's division back from guarding Snavely's Ford for commitment on the left.[31]

2

The West Woods

I

When the Confederate left col-lapsed, a little after 8:30 A.M., the one remaining brigade of Jackson's command that had not been seriously engaged was Jubal Early's. Early's brigade had arrived the evening before with the rest of Lawton's division but had been personally positioned by Jackson, along with Hays's brigade, on the west side of the West Woods near the Alfred Poffenberger farmstead on the left of J. R. Jones's division "so as to prevent its being flanked." When the battle opened on the morning of the 17th, Lawton called for Hays to join the rest of the division fighting on the east side of the cornfield quadrangle, while Jackson, again in person, directed Early to take his brigade farther to the west "to support some pieces of artillery, which Maj.-Gen. Stuart had in position to the left of our line."[1]

Early marched northwest along a route that Jackson had designated for him. Not long after leaving the West Woods and passing through another smaller woodlot and into some fields, he encountered a body of Federal skirmishers, which he believed were "moving around our left." Early responded by sending out skirmishers of his own "to hold them in check until I had passed." These Federal troops were from the 23rd New York of Patrick's brigade, which was following in support a part of Gibbon's brigade as it moved into the northern extent of the West Woods. Patrick spotted Early's brigade as it marched to the northwest and sent the 23rd New York "to head off the enemy in that direction."[2]

After marching about a mile, Early found Stuart on Nicodemus Heights directing an assemblage of no less than five batteries, "very adventageously [sic] posted so as to bring an enfilading fire upon the enemy's right." The batteries were Captain John Pelham's from Stuart's own division horse artillery; Captain Louis E. D'Aquin's Louisiana Guard Artillery and Lieutenant A. W. Garber's Staunton, Virginia, Battery (Balthis's battery) from Lawton's division; and Captain Joseph Carpenter's Alleghany, Virginia, Battery and Captain George W. Wooding's Danville, Virginia, Battery from J. R. Jones's division. As these batteries were engaged in an exchange of fire with some Federal batteries north of the North Woods, Stuart suggested that Early form his brigade in line to the rear of the ridge.[3]

After about an hour in this position, Early reported that Stuart "discovered a body of the enemy's troops making their way gradually between us and the left of our main line, [and] determined to shift his position to an eminence nearer our line and little to the rear." Early, at Stuart's direction, also moved his brigade to the rear, taking up a position in line in the southern edge of the small woodlot he had marched through on the way out. It was at this point that Stuart informed Early that Lawton was wounded, "and that Gen. Jackson had sent for me to carry my brigade back and take command of the division." At Stuart's request, Early left the 13th Virginia, which numbered less than one hundred men, to support the batteries, and started the rest of his brigade back toward the West Woods.[4]

Arriving back at the West Woods (Map 2.1: Situation 0830) where his brigade had been posted the previous night, Early found Colonel A. J. Grigsby, who had succeeded Brigadier General William E. Starke in command of J. R. Jones's division, and Colonel Leroy A. Stafford attempting to rally what was left of the division. They had only two hundred to three hundred men with them. Federal skirmishers were gaining a foothold in the northern part of the woods, and as Early arrived Grigsby and Stafford were pushing their small command forward to drive them out. Early reported, "I immediately formed my brigade in line and advanced in their rear, the enemy giving way as the advance was made." The advance went about two hundred yards to a small ridge in the woods. Here Early directed Grigsby and Stafford to move to the left, which placed their command just out of the woods a little north of the Poffenberger farmstead, while Early moved his brigade up to take position on their right, remaining in the woods.[5]

At this point, Early turned command of his brigade over to Colonel William Smith of the 49th Virginia, ordering him to resist any further advance of the enemy "at all hazards." Early then rode off to find and take command of the

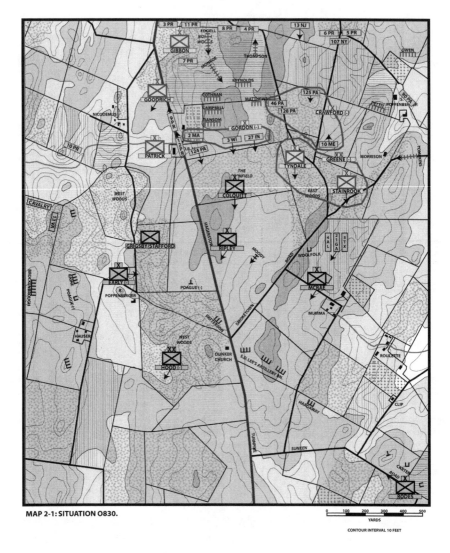

MAP 2-1: SITUATION 0830.

remaining brigades of Lawton's division, but quickly discovered that they "had fallen back some distance to the rear for the purpose of reorganizing, and that they were probably not in a condition to go into the fight again." Nevertheless, he sent Major John P. Wilson, a volunteer aide on Lawton's staff, "to find out where these brigades were, and to order them up." Early also "observed that our troops, who were engaged on this part of the line, were giving way before the enemy." What Early was witnessing was the precipitous withdrawal of the last of Hood's division and Ripley's and McRae's brigades of D. H. Hill's division from the cornfield quadrangle through the West Woods. Alarmed, Early rode to find Jackson to inform him of the situation and to request reinforcements. Jackson told Early "that he would send for re-enforcements, and directed me to keep the enemy in check until they arrived." Early then returned to his brigade and resumed command.[6]

Back with his own brigade (Map 2.2: Situation 0840), Early discovered that a strong enemy column was entering the woods from the north and coming toward his position. He immediately sent Major Samuel Hale, his acting assistant adjutant general, to Jackson requesting that he send reinforcements immediately. Hale returned soon enough with assurances from Jackson that the reinforcements were on the way. Just as Hale arrived, though, a battery to the right and rear of Early's position opened fire. Judging by the sound of the guns, Early guessed that the battery was probably some two hundred yards distance on the Hagerstown Pike near the point where the woods bordered the pike. He assumed that it was a Confederate battery. A soldier, however, who was at the edge of the woods and could see in that direction informed Major Hale that it was an enemy battery. Hale told Early, but Early did not believe it, so he rode himself to the edge of the woods to discover that, sure enough, an enemy battery was positioned near the pike and firing south toward Sharpsburg. Even worse, a large body of infantry supported the battery. Early reported, "This made me aware of the fact that our troops which I had seen giving way had fallen back, leaving the enemy entire possession of the field in front."[7]

Early was fortunate that he occupied a concealed position in the woods on the western slope of the height of land, so the enemy did not know that he was there. Had they known, the "battery could have raked my flank and rear." His situation was now exceedingly critical and desperate. He had an enemy column approaching his front, and another on his right rear that could effectively cut him off from the rest of the army, which had fallen back well south of his position. But Early also "saw the vast importance of maintaining my ground, for, had the enemy gotten possession of this woods, the heights immediately in rear, which commanded the rear of our whole line, would have fallen into his hands." He determined, therefore, to maintain his position hoping that the reinforcements promised by Jackson would arrive in time. Quietly, carefully, Early bent back his right flank "so as not to have my rear exposed in the event of being discovered."[8]

The Federal column that had entered the northern extremity of the West Woods and was advancing toward Early's and Grigsby's line was composed of

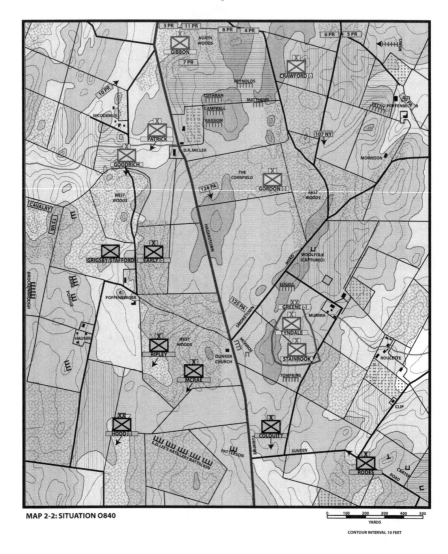

MAP 2-2: SITUATION 0840

0 100 200 300 400 500
YARDS

CONTOUR INTERVAL 10 FEET

the brigades of Goodrich and Patrick operating in tandem with Goodrich in front and Patrick in the rear. The battery to Early's right rear was Battery D, 1st Rhode Island Light Artillery, under the command of Captain J. Albert Monroe. Although Early thought the battery was only two hundred yards distant, its actual position was some six hundred yards to the south on the east side of the Hagerstown Pike directly across from the Dunker Church. Two of this battery's guns were firing at snipers that had secured a covered position below a ridge line ahead of the battery. The battery's remaining four guns were firing into the woods on the fleeing survivors of Hood's division and D. H. Hill's brigades. The "very heavy column of infantry" that Early believed was supporting the battery was the 125th Pennsylvania. This regiment was indeed large, as it had been recruited during the summer and only entered active service with the Army of the Potomac at the beginning of the campaign. Accordingly, it had nearly its full complement of one thousand men, making it as large as most brigades made up of veteran regiments.[9]

What Early did not see—or did not mention seeing—was another new and very large regiment, the 124th Pennsylvania, that was making its way through Miller's cornfield. It was about to take position on a crest just south of the cornfield, only three hundred yards from Early's right front. To the left of the 124th, below the crest on the eastern slope of the height of land, where Early could not have seen it, was Gordon's brigade that had been instrumental in clearing the East Woods and the cornfield quadrangle. Also below the crest to the east of Monroe's battery were the two brigades of Greene's division that had driven through the East Woods and across the Mumma farm and were now lying down while awaiting a resupply of ammunition. Backing up Greene's position was a second battery that had come forward with Monroe's. The 1st Battery, New Hampshire Light Artillery, under the command of Lieutenant Frederick M. Edgell, was in position to Greene's rear on the high ground just south of the junction of the Mumma farm lane and Smoketown Road. And a third battery was in position on the left front of Greene's division, Battery A, 1st Rhode Island Light Artillery, under Captain John A. Tompkins. Indeed, Early was right when he concluded that "the troops which I had seen giving way had fallen back, leaving the enemy entire possession of the field in front." Early's position in the West Woods was even more desperate than he imagined.[10]

As Early continued watching, the infantry column to his rear, the 125th Pennsylvania, suddenly moved into the woods in the vicinity of the Dunker Church. Early said he "looked to the rear for the re-enforcements, and could not see them coming. I was thus cut off from the main body of our army on the right, and a column was moving against me from the left." Immediately, he decided that he must confront the 125th Pennsylvania in the woods near the church, so he started his brigade south, marching by the flank, using the Poffenberger farm lane along the western boundary of the woods. To replace his brigade in confronting the Federal force entering the woods from the north, Goodrich's and Patrick's brigades, Early ordered Grigsby and Stafford to extend their line again into the woods to their right.[11]

Being well below the height of land and on the opposite side of the woods from the 125th, Early's brigade remained concealed. He marched the brigade south about four hundred yards until he was opposite a small hill just inside the edge of the woods. Here he "discovered the enemy moving with flankers thrown out on his right flank." Early "directed Colonel William A. Smith, whose regiment, the 49th Virginia, was in the lead, to open fire on the flankers, which was promptly done, and they ran in on the main body, which was taken by surprise by the fire from the unexpected quarter from which it came." Early reported that he then "continued to move by the flank until my whole force was disclosed." Facing to the front and moving into the woods, he ordered the brigade to "open fire, which was done in handsome style and responded to by the enemy."[12]

As his brigade was entering the woods, Early personally took command of the 49th Virginia and led it in a charge up the slope toward the main body of the 125th Pennsylvania (Map 2.3: Situation 0850). The 49th withdrew back down the slope soon enough, but Early led it in a second and then a third charge up the hill. When Lieutenant Colonel Jonathan C. Gibson of the 49th asked Early "what in the heaven he was doing that for he said it was to prevent a battery which was firing most fiercely into our ranks from getting our exact range." The battery to which Early was referring was Monroe's, which was still in position near the Dunker Church. Even though Early believed that the regiments of his brigade to the left of the 49th were in the woods and firing toward the 125th Pennsylvania, the sudden move to the south and into the woods had actually left them in considerable confusion. Lieutenant Colonel Gibson observed that "Early's charges and fall backs on the extreme right necessarily threw his left in great confusion. As far as I could see they were trying to get into line, but could not do so. They were not in line but straggling to the front."[13]

As Early was attempting to deal with the 125th Pennsylvania, Grigsby's and Stafford's small command continued to oppose the advance of Goodrich's and Patrick's brigades. All seemed to be going well enough until a new line of Federal troops appeared suddenly on their right flank, attacking into the woods from the higher ground (Map 2.4: Situation 0900). Grigsby and Stafford had no alternative other than to withdraw from the woods toward the southwest and attempt to take up a new position among the buildings, haystacks, fences,

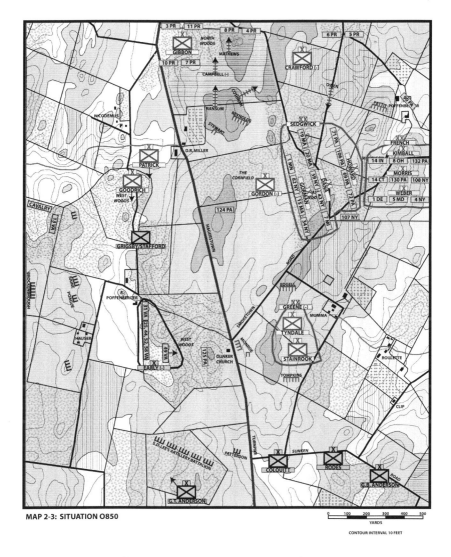

MAP 2-3: SITUATION 0850

0 100 200 300 400 500
YARDS

CONTOUR INTERVAL 10 FEET

and orchard trees of the Poffenberger farmstead. But Grigsby and Stafford were fortunate, because in their new position they would be supported by three batteries of artillery from J. R. Jones's division that Jackson and Stuart were putting in place on Hauser's Ridge, "the heights immediately in rear" of the woods that Early recognized as being key to the survival of the Confederate army. The batteries, all of which had been engaged in the fight for the cornfield quadrangle, were Captain John B. Brockenbrough's Maryland Battery, Captain Charles J.

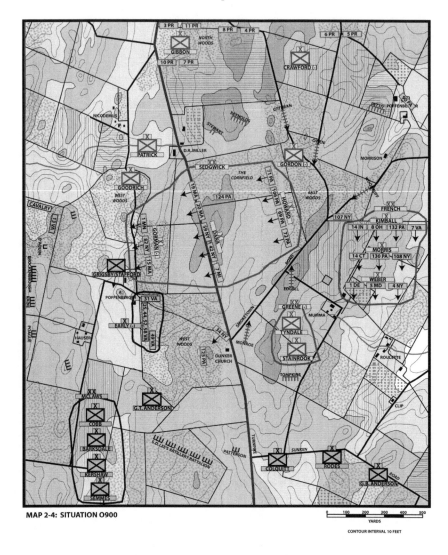

MAP 2-4: SITUATION O900

0   100   200   300   400   500
YARDS

CONTOUR INTERVAL 10 FEET

Raine's Lee Virginia Battery, and Captain William T. Poague's Rockbridge Virginia Artillery. In addition, Stuart called on D'Aquin, whose battery he had sent to Cox's farm to support the cavalry, to send back his two howitzers. These batteries were supported by the 13th Virginia, the regiment that Early had left on Hauser's Ridge.[14]

Early noticed this new enemy column as well, "moving across the plateau on my left flank, in double-quick time" and watched in amazement as it brushed past his own left. Suddenly he had to contend not only with the enemy in the woods to his front, but also an enemy column that was in position to attack his flank and rear.[15]

II

The new Federal line driving through the West Woods was the brigade of Brigadier General Willis A. Gorman, the lead brigade of Major General John Sedgwick's division of the Second Army Corps, commanded by Major General Edwin V. Sumner. Sumner's corps had been placed on alert on the evening of the 16th at the same time that Mansfield's corps was sent across Antietam Creek to support Hooker. Under a temporary command arrangement, Sumner, the second-ranking officer in the Army of the Potomac, was responsible for both his own and Mansfield's corps. The order for Mansfield to cross the creek the evening before had gone through Sumner, and it also directed Sumner to have his own corps "ready to march one hour before daylight tomorrow morning." The implication was clear. Under McClellan's plan of battle, it would be Hooker's, Mansfield's, and Sumner's corps that would combine "to make the main attack upon the enemy's left."[16]

As the battle began on the morning of the 17th, however, McClellan held Sumner's corps on the east bank of the Antietam. Although Sumner had the corps up by 2:00 A.M., and was ready to march to join Hooker and Mansfield before first light, he did not receive orders to do so until 7:20 A.M. Even then McClellan allowed Sumner to take only two of his three divisions, Sedgwick's and the division under Brigadier General William H. French. Sedgwick's division led the march and French's followed. After crossing the Antietam at Pry's Ford, Sumner encountered Hooker being carried by ambulance to the Pry House, McClellan's headquarters, with a painful wound in the foot. Although Hooker later recalled that he was upbeat about the course of the battle, in his half-conscious state he probably communicated little to Sumner concerning the situation at the front. As Sumner continued west, climbing toward the height of land, a courier from headquarters reached him with orders for him to get "possession of the woods to the right as soon as possible" and "push on towards Sharpsburg and a little to its rear as rapidly as possible."[17]

Sumner and his two divisions finally reached the front near the East Woods at approximately 8:45 A.M. as the last of D. H. Hill's three brigades were withdrawing from the cornfield quadrangle. The battlefield at that point was relatively quiet and Sumner had time to make a reconnaissance as Sedgwick's division moved into the East Woods. From the western edge of the woods, Sumner could see the line formed by the 124th Pennsylvania and Gordon's brigade, as well as some batteries on the hill north of D. R. Miller's cornfield firing toward the West Woods. Although he could not see it because of the intervening height of land, Sumner could tell from the noise and smoke that a firefight was going on in the northern end of the West Woods, the fight between Grigsby and Goodrich and Patrick. Cantering along the western edge of the woods as far south as the junction of Smoketown Road and the Mumma farm lane, he was able to observe Monroe's, Edgell's and Tompkins's batteries, and Greene's division. He could also see the 125th Pennsylvania as it entered the West Woods in the vicinity of the Dunker Church and the last two of D. H. Hill's brigades moving into position in a sunken farm lane to the southeast.[18]

Sumner's conclusion concerning the West Woods was the same as the one that Early was drawing at that very moment: they were the key to the battlefield. If he were to continue the attack to the south and west of Sharpsburg as he had been ordered, he would first need to secure those woods. From his perspective that would not be a problem, as no significant enemy force appeared to occupy the woods. The 125th Pennsylvania had entered the woods near the Dunker Church without opposition. The fighting in the northern end of the woods was on a north-south axis, so he was on the flank of whatever Confederate force was in the woods at that point. He could not, of course, see Early's brigade, which was just beginning to move toward the southern end of the woods.

Sumner decided to order Sedgwick's division to attack across the quadrangle to secure the woods, and then to continue the attack to the south and west. Sedgwick's flanks would be secured by Greene's division and the 125th Pennsylvania on the left, and on the right by whatever Federal forces were already in the northern end of the woods. As he could not leave the Confederate force taking position in the Sunken Road to the southeast unattended, he decided to have French's division attack it, and then continue the attack toward Sharpsburg, again linking up with Sedgwick. Greene's division and whatever other Federal forces that might be available could support the whole operation.

Sedgwick's division was already in formation for an attack to the west, a column of brigades with the regiments of each brigade in line of battle. Gorman's brigade was in the lead, followed by Brigadier General Napoleon J. T. Dana's and Brigadier General Oliver O. Howard's. The three brigade lines were to be approximately sixty to seventy yards apart. On leaving the East Woods, however, Dana mistook Gordon's brigade, which was then lying down, for Gorman's and stopped. While this error was being corrected, Gorman continued on well ahead of Dana. When Dana started off again across the quadrangle, Howard did not immediately follow. One of Sumner's staff officers had ordered Howard to send a regiment to support the troops fighting in the northern end of the West Woods, and Howard stopped his brigade to send off the 71st Pennsylvania. Seeing that Howard was not following, Sedgwick rode back and ordered him to move his entire brigade forward. But Howard waited to get the 71st back in line before he continued on after Dana.

Despite these problems, Gorman's brigade advanced easily through the West Woods. But it halted when it met stiff resistance from Grigsby and Stafford at the Poffenberger farm, supported by Jackson's and Stuart's batteries and the 13th Virginia on Hauser's Ridge. The two howitzers of D'Aquin's battery, which were just arriving, went into position in some woods at the northern end of the ridge and opened with canister. To their right, Brockenbrough's Maryland Battery was also just getting into position. Captain Brockenbrough was surprised when one of his soldiers, John A. Walters, pointed out the U.S. flags emerging from the West Woods. He had to hurriedly complete the positioning of his six guns and open fire. To his right, Raine, commanding the Lee Virginia Battery, which was already in position, reported that his four guns "opened on [the enemy] with grape and canister at about 300 yards distance and succeeded in mowing them down at every fire and prevented their further advance." A little over one hundred yards to Raine's right were the three guns of Poague's Rockbridge Virginia Artillery. These guns had been in position long enough that Edward A. Moore, a sergeant in charge of one of the guns, recalled Jackson being close by and making "efforts to stop the stream of straglers [sic] passing by us from the north end of the woods."[19]

As his brigade reached the west side of the woods, Gorman was unaware that one of his regiments was not with the brigade. At some point while crossing the open quadrangle, he had ordered a right oblique to bring the brigade in on the flank of the Confederate force fighting Goodrich and Patrick. This order did not reach his left regiment, the 34th New York, and it continued to guide on Smoketown Road. This brought it into the woods in the vicinity of the Dunker Church directly in the rear of the 125th Pennsylvania, creating a gap of about three hundred yards between the 15th Massachusetts, now the left most regiment of Gorman's line, and the 125th Pennsylvania and 34th New York. Had the 34th New York maintained its position on the brigade left during the movement across the quadrangle, it would have filled that gap and directly confronted Early's brigade in the west end of the woods.

III

As Early watched Gorman's line push to the west side of the woods and take position on his left and rear, his first counteraction was to break off the fight between his brigade and the 125th Pennsylvania. "I succeeded in arresting my command and ordered it to retire, so that I might change front and advance upon this force." Just as he was about to do so, however, Early "observed the promised re-enforcements coming up toward the woods at the farther [southern] end." Suddenly, maneuvering his brigade either to change front and attack the flank of the newly arrived Federal column or to again move forward against the 125th Pennsylvania would be dangerous. Early observed that the reinforcements were preparing "to advance into the woods from the direction of my right flank, and [I] was afraid of exposing my brigade to their fire, and that the two movements would throw us into confusion, as they would have been at right angles." Early had no choice, therefore, other than to maintain his position for the time being. He did, however, have his left flank regiment, the 31st Virginia, change front to face north and secure that flank.[20]

The reinforcements that Early saw preparing to move into the West Woods on his right were G. T. Anderson's brigade of D. R. Jones's division and the brigades of McLaws's division. Anderson's brigade was the first of the reinforcements that Lee had sent to the left. Since arriving near Sharpsburg on the 15th, this brigade had been in position to the right of the Boonsboro Pike on the high ground at the eastern edge of the town. Anderson's release to go to the left was based on D. H. Hill's initial request to Lee at about 7:30 A.M. to be allowed to commit his whole division to the battle on the left and for some reinforcements. Anderson's orders were to go to the support of Hood's division, but he was given no directions and no guide. Consequently, he simply marched to the northwest directing "my course by the sound of the musketry."[21]

Anderson finally reached the vicinity of the West Woods and found Hood, "who pointed out the position he wished me to occupy." The position was be-hind a rail fence at the extreme southwestern face of the woods. It was a posi-tion from which Anderson's brigade could cover the final withdrawal of Hood's and D. H. Hill's men from the woods, as well as resist any further advance of the enemy. Anderson moved his brigade toward the woods in line of battle. A member of the 1st Georgia Regulars, W. H. Andrews, recalled that "when within 300 yds. of the Wood the Federal Sharp Shooters opened fire from the woods. Genl. Anderson ordered the brigade Sharps Shooters to charge to the front, which they did quickly entering the woods & engaging the enemy. When we arrived at the woods we were halted & ordered to tear down the fence mak-ing temporary works by placing the rails end wise. We were then ordered to lye [*sic*] down behind them as the bullets from the Sharp Shooters were flying pretty thick one of them striking a rail in 3 inches of my head while trying to see what was going on in front. In our front the Federal line of battle was be-yond a ridge & invisible from our position."[22]

McLaws's division had been resting near Lee's headquarters west of Sharps-burg since its early-morning arrival. Based on Jackson's 8:30 A.M. request for reinforcements carried by his adjutant, Captain Pendleton, Lee finally decided the situation on the left called for committing the division he was holding in reserve. Accordingly, he sent one of his aides, Major Taylor, to deliver orders to McLaws to march the division immediately to the left. Taylor, however, could not find McLaws because he had fallen asleep in some tall grass, so the order was delivered to McLaws's adjutant, telling him to start the division at once. Continuing his search for McLaws, Taylor finally did find him sometime after the division had started off, so McLaws had to ride quickly to catch up with it.

Even though McLaws's brigades started well after G. T. Anderson's, they had less distance to go, so they reached the vicinity of the West Woods not long after Anderson did. As McLaws's caught up with the division he halted it in a plowed field about four hundred yards southwest of G. T. Anderson's brigade and the West Woods. At this point, the brigade of Brigadier General Howell Cobb was in the lead, followed by the brigades of Brigadier Generals William Barksdale, Joseph B. Kershaw, and Paul J. Semmes. The first person that McLaws encountered was Major James W. Ratchford of D. H. Hill's staff, who pointed out the West Woods as the position that the division was to occupy. McLaws, however, recalled in his official report that he was "entirely ignorant of the ground and of the location of the troops. Gen. Hood, however, who was present, pointed out the direction for the advance." The direction pointed out by Hood was the same as that indicated by Ratchford, toward the West Woods. Looking in that direction, McLaws noted "a large body of woods, from which parties of our troops, of whose command I do not know, were seen retiring, and the enemy, I could see, were advancing rapidly, occupying the place. . . . As the enemy were filling the woods so rapidly, I wished my troops to cross the open space between us and the woods before they were entirely occupied."[23]

McLaws's plan was to send his division into the woods with Semmes's brigade on the left, then Barksdale's and Kershaw's and Cobb's on the right. Getting the whole division on line, however, would take time, time at that point McLaws did not have. To blunt what he perceived was a Federal move to the extreme south end of the woods, McLaws ordered Kershaw "to occupy that part of the wood in advance of them while our lines were being formed. For this purpose I [Kershaw] ordered forward, at double-quick, Col. Kennedy's Second South Carolina Regiment to march by a flank to the extreme point of the wood; then by the front to enter it." The route of the 2nd South Carolina required crossing several rail fences at odd angles. Kershaw reported, "Before the head of the regiment had reached the point, and when entangled in a rail fence, the enemy opened fire upon them from a point not more than 60 yards distant. They promptly faced to the front, and returned the fire so rapidly as to drive the enemy almost immediately." On reaching the woods, the 2nd had to cross over the right of G. T. Anderson's brigade lying down behind its makeshift breastwork of fence rails. Entering the woods, the 2nd started for the high ground and the left of the 125th Pennsylvania. W. H. Andrews of the 1st Georgia Regulars, watching from behind the breastwork of rails, remembered that "soon after we arrived at the fence Kershaws [*sic*] South Carolina Brigade marched up within twenty feet of our line and halted. Just at the right of our brigade a regiment moved in by the right flank, the enemys [*sic*] line of battle was beyond the ridge in a bottom and not visible from our position at the fence. As the head of the column rose the ridge the enemy opened fire on them. The regiment was ordered to right wheel into line which was promptly executed under the enemys fire and on reaching the crest of the ridge opened fire."[24]

At the time that the South Carolinians were beginning to push into the woods, Cobb's and Barksdale's brigades were also beginning to move toward the woods (Map 2.5: Situation 0910). Cobb's brigade, which on this day was under the command of Lieutenant Colonel C. C. Sanders, was to be the ex-

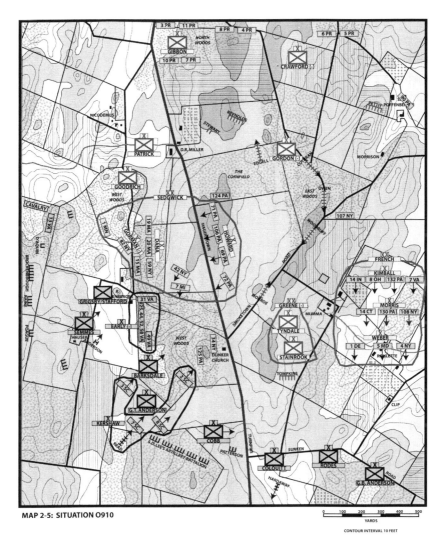

MAP 2-5: SITUATION O910

0 100 200 300 400 500
YARDS

CONTOUR INTERVAL 10 FEET

treme right of the division. McLaws ordered Sanders to march the brigade to the right by the right flank with the intent that once it was due south of the woods, it would face front (left), forming line of battle and attack due north into the woods guiding on the Hagerstown Pike. As the head of the brigade column approached the pike, McLaws gave the signal for all the brigades to commence their move toward the woods by waving his handkerchief. This was the signal for Sanders to have his brigade face front and move toward the woods in line.

But, according to Lieutenant Colonel William MacRae of the 15th North Carolina, who would write the brigade's official report, "Colonel Sanders, being in
front, did not hear [or see] the order, but marched on and joined the left of
General Rodes' command," which at that point was establishing itself in the
sunken farm lane east of the pike. "We were thus separated from the division,
and did not join it until the next morning."[25]

Barksdale's brigade, just behind Cobb's in the division column, was ordered
to head directly for the woods. Barksdale reported that he "formed a line of
battle in an open field, which was at that time being raked by a terrible fire of
grape and canister from the enemy's artillery." Once the brigade was in line
Barksdale made a brief speech. "The enemy is driving back our center. We must
check them. Stonewall Jackson and General Lee expect you to do so. I have
promised that you will, and I want every man to do three men's duty. If there
is a man before me who cannot, let him step out. I will excuse him." When no
one asked to be excused, Barksdale told them, "Leave everything, except guns
and cartridge boxes, under that tree."[26]

When the signal to move forward came, Barksdale's brigade "advanced upon
the enemy, who occupied the woods immediately in front, and from which
they had just driven a portion of our forces." To get into the woods, Barksdale
had to go around the left flank of G. T. Anderson's brigade. This meant that
the brigade would enter the woods at the mouth of a wide ravine that would
channel it through the woods in a northeasterly direction. The brigade, therefore, would cross obliquely in front of Early's brigade, which was still in position on the western edge of the woods. The ravine would also lead the brigade
past the right flank of the 125th Pennsylvania.[27]

Kershaw, in the division column behind Barksdale, still did not have all of
his remaining regiments on line when the signal to advance came. Nevertheless he started off the 7th and 8th South Carolina, which were nearly deployed,
followed by the 3rd South Carolina deploying into line as it moved forward.
The 7th and 8th followed the path of the 2nd South Carolina, partly skirting
and partly going over the right of G. T. Anderson's brigade. W. H. Andrews in
Anderson's brigade, still behind the makeshift breastworks of rails at the southwest side of the woods, recalled, "Kershaws [*sic*] South Carolina Brigade was
then ordered in[,] passing over us[.] General Kershaw asked what command
and being told Andersons [*sic*] Georgia Brigade called for three cheers for the
Georgians which his men gave with a vim and moved forward into the fight.

It made the Georgia boys feel good to watch the Palmetto boys move into action. As their heads rose over the ridge the enemy opened fire on them, but not a man flinched or a gun fired until they reached the crest and then such a volley of musketry as would scare a weak kneed soldier to death." The 3rd South Carolina, however, which was to be the left regiment of the brigade line, moved around the left of Anderson and entered the woods "immediately after a regiment of Gen. Barksdale's brigade," according to the regimental commander, Colonel James D. Nance. Following in the wake of the Kershaw's brigade was one of the division batteries, the Pulaski (Georgia) Artillery, commanded by Captain John P. W. Read.[28]

McLaws's last brigade, Semmes's, was ordered by McLaws "to move forward in line to the support of Maj.-Gen. Stuart." The brigade would thus advance as the left flank of the division. Semmes had his regiments march by the flank into a cornfield to the left of the plowed field in which McLaws's other brigades were forming, and there go into brigade line of battle with the 53rd Georgia on the left, then the 15th Virginia, 10th Georgia, and the 32nd Virginia on the right. Moving along to the right of the brigade was a section of the 1st Company, Richmond Howitzers under Lieutenant R. M. Anderson. The deployment of the brigade on the left of the division brought it onto Hauser's Ridge, the same ridge from which Jackson's and Stuart's artillery and the 13th Virginia were resisting the further advance of Gorman's brigade from its position at the edge of the woods. Following the high ground, the brigade advanced some two hundred yards north to the Hauser farmstead "under a fire occasioning severe loss in killed and wounded." At this point, the brigade wheeled partially to the right, halted behind the fence bordering Hauser's farm lane, and was ordered to commence firing even though the enemy line ahead in the West Woods was still some four hundred yards distant. In his official report Semmes explained, "This order was then given at long range for most of our arms, for the purpose of encouraging our troops and disconcerting the enemy." It apparently had the desired effect, for Semmes reported that the result was "distinctly visible in the diminished numbers of killed and wounded." Still much damage had already been done to the brigade. Captain S. W. Marshborne of the 53rd Georgia had to assume command of his regiment at this point, because "it was here that Lieut.-Col. [Thomas] Sloan was seriously wounded. His calmness and bravery deserve special notice. Here, also, Lieut. [C. C.] Brown fell. His captain informs me that his last words were those of encouragement to his company."[29]

With the fire from Gorman's brigade somewhat suppressed, Semmes decided to continue "to press steadily forward, pouring a deadly fire into his [Gorman's] ranks." Marshborne reported that his "regiment was ordered forward, and officers and men leaped over the fence, determined to do or die." This advance took the brigade northeast across an open pasture to the Poffenberger farmstead. Reaching the farmstead, the brigade was forced to halt where it was somewhat sheltered by the haystacks and rock outcroppings around the main house, and here it remained for some time exchanging fire with the 15th Massachusetts and 82nd New York of Gorman's brigade. Ensign John T. Parham, who was with the colors of the 32nd Virginia on the right of the brigade, recalled that "as we started across the field Barksdale's men were a little ahead and [in] front of us. They got to the piece of woods in their front about the time that we started across the field. We were under a severe fire going over the field. When we got to the [rocky] knoll, the fire was so severe that we could go no further. There was a wheat stack & a barn on our left & rear where our wounded got. We lost very severe at this point. The federals were in our front behind a *stone* fence. I think just in rear of the fence was a piece of woods. . . . My Regt. lost half its men at that point." Lieutenant Anderson with his two guns kept with the brigade as far as the Poffenberger farm and even unlimbered to add supporting artillery fire. But being to the right of the brigade in the open field and exposed to the fire of Gorman's line, he was soon forced to retire to the greater safety of Hauser's Ridge. D. S. McCarthy, a member of Anderson's section, recalled, "We did not advance beyond this point, but received orders to put our guns in position, on a piece of elevated ground a short distance to the rear, and right of this point, where we remained, until our army left the field."[30]

IV

Once in the woods, both Kershaw's and Barksdale's brigades began to press the flanks of the 125th Pennsylvania (Map 2.6: Situation 0920). The first to attack was Kershaw's leading regiment, the 2nd South Carolina, which struck the left of the 125th on the high ground a little to the southwest of the Dunker Church. A member of the 2nd, Creswell A. C. Waller, believed that his regiment had an advantage over the 125th in that "we had two 'crack' rifle companies on the right of the regiment composed of good shots [and] we had two on the left, one of which was the Palmetto Guards of Charleston & the other the Brooks Guards

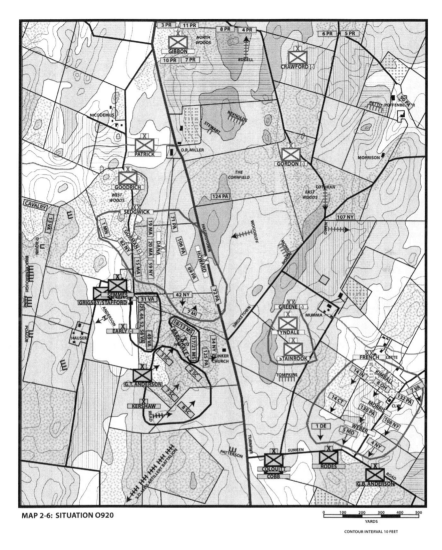

MAP 2-6: SITUATION O920

0 100 200 300 400 500
YARDS

CONTOUR INTERVAL 10 FEET

of the same place." Waller recalled that at first the Pennsylvanians stood their
ground. "I cannot say how long it took to drive them. We shot several times, so
often that some guns became foul & clogged." Waller noted that the Pennsylvanians were armed with "new guns[,] dark enfields & new *covered* canteens."
Eventually, he managed to secure one of the Enfields for himself, and got several canteens, which he gave to his friends.[31]

As the 2nd South Carolina engaged the left of the 125th, Barksdale's brigade was pushing up the ravine west of the Dunker Church. This brought the Mississippians into the three-hundred-yard-wide gap between the right of the 125th and the left of the 15th Massachusetts of Gorman's brigade at the western edge of the woods. This was the gap that would have been covered by the 34th New York had that regiment executed the right oblique with the rest of Gorman's brigade as it crossed the open area between the East and West Woods. Following this ravine brought Barksdale's regiments nearly around the right of the 125th. Ensign Parham of the 32nd Virginia in Semmes's brigade witnessed the advance of Barksdale's brigade as his regiment was charging across the open fields between the Hauser and Poffenberger farms. He later recalled, "Their fire was so steady and severe that it looked like a whirlwind was passing through the leaves on the ground and woods." The combined attacks by the 2nd South Carolina and Barksdale's brigade proved too much for the 125th Pennsylvania, and it began to withdraw from the woods in confusion. Colonel Jacob Higgins, who commanded the regiment, reported "looking around and finding no support in sight, I was compelled to retire. Had I remained in my position two minutes longer I would have lost my whole command."[32]

At that point, another Federal regiment appeared coming forward through the woods on the opposite side of the ravine from the 125th. This regiment was the 7th Michigan and it was closely followed by the 42nd New York. These were the two left regiments of Dana's brigade. Crossing the quadrangle at some distance behind Gorman, Dana, on reaching the West Woods, had detected the fight between Early and the 125th in the woods to his left. Realizing that an enemy force in the woods to his left would pose a threat to the advance of Sedgwick's division, Dana turned the 7th Michigan and 42nd New York in tandem and started them down into the woods just as Barksdale's regiments were starting up the ravine. To deal with this new threat, Barksdale allowed his right wing, the 17th and 21st Mississippi, to continue the attack on the right of the 125th, but turned his left wing, the 13th and 18th Mississippi, to attack the 7th Michigan. The 7th broke and began to flee the woods, throwing the 42nd New York into some confusion.[33]

With the collapse of the 125th, the 34th New York, behind it and a little north of the church, was now fully exposed on both flanks. Faced with the threat of the 7th Michigan and 42nd New York on his left, Barksdale held back from immediately advancing against the right of the 34th New York. The 2nd South Carolina, however, continued its advance. In doing so, it moved alone against the 34th and was driven back by a well-directed volley from a regiment more experienced than the 125th. A member of the 2nd South Carolina remarked, "The first Union line was very quickly driven, but an oblique line [34th New York] apparently older soldiers, was not so easily moved and checked us."[34]

The repulse of the 2nd South Carolina by the 34th New York was only temporary, for coming up on the left of the 2nd was G. T. Anderson's brigade (Map 2.7: Situation 0930). Anderson had maintained his position at the fence at the southwest face of the woods while Kershaw and Barksdale passed over and around him entering the woods. Once Barksdale was in the woods, though, Anderson "moved by the left flank some 200 yards" north along the edge of the woods. As W. H. Andrews in the 1st Georgia Regulars remembered it, "General Anderson then ordered his brigade by the left flank double quick and away we went at the right shoulder shift, how steady the boys moved as though on drill. As we were well under way the enemy opened fire on us, their line being on top the ridge and not more than sixty yards from the fence. What a move under the enemy's fire, but not a bobble or a break until we gained our brigade distance to the left."[35]

Facing front, the brigade then entered the woods at approximately the same point as Barksdale and the 3rd South Carolina. Andrews wrote, "General Anderson then gave the order by the right flank and [as] we jumped the fence it would then have done your heart good to hear the rifles of the Georgia boys." Instead of following the course of the ravine, however, Anderson sent his regiments directly up the hill to the right of the ravine. They reached the top of the hill just at the point that Barksdale was beginning to turn his right wing back to the left to deal with the 7th Michigan and 42nd New York. Anderson continued forward and joined with the 2nd South Carolina in the assault on the 34th New York. Andrews remembered that as the brigade advanced up the hill:

I saw directly in front of me the stars and stripes how defiant that flag looked as it unfurled to the breeze then gradually wound itself around the staff to be lifted again by the powder exploding around it. Right then and there I thought it would be the greatest feat of my life if I could topple that flag in the dust by shooting the color bearer. In placing my rifle to my shoulder I pressed the trigger, but instead of the colors falling my gun snapped[;] my feelings can better be imagined than described. I had to pick the trobe [tube] and recap before I knew what was going on about me.

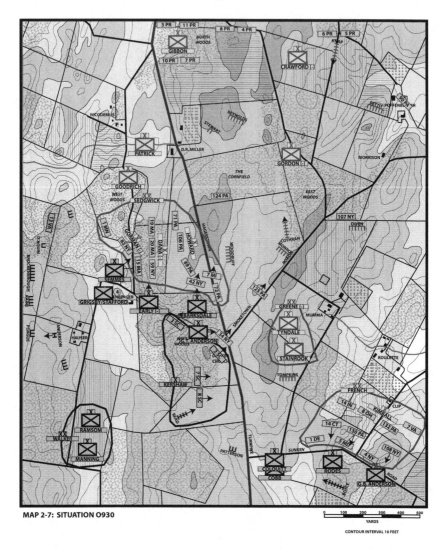

MAP 2-7: SITUATION 0930

0   100   200   300   400   500
YARDS

CONTOUR INTERVAL 10 FEET

On looking up I saw that the line had passed me the order to charge had been given and I saw Lieut. G.B. Lamar, Captain [Richard A.] Wayne and several other officers with swords aloft calling on the men to follow them. The line had fired about two volleys when ordered to charge. The enemy were generally routed leaving the ground covered with the dead and wounded (I was on many battlefields during the war but never saw the ground covered so thick with the fallen) it then became a tree to tree fight. Anderson's Brigade sweeping everything before it. During

the fight I passed Captain Wayne and one or two other officers supporting Captain [J. G.] Montgomery who was wounded in the head. He was
promptly sent to the rear. It seemed like it was only a few minutes that
we were driving the enemy out of the woods, it being a total rout as the
last squad I saw only amounted to three men.[36]

As G. T. Anderson's brigade and the 2nd South Carolina were making their
determined attack against the 34th New York, Sedgwick was himself directly
behind the regiment and realized that it could not hold such an advanced position. The 34th's commander, Colonel James Suiter, reported:

At this time I discovered that the enemy were making a move to flank
me on the left. Lieut. [Church] Howe [aide-de-camp to Sedgwick] arriving at this time, I informed him of my suspicions. He replied that he
thought they were our friends. Lieut. [William R.] Wallace, of Company
C, proposed going to the front, to make what discovery he could, which
I granted. He returned, saying that the enemy were moving upon my left
flank with a strong force. I turned and discovered Lieut. Richard Gorman, of Gen. Gorman's staff, and requested him to inform the general
that the enemy were flanking me. He immediately returned for that purpose. Presently Gen. Sedgwick arrived upon the ground. Moving down
my line, he discovered the situation of my command, and that the point
could not be held by me, and gave the order for me to retire, which I did.
Rallying my command, I formed them in line of battle, supporting a battery some 400 yards in rear of the battle-field.[37]

Back in the center of the woods, Barksdale now had his entire brigade facing north and driving against the 7th Michigan and 42nd New York. Coming up in support of Barksdale's brigade was the 3rd South Carolina of Kershaw's brigade, which had followed Barksdale into the woods. The commander
of the 3rd reported that his regiment "advanced steadily, with spirit, under a
heavy fire drawn by the troops in front." As Barksdale's brigade changed direction to the left, so did the 3rd South Carolina. Dana, who was with the 42nd
New York, reported that "the fire which was poured upon it and the Seventh
Michigan was the most terrific I ever witnessed." Both of these regiments retired from the woods and into the open quadrangle that they had crossed only
a few minutes before.[38]

Early, who had been unable to maneuver his brigade as Barksdale and G. T. Anderson entered the woods and marched partially across his front, now saw his opportunity. With the area to his front clear, he swung his remaining regiments around to the left and came on line with the 31st Virginia, which was already facing north. The entire brigade was now on Barksdale's left. This maneuver placed Early squarely on the left flank of the 59th New York of Dana's brigade, exposed by the withdrawing 7th Michigan and 42nd New York. It also placed Early on the flank and rear of the 15th Massachusetts, the left regiment of Gorman's line at the western edge of the woods.

Gorman's line was already hard-pressed from the front. His three regiments had now been in a heavy firefight for approximately thirty to forty-five minutes, and each soldier had "expended from 40 to 50 rounds at the enemy." Just at the point that Early's brigade was finding the flank and rear of Gorman's line, Semmes's brigade at the Poffenberger farmstead renewed its advance. Ensign Parham in the 32nd Virginia, still at the rocky knoll, remembered:

> General Semmes came to our colors, and saw me still shooting away as fast as I could load, and asked where the enemy was located. I told him behind that fence in front. He said, "Yes, and they will kill the last one of us, and that we must charge them." He gave the command to charge. Bob Forrest went forward several paces in front and waited for the line of battle to come up, and Lieutenant Henry St. Clair, of Company I, ran up to him and said, "Bob Forrest, why in the h-ll don't you go forward with the flag; if you won't go, give it to me," and started for it. Bob Forrest, as brave a man as ever lived, said to him, "You shan't have it; I will carry this flag as far as any man; bring your line up and we will all go together." They did come up, and took the fence and drove the enemy up the hill.[39]

Semmes reported, "Our troops continued to press steadily forward, pouring a deadly fire into his [the enemy's] ranks." Gorman remembered that the "attack of the enemy on the flank was so sudden and in such overwhelming force that I had no time to lose, for my command could have been completely enveloped and probably captured, as the enemy was moving not only upon my left flank but also forcing a column toward my right." Lieutenant Colonel John W. Kimball commanding the 15th Massachusetts was in the same predicament. He reported the enemy appearing "in heavy columns, advancing upon my left and rear, pouring in a deadly cross-fire on my left. I immediately and without orders ordered my command to retire, having first witnessed the same movement on the part of both the second and third lines."[40]

V

The arrival of the reinforcements sent by Lee successfully arrested the disaster menacing the Confederate left. The West Woods had been the rampart of Jackson's initial defensive line. Without it there was only one remaining ridgeline on which to make a last desperate stand before reaching the Potomac. Driven back to that line, Lee would have had no choice other than to begin an immediate withdrawal from the field and a crossing of the Potomac at Boteler's Ford while under attack. At the time of the arrival of Sedgwick's division, the only organized force remaining on the Confederate left was Grigsby's and Early's small brigades and the batteries that Jackson and Stuart had assembled on Hauser's Ridge. Sedgwick's advance across the cornfield quadrangle and into the West Woods had given the Federals possession of the woods—except for the toehold held by Early—and a launch point for continuing the attack to the south and west. The timely arrival of McLaws's division and G. T. Anderson's brigade and their precipitous attack into the woods against Sedgwick had not only returned control of the woods to the Confederate side, but offered Lee the opportunity to reverse the momentum of the battle and to reseize the initiative.

As Sedgwick's division withdrew from the West Woods, the Confederate brigades that had forced the withdrawal continued their attack (Map 2.8: Situation 0940). On the left of the woods Semmes's, Early's, and Barksdale's brigades drove against the withdrawing regiments of Gorman's and Dana's brigades. Semmes's brigade, somewhat in advance of Early and Barksdale, moved north from the Poffenberger farm along the lane leading to the Nicodemus farm. When his regiments reached the woods, however, they separated. The 53rd Georgia on the left continued due north and entered the extreme northern extension of the woods generally following the lane running between the Poffenberger and Nicodemus farms. This brought it up against three Federal regiments, the 82nd New York, 1st Minnesota, and 19th Massachusetts, which had rallied under the command of Colonel Alfred Sully of the 1st Minnesota. This ad hoc brigade took position behind a stone wall just north of the woods, and probably would have been able to maintain its position against the 53rd

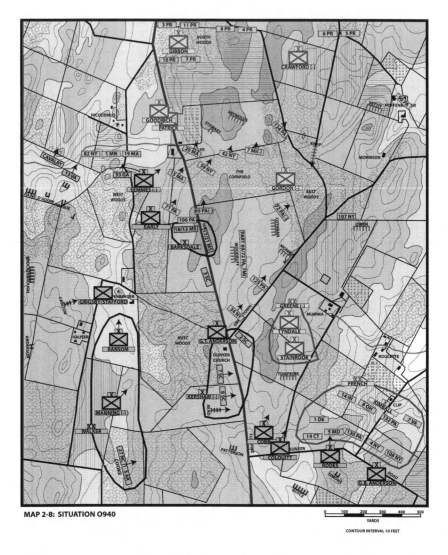

MAP 2-8: SITUATION 0940

had Sully not perceived that "the enemy were turning my right" and withdrawn to a second position at the Nicodemus farm and eventually a third even farther to the north.[41]

Sully's perception that his right was being turned was created by Stuart, who started north with some of the batteries that he and Jackson had collected on Hauser's Ridge, keeping them on the flank of Sedgwick's withdrawing regiments. D'Aquin's two howitzers were repositioned to the right and out of the woods at the north end of the ridge, while two of Poague's guns moved in on their right at the eastern edge of the same woodlot, his third gun being positioned farther to the right. Poague reported that from this position the battery "kept up an advancing fire on the retreating enemy until he found shelter under a number of reserve batteries." Sergeant Moore, who was with the right gun at this point, remembered seeing Stuart "riding to & fro in our front with a line of skirmishers." Raine's battery also came up to the head of the ridge taking position a hundred yards to D'Aquin's left. In addition to these batteries, Stuart also had some of his cavalry and the 13th Virginia supported by a battery of three guns maneuvering against the right of Sully's line. Eventually, two batteries from Walker's division, Captain Thomas B. French's Virginia Battery and Captain James R. Branch's Virginia Field Artillery, would get into position on Nicodemus Heights to the right and rear of Sully's line.[42]

Semmes's three right regiments, the 32nd Virginia, 10th Georgia, and 15th Virginia, on reaching the woods turned to the northeast following the route of withdrawal of the 15th and 20th Massachusetts and 59th New York. This took them through the narrowest part of the woods, and they emerged into the pasture field south of the D. R. Miller farm. They continued to pursue the withdrawing Federal regiments, which now included the remains of Goodrich's and Patrick's brigades, as far as the Miller farmstead. Colonel Edgar B. Montague of the 32nd Virginia reported that here the enemy succeeded "in forming a new line in a strong position behind a stone wall, with batteries raking us on our right and front. We advanced, however, within less than 150 yards of his line, where we were compelled to get under shelter of a barn and hay-stacks, ready to advance again when our flank should be supported." While awaiting support, members of the 10th Georgia searched the buildings of the farmstead finding "in the house and barn a number of the enemy, who surrendered without resistance, [and] who were sent to the rear, prisoners."[43]

Captain William J. Stores, commanding Company I, 32nd Virginia, took position with his company in vicinity of the Miller barn and the haystacks to its right. He recalled that "we captured some prisoners at the barn," although he "did not learn from what regiment they came." He also remembered "distinctly that we had a man killed standing on an old wagon frame between the barn and the stacks." While waiting at the barn with the rest of the brigade for support, Stores saw General Stuart come "from the woods across an open field at full speed to the barn and stacks where we were and asked to what command we belonged and inquired for General Semmes. Just then a battery from the enemies' side opened fire on the barn and stacks. Anxious to hear what so distinguished a General as Stuart would have to say to our brigade commander, I slipped up close and heard him say 'General that battery must be taken.' Semmes replied, 'General, my men have been in the engagement all this morning. Barksdale's brigade is through the woods there unemployed.' Stuart dashed off as if in search of Barksdale. I turned about and found that my right had returned through the woods to a less exposed position, where ammunition was brought and the cartridges boxes were refilled."[44]

Semmes by this time realized that no one was coming to support him in his advanced position and that his troops "having been under an incessant musketry and artillery fire for two hours and twenty minutes were so thoroughly exhausted and their ammunition so nearly expended as to render necessary the order to retire for the purpose of reforming and obtaining a fresh supply of ammunition." Semmes himself remained for a time at the farmstead with Lieutenant Benjamin F. Davis and six men from the 10th Georgia before withdrawing to see to the reassembling of his brigade as a reserve behind the West Woods. Colonel Montague of the 32nd Virginia reported that "after remaining in this position some twenty or thirty-minutes, that there was no support on our right, but, on the contrary, that the enemy was again enfilading us from that point, and that my command at this time was reduced to 60 or 80 men, nearly without ammunition, and that there was no supporting force even in sight, I reluctantly determined to withdraw to a less exposed position, which was accordingly done in tolerable order." The 53rd Georgia to the left of Semmes's other regiments also withdrew when Captain Marshborne, finding the regiment out of ammunition thought it "prudent to fall back to the lines for a new supply."[45]

Early's brigade in the meantime continued its advance through the West Woods somewhat on the right rear of Semmes and due north through the center section of the woods. This took the brigade across the position it had held earlier in the day, when it first returned to the woods and was supporting Grigsby and Stafford. Coming to the northern edge of this section, the brigade came just a little way out into the pasture, but on Early's orders halted and went no farther. Cyrus B. Coiner, commanding a company in the 52nd Virginia, recalled that Early's order was quite imperative, "to halt, or we would be cut off and captured." The brigade, Coiner thought, "was not demoralized, but badly disorganized." In his memoir Early said, "As soon as the enemy had been repulsed, I recalled my regiments and caused them to be re-formed." He then withdrew the brigade back through the woods and posted it in position in the extreme western edge of the woods in front of the Poffenberger farmstead.[46]

Barksdale's brigade was to the right and perhaps a little to the rear of Early's advance moving in a northeasterly direction. After driving the 7th Michigan and 42nd New York out of the woods, the brigade debouched into the pasture field east of the center section of the woods and on to the Hagerstown Pike squarely on the left flank of Howard's brigade. Howard's left regiment, the 72nd Pennsylvania—already somewhat disrupted by the rush of the 7th Michigan and 42nd New York out of the woods on its right front—collapsed immediately, its soldiers streaming off toward the East Woods. The next regiment to the right, the 69th Pennsylvania, did not collapse as did the 72nd, but turned and marched for the North Woods. Barksdale remembered, "At this point I discovered that a very large force of the enemy were attempting to flank me on the left. I therefore ordered the Eighteenth and Thirteenth [Mississippi] to wheel in that direction, and not only succeeded in checking the movement they were making, but put them to flight, and pursued them for a considerable distance." This enemy force was the 106th Pennsylvania, the third regiment from Howard's left. Howard was near this regiment when he was made aware of the attack on his flank by Sumner himself motioning frantically for Howard to change front. Howard was able to get the 106th to come around and take position behind the fence at the northern end of the pasture. From this position they fired several volleys, momentarily checking the advancing Mississippians. The short respite created by the stand of the 106th allowed Howard to get control of the 71st and 69th Pennsylvania on the right and left of the 106th, respectively, and the three were able to make a fighting withdrawal toward the North Woods pursued by the 18th and 13th Mississippi. Barksdale reported, "As we advanced, the ground was covered by the dead and wounded of the enemy. I did not deem it prudent, however, without more support, to advance farther, and, I therefore ordered these regiments to fall back to the woods in front of my first position."[47]

On the right of the 18th and 13th Mississippi, Barksdale's remaining two regiments, the 17th and 21st Mississippi, with the 3rd South Carolina on their right, continued to advance across the open field toward the Hagerstown Pike pursuing the remnants of the broken 7th Michigan, 42nd New York, and 72nd Pennsylvania. On approaching the pike, however, Colonel Nance of the 3rd South Carolina realized that he was leaving some enemy forces "on my right to my rear, which, together with the fire then opened on me from his batteries on their right and which enfiladed my line, rendered my position hazardous." What Nance was seeing to his right was the 125th Pennsylvania and 34th New York withdrawing along Smoketown Road toward the East Woods. The batteries that he referred to were Monroe's and Battery I, 1st U.S. Artillery, under the command of Lieutenant George A. Woodruff. After withdrawing from his advanced position opposite the Dunker Church, Monroe had taken up a new position just outside the East Woods on the north side of Smoketown Road. Woodruff's battery had been brought forward by the Second Corps chief of artillery, Major Francis N. Clarke, to support Sedgwick's advance, and was some two hundred yards in advance of Monroe's right front, only one hundred and fifty yards east of the pike. Nance reported, "No enemy was then visible to me in my front; so I effected a change of front on my first company, which threw my line in a slight hollow that afforded me protection from the artillery fire then raging, and left me in a position to co-operate on the enemy's flank and in any movement against his force in that direction. I directed my men to lie down under cover of the hill in front, while I kept a strict watch for any demonstration of our forces in his front."[48]

As the 3rd South Carolina dropped off into the protective hollow to the right, the 17th and 21st Mississippi "pursued the enemy across the open field." Both regiments reached and crossed the Hagerstown Pike by climbing the post and rail fences and then continued on toward the East Woods. Suddenly, though, Barksdale saw "a very strong force moving to the right and attempting to flank them." This Federal force was essentially the same as seen by Colonel Nance. The 34th New York and the 125th Pennsylvania both rallied after passing Woodruff's battery and reaching Monroe's. In addition, parts of some of the other regiments that had been driven from the West Woods, the 69th and 72nd Pennsylvania and the 7th Michigan, were rallying behind Woodruff. Barksdale reported that with "all of our forces having retired from that part of the field," the 17th and 21st Mississippi "fell back, under protection of a stone fence, in good order." The stone fence that Barksdale referred to was some five hundred yards south of the West Woods bordering the east side of the plowed field from which McLaws's division had originally deployed.[49]

Coming to the support of Semmes, Early, and Barksdale at this time was the brigade of Brigadier General Robert Ransom of Walker's division (Map 2.9: Situation 0950). Walker, it will be recalled, had been posted by Lee early

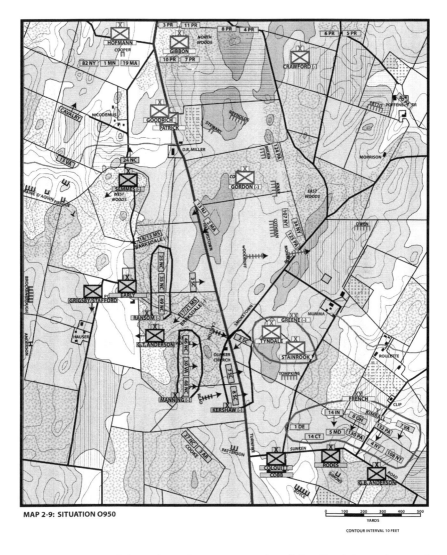

MAP 2-9: SITUATION 0950

on the morning of the 17th to the extreme right of the Confederate line and
had taken position overlooking Snavely's Ford. At the same time that Lee ordered McLaws's division to the left, he also sent a staff officer to recall Walker.
Walker later said, "Soon after 9 A.M., I received orders from Gen. Lee, through
Col. [Armistead L.] Long, of his staff, to hasten to the extreme left, to the
support of Maj.-Gen. Jackson. Hastening forward as rapidly as possible, along
the rear of our entire line of battle, we arrived, soon after 10 o'clock, near the

woods which the commands of Gens. Hood and Early were struggling hero-
ically to hold but gradually and sullenly yielding to the irresistible weight of
overwhelming numbers."[50]

Walker's route of march to the left took him through the town of Sharpsburg and out the Landing (now Mondale) Road, which led north from the
town center. About three quarters of a mile out of town, where the road made
a right angle turn to the left, Walker entered the same plowed field in which
McLaws's division had deployed for its move toward the woods. As McLaws
had done, Walker immediately ordered his regiments into line of battle. Ransom's brigade, which was in the lead, moved forward as the left of the division,
the brigade of Colonel Van H. Manning as the right. Ransom noted, "The line
was formed under a severe fire and in the presence of some of our troops who
had been driven back. As soon as formed, the whole brigade was pushed rapidly forward."[51]

Ransom's route from the plowed field was due north to the Poffenberger
farmstead with the brigade in a column of regiments, the 49th North Carolina
in the lead followed by the 35th, 25th, and 24th North Carolina. As the brigade
reached the Poffenberger farm, Ransom said he "received orders to form to the
right and resist the enemy, who were in possession of a piece of woods." To make
the change of direction, he had his regiments wheel to the right in turn so that
the 49th was on the right of the brigade line with the 35th and 25th to the left
in that order. The 24th, however, which would have been on the extreme left of
the brigade, failed to make the turn. Ransom reported that it "had come upon
the enemy and opened fire, and continued in the first direction upon the left
of Gen. Barksdale's brigade." The other three regiments of the brigade moved
into and through the woods to the east. In his official report, Walker credited
them with advancing "in splendid style, firing and cheering as they went, and
in a few minutes cleared the woods, strewing it with the enemy's dead and
wounded." These descriptions of a fighting advance through the West Woods
by Ransom's regiments, however, are greatly exaggerated, given that Semmes's,
Early's, and Barksdale's brigades had already passed through and cleared the
woods. The 25th and 35th North Carolina stopped and took position as they
reached the eastern edge of the center section of the woods. The 49th North
Carolina on their right also stopped, but it was still inside the most southern
section of the woods, which extended at that point all the way to the pike. All
three regiments were protected by a rock ledge in their front. It was to posi-

tions behind this line that Early's brigade and the 18th and 13th Mississippi of Barksdale's brigade withdrew when they fell back into the woods.[52]

Ransom reported, "At this time I determined to charge across a field in our front and to a woods beyond, which was held by the enemy, but he [the enemy] again approached, in force, to within 100 yards." The Federal force that Ransom encountered coming toward the position of his three regiments in the West Woods was Gordon's brigade of the Twelfth Corps. After the advance of Sedgwick's division from the East Woods this bloodied brigade had withdrawn back into the woods to reorganize. As Sedgwick's division was driven from the West Woods, corps commander Williams ordered Gordon forward to stop the pursuing Confederates. Deeming "it of the utmost importance that my command should move forward with the least possible delay," Gordon sent out the 2nd Massachusetts and 13th New Jersey, which went as far as the Hagerstown Pike and attempted to cross it at the point where it passed over the highest part of the height of land. Here they met such a galling fire laid down by Ransom's concealed and protected regiments that they withdrew to the east side of the ridge, where they were protected and supported by the remaining three regiments of Gordon's brigade. Gordon reported, "So strong was the enemy, that an addition of any force I could command would only have caused further sacrifice, without gain." Consequently, Gordon withdrew his brigade once again to the East Woods.[53]

VI

As already discussed, G. T. Anderson's brigade entered the West Woods behind Barksdale. But where Barksdale followed the ravine to the northeast and then turned north to find the flank of Dana's and Howard's brigades, Anderson maintained a due east course through the woods, where he joined the 2nd South Carolina in driving the 34th New York from its position in the woods north of the Dunker Church. Reaching the eastern edge of the woods where it bordered the Hagerstown Pike, Anderson halted his brigade and did not pursue the 34th New York across the open area. In his official report, he wrote, "By this time the enemy had disappeared from before us." Anderson then proceeded to check his line, but while he was doing so "some mounted officer (unknown) reported the enemy turning our right flank, and ordered the men to fall back." This created considerable confusion as the regiments fell back through the woods. W. H.

Andrews in the 1st Georgia Regulars recalled, "When our brigade was nearly through the woods a staff officer dashed down the line and ordered our line to fall back as the South Carolina boys had failed to move the enemy in their front and we were in a position to be cut off. The line ceased firing[,] about faced and returned to where we jumped the fence." Anderson himself had to rush to catch up with his withdrawing brigade, reporting that "I soon reformed the line and moved to the right, near the first position I had held."[54]

Unlike Anderson's regiments, the 2nd South Carolina did not stop when it reached the eastern edge of the woods. Rather, moving in a northeasterly direction nearly perpendicular to the pike, it passed around both sides of the church—the greater part of it to the south—and began crossing the pike, all the while firing on the retiring 34th New York and 125th Pennsylvania. While climbing the post and rail fences of the turnpike, the regimental commander, Colonel John D. Kennedy was wounded in the foot, and command of the regiment devolved upon Major Franklin Gaillard. Once beyond the pike, the regiment advanced another hundred yards, finally taking position behind a rock ledge in the obtuse angle created by the junction of Smoketown Road and Hagerstown Pike. In this position it continued to harass the retiring Federal infantry and Woodruff's battery, which C. A. C. Waller thought "was getting ready to fight or move." Captain George B. Cuthbert, who as acting field officer was in charge of the right wing of the regiment, determined to continue the advance to the crown of the height of land and re-formed his wing to the right for that purpose. Just as he was starting off, however, a new line of Federal infantry came up from behind the ridge and opened fire on the divided regiment, causing the South Carolinians to precipitously withdraw back across the pike to the safety of the woods, south and west of the church. This new line of Federal infantry was Tyndale's brigade of Greene's division, which, re-supplied with ammunition, had re-formed their line to the right and advanced to the top of the ridge.[55]

Also taking position near the Dunker Church was a three-gun battery from McLaws's division, the Troup Georgia Artillery, under Captain Henry H. Carlton. As the division marched north from the vicinity of Lee's headquarters, this battery had been on its left. As McLaws's brigades deployed and started for the West Woods, Carlton led the battery north along Hauser's Ridge to the vicinity of the Hauser farmstead. There he reported to McLaws for orders. Before

McLaws could give him any, however, General Stuart rode up and asked for the release of Carlton's battery so that Stuart could lead it into the West Woods to hold them until the infantry could arrive. McLaws objected that this would mean sending the battery too far forward without infantry support, but Jackson, who was also present, ordered McLaws to release the battery to Stuart anyway.[56]

Together Stuart and Carlton led the battery northeast across the pasture field to the Poffenburger farm. Near the Poffenburger barn they found an old road that led them through the woods to the Hagerstown Pike at its junction with Smoketown Road, just north of the Dunker Church. Carlton recalled, "Genl. Stuart and I rode up in front of [the] church in advance of [the] battery, and as we stood there on [the] edge of [the] grove, looking across [the] open space, we discovered [a] heavy line of Federal Infantry behind a fence beyond the open space, and counted some two or three batteries of artillery on the ridge just opposite us. As we stood there a courier who accompanied us was killed outright by sharp shooting. Genl. Stuart's horse and mine also were shot." Despite the withering fire, Stuart ordered Carlton to put his three guns into position and "not to let the loss of my men or horses cause me to give up the position, but to hold it until re-inforced by Genl. Kershaw and others." Carlton recalled, "In attempting to take position I lost 18 horses killed and wounded by Federal artillery and finally had to push [the] guns in position by hand."[57]

Coming up on the right of Carlton and the 2nd South Carolina at this point were the remaining two regiments of Kershaw's brigade, the 7th and 8th South Carolina. After passing over and around G. T. Anderson's right as the 2nd had done, the 7th entered the woods behind that regiment. Instead of following the northeasterly course of the 2nd, however, the 7th continued east, keeping the southern edge of the woodlot on its right. This brought the 7th out of the woods about one hundred yards south of the Dunker Church and the 2nd South Carolina. Moving on the right of the 7th, but not entering the woods, was the 8th South Carolina, its left guiding along the wood line. Behind the 8th was the Pulaski (Georgia) Artillery under the command of Captain Read. Read brought with him four guns, one 10-pounder Parrott rifle, one 3-inch Ordnance rifle, and one 6-pounder and one 12-pounder smoothbore. Waller of the 2nd South Carolina remembered that the 7th and 8th South Carolina advanced "in splendid order & condition in column of division . . . to reduce front until ready for extension." As the two regiments approached the pike, the colors of the 2nd South Carolina were advanced to the turnpike fence, unfurled and waved to ensure that it would be recognized as a friendly unit. On reaching the pike, the 7th and 8th South Carolina paused only momentarily before climbing the turnpike fences and continuing into the open field and up the slope beyond. The 2nd South Carolina followed, and moved forward to again cross the pike in the vicinity of the church.[58]

Three hundred yards to the northwest, the 3rd South Carolina was still in its protective hollow with regimental commander Nance watching for any sign of a forward movement of friendly forces to his right front. The movement of the other three regiments of Kershaw's brigade out of the woods near the Dunker Church and their crossing of the Hagerstown Pike was exactly what he was looking for. Nance reported that he immediately advanced his regiment "up the hill across a small road, climbed a fence, and passed to the summit of a hill in a freshly plowed field, where I opened fire upon the enemy." This movement brought the regiment into the acute angle of the junction of the Hagerstown Pike and Smoketown Road.[59]

The movement of Kershaw's regiments, especially the 3rd South Carolina, east of the pike caused Woodruff to withdraw his battery to the edge of the East Woods, where it took the position being vacated by Monroe's battery. Woodruff reported, "A heavy mass of rebel infantry soon moved to our left in such a way as to be almost entirely covered from our fire by the peculiar nature of the ground. A change of front was impracticable from the want of time, and the fact that while protecting one flank we should expose another. Being still without supports, our only course was to retire, and accordingly I fell back about 200 yards to the edge of the woods, where we were supported on the right and could protect our left." The support on Woodruff's right consisted of three newly arrived Twelfth Corps batteries, Battery M, 1st New York Light Artillery, under the command of Captain George W. Cothran; Battery E, Pennsylvania Light Artillery, under the command of Captain Joseph M. Knap; and 10th Battery, New York Light Artillery, under the command of Captain John T. Bruen. These batteries were also supported by four regiments of infantry: the rallied 34th New York, 125th Pennsylvania, and 107th New York, and the 124th Pennsylvania.[60]

Once across the turnpike, the 2nd, 7th, and 8th South Carolina found themselves facing Tyndale's line on the crest of the height of land just to the east of them (Map 2.10: Situation 1000). This line, however, appeared to be withdrawing, so Kershaw ordered his regiments to charge and for Read's battery to sup-

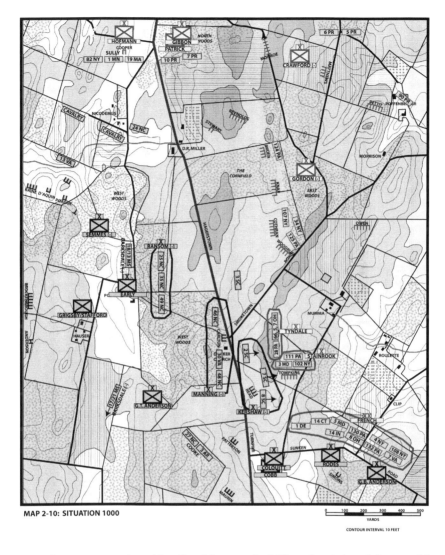

MAP 2-10: SITUATION 1000

0 100 200 300 400 500
YARDS

CONTOUR INTERVAL 10 FEET

port the movement by taking "position on the hill to the right of the wood." Not all of Kershaw's four regiments, however, were able to execute the order to charge. For the 3rd South Carolina any additional move forward would mean advancing directly into the fields of fire of both Cothran's and Woodruff's batteries and their infantry supports, so the 3rd remained in position just east of the pike, if indeed it received the order to charge at all. South of Smoketown Road, the 7th South Carolina led the way. Its commander, Colonel D. Wyatt

Aiken, had been wounded as the regiment left the woods, so the charge was led by Major William C. White. The 7th was supported on its right by the 8th South Carolina, and on its left by the 2nd.[61]

As H. W. Addison remembered it, the 7th South Carolina charged "right over the crest of the hill . . . where we found the Federals, who had fallen back under it, with innumerable Cannon and numbers of lines of Infantry ready and waiting for us. So rapid was the Federal fire of grape, canister and cannon balls of large size together with infantry fire, that we lost in killed and wounded about three fourths of our number in fifteen minutes." The Federal artillery and infantry, he thought, "belched forth such destruction as I had never seen before, though no novice in the business." Addison himself was wounded by grape shot and had to leave the field, and one of those killed was Major White, who Kershaw credited with leading the regiment to "within 30 yards of one of the batteries, driving the men from the guns."[62]

The Federal forces encountered by the 7th as it crested the ridge were the two brigades of Greene's division that were indeed not withdrawing but waiting for the charge. Major Orrin J. Crane of the 7th Ohio, who would write the official report of the First Brigade for the wounded Tyndale, said that when Kershaw's regiments left the West Woods and began advancing toward his position, "we received orders to fall back under the cover of the hill, and awaited the advance of the enemy; when within a short range our troops were quickly thrown forward to the top of the hill, where we poured into their advancing columns volley after volley. So terrific was the fire of our men that the enemy fell like grass before the mower; so deadly was the fire that the enemy retired in great disorder, they not being able to rally their retreating forces."[63]

Still in position on the left of Greene's two brigades was Tompkins's battery of the Second Corps. Tompkins's position was well below the crest of the ridge, so he did not see Kershaw's regiments coming. In his official report Tompkins wrote, "I was not aware of their approach until the head of the column gained the brow of a hill, about 60 yards from the right gun of the battery. The pieces were immediately obliqued to the right, and a sharp fire of canister opened upon them causing them to retire in confusion, leaving the ground covered with the dead and wounded, and abandoning one of their battle-flags." What Tompkins left out of his report was what Kershaw had included in his, that the 7th South Carolina came so close to Tompkins's guns that his three right pieces had to be abandoned for a time. Theodore Reichardt, a member of the battery, recorded in his diary, "There was a time when half of the battery was compelled to cease firing. The order, 'limber to the rear,' was given; but, fortunately, not heard, as it would have resulted in the certain capture of the battery. At that critical turn, Captain Tompkins called on our infantry support to advance and do their duty, which they did, enabling us to load again. The enemy, after failing to take the battery, retreated slowly."[64]

As the 7th South Carolina began to recoil from its initial encounter with Greene's brigades, the 2nd and 8th South Carolina came to its support. These three regiments of Kershaw's brigade established themselves just below the crest of the height of land to resist any further advance of the Federal line (Map 2.11: Situation 1010). Joining them at this point were two regiments of Manning's brigade of Walker's division. Manning's brigade was to be the right of Walker's division as it advanced into the West Woods. Accordingly, Manning with three of the brigade's five regiments, the 46th North Carolina, 30th Virginia, and 48th North Carolina in that order, followed Ransom turning east on Ransom's right flank and advancing through the West Woods toward the Dunker Church behind Kershaw's brigade. The remaining two regiments, the 27th North Carolina and 3rd Arkansas under the direction of Colonel John R. Cooke of the 27th, were sent by Walker east through the cornfield south of the woods "to hold the open space between the woods and Longstreet's left."[65]

Manning with the three remaining regiments arrived in the vicinity of the Dunker Church and found Kershaw just as he was about to order his regiments to charge toward the height of land. Kershaw told Manning that he needed a regiment to fill the gap on the left of his brigade between the 3rd and the 2nd South Carolina, and for the remainder of Manning's brigade to go in "to the right of my brigade." To fill the gap on the left, Manning sent Colonel Edward D. Hall with the 46th North Carolina, which was guided into position about two hundred yards north of the church by Lieutenant Y. J. Pope, adjutant of the 3rd South Carolina. On arriving at the edge of the woods, Hall reported finding "the enemy in heavy force on an elevation, distant about 200 yards, with a battery of artillery in position on the crest of the hill. Between the enemy and the woods were two heavy panel fences, running obliquely. In face of such difficulties I thought it inexpedient to charge farther. I therefore placed my regiment behind a breastwork of rails, which I found just beyond the woods, in short range of the enemy, and commenced firing, my men being well protected."[66]

Manning then ordered his remaining two regiments, the 30th Virginia and

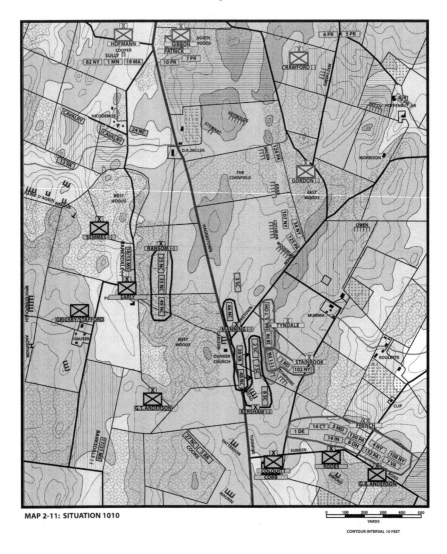

MAP 2-11: SITUATION 1010

0   100   200   300   400   500
YARDS

CONTOUR INTERVAL 10 FEET

the 48th North Carolina, to follow Kershaw's regiments in a charge across the pike and up the slope toward the height of land. As Lieutenant Knox of the 30th remembered it, Manning "came tearing up on horseback & waving his sword around his head & clearing the fence at a bound called to us . . . to follow him & where was the Confederate soldier then that would have held back[?] We charged over the fence & across the field with a yell fixing bayonets at a full run." The heavy post and rail fence of the Hagerstown Pike proved to be no problem for the 30th. "Our boys went flying over it scarcely considering it an obstacle. Oh, it was a glorious sight, our flag [carried] to the front by Segt. Haney, and there we stood, a handful against a host. The enemy were in massive columns in our front & two twelve gun batteries enfilading our advance." As the regiment charged up the slope, Knox saw what he believed to be four Federal regiments, one in front of the other, rise up in front. "Our men were halted and then and there poured [out] a fire as cool and calm . . . as if on parade." As Knox watched, the regimental colors fell "from the hands of the last of our colour sergeants[,] 9 all killed or wounded." Knox himself rushed to pick up the color and "wave it so our boys could see we were there[,] in [the] meantime our men were falling every minute."[67]

In leading the charge of these two regiments, Manning suffered a serious wound that would force him from the field. He rode over to the 46th North Carolina to inform Colonel Hall that as the ranking officer he was to take command of the brigade. For Hall, this was problematic because he was now so far to the left that he had lost contact with the other regiments of the brigade. He would learn later of the charge of the 30th Virginia and the 48th North Carolina and as brigade commander would report that these two regiments "in attempting to charge over the fences and up the ascent, found themselves so massed up that they were compelled to lie down in the face of the enemy and under a withering fire."[68]

At this point, almost all of the regiments of Tyndale's and Stainrook's brigades were on the ridge pouring fire into the regiments of Kershaw's and Manning's brigades. Tompkins brought at least two of his guns to the crest of the ridge, reporting that the "enemy now opened a fire upon us from a battery in front, and also from one on the right, near the white schoolhouse. Two guns were directed to reply to the battery on the right, while the fire of the rest was directed upon the guns in front, which were silenced in about twenty minutes, and one of their caissons blown up." The battery to Tompkins's front was Read's, while the one at the schoolhouse was Carlton's. Both of these batteries suffered the loss of significant numbers of men and horses. McLaws reported that Read was "exposed to such a severe fire, Gen. Kershaw ordered it back after losing 14 officers and men and 16 horses. Another battery, Capt. Carlton's, . . . was so severely cut up in a short time by the direct and cross-fires of numerous batteries that I ordered it to retire." Carlton recalled that he "succeeded in firing 109 rounds" before "all three of my guns were disabled by Federal artillery."

His "loss in killed and wounded was very heavy," but he remained proud of the fact that "I succeeded in taking all of my guns off [the] field, also all of my dead and wounded." One of the dead he had to evacuate was his own brother.[69]

The infantry regiments of Kershaw's brigade had also had enough (Map 2.12: Situation 1020). The first to withdraw was the 7th South Carolina, which, as already noted, had lost three quarters of its strength in just a few minutes of combat. It was followed quickly by the 2nd on its left. On the right of the brigade, Captain Duncan McIntyre, commanding Company H of the 8th South Carolina, recalled that his regiment had not been east of the pike for very long when someone "announced that the left of the brigade was giving way. On looking down the line I saw that the other Regts., had been repulsed, and were hurrying in, in confusion to the cover of the woods. The 8th then fell rapidly back also." Colonel Nance of the 3rd South Carolina across Smoketown Road from the rest of the brigade noted that "under the heavy fire of artillery and the press of fresh troops, our line on my right, that just before advanced in such admirable style, fell back so far that I retired to the road I had just crossed. There I halted and fired for a time, until a farther retirement required me to fall back to the hollow in which I had before changed my front."[70]

The three regiments of Kershaw's brigade that crossed the pike near the Dunker Church, although repulsed and forced to withdraw to the woods in some confusion, rallied and re-formed once back in the woods. As C. A. C. Waller remembered it, the brigade remained in the woods for "sometime not pursued there by infantry but catching it hot from artillery." McLaws in his official report referred to the artillery fire as "an incessant storm of shot and shell, grape and canister, but the loss inflicted by the artillery was comparatively very small. Fortunately, the woods were on the side of a hill, the main slope of which was toward us, with numerous ledges of rocks along it." Despite this relatively "safe" position, and Waller's recollection, these regiments tarried only briefly in the woods before Kershaw ordered a further withdrawal, taking them some five hundred yards southwest of the West Woods, where the "lines were reorganized behind the fences, near where they entered the fight, and their exhausted cartridge-boxes replenished."[71]

The 3rd South Carolina was also forced to abandon its position in the protective hollow, withdrawing into and then beyond the woods, but it did not join the other regiments of Kershaw's brigade. Colonel Nance reported: "I sent officers out to ascertain the position of our forces. They could find no force, and

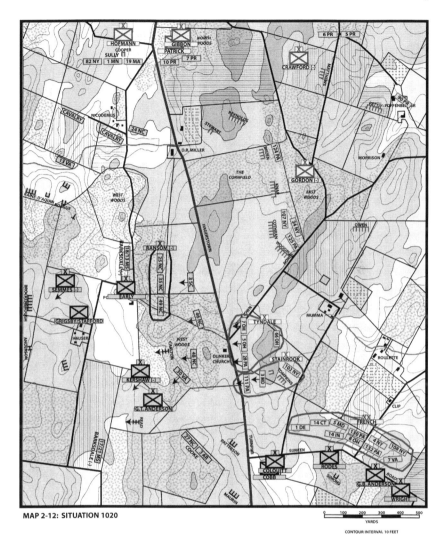

MAP 2-12: SITUATION 1020

CONTOUR INTERVAL 10 FEET

I retired into the open field near where our line was first formed. There Lieut. W[illiam]. D. Farley, aide-de-camp [to Major General Stuart], informed me that I was without proper support, and advised . . . me to take up my position there behind a rail fence, running about parallel to the woods. I then acquainted both Brig.-Gen. Kershaw and Maj.-Gen. McLaws with my position, and requested orders. I was directed to remain in my position, and, at my request, Gen. McLaws assisted in replenishing my cartridge-boxes." The rail fence be-

hind which the 3rd took position was just south of the Hauser farmstead, but it
would not prove to be a comfortable position. Lieutenant Pope, the regimental
adjutant, explained, "Here the Federal artillery concentrated one of the heaviest and most prolonged firing of shot and shell I can recall as coming from
Field batteries. I recall seeing round cannon balls dancing over the ground!"[72]

Kershaw's regiments were not immediately pursued into the woods by Greene's
regiments because after their withdrawal, the 30th Virginia and 48th North
Carolina continued to hold the line for a short time. Watching from his position north of the Dunker Church, Colonel Hall of the 46th North Carolina reported that beyond the pike these two regiments "suffered severely, and
in a short time were compelled to retire. Owing to the nature of the ground,
their maneuvers were accompanied by some disorder." Lieutenant Knox in the
30th Virginia remembered that the enemy at this point "poured a perfect hail
of bullets into us, mortal man could not stand it," so "Col. Chew ordered us
to fall back."[73]

Unlike Kershaw's regiments, with Manning wounded and out of action and
Colonel Hall too far to the left to effectively exercise command of the brigade,
the 30th Virginia and 48th North Carolina were left on their own. For a short
time, the 30th sheltered behind the stone ledge across the pike from the Dunker
Church, but was soon forced to continue its withdrawal into the woods. There
Lieutenant Knox remembered "having no orders & no one in command [of
the brigade, we] fell still farther back—having only some 74 men left & nearly
everyone was helping off some wounded friend & comrade." Eventually, the
30th withdrew some three hundred yards south and a little west of the woods.
Knox saw nothing of the other regiments of the brigade, and assumed that "the
rest of our brigade must have remained in those Dunker Church woods."[74]

The 48th North Carolina did, perhaps, remain a little longer in the woods
than the 30th Virginia, but certainly not long. The 48th retired into the woods
about the same time as the Virginians, but very quickly left the woods altogether, taking up position in the plowed field about one hundred yards behind G. T. Anderson's brigade. Colonel Hall was aware of the withdrawal of
the 30th Virginia and 48th North Carolina, but had no idea as to where they
had gone. He admitted in the brigade official report, "I saw no more of these
regiments during the day." Still, he attached no blame to their conduct. "All
things considered, that portion of the Forty-eighth Regiment and the Thirti-

eth Virginia behaved as well as any troops could who were in such an exposed and fatal position."[75]

Their withdrawal, however, left Hall and his regiment in a precarious position. He reported, "The falling back of the Forty-eighth North Carolina and Thirtieth Virginia, on the immediate right of the Forty-sixth North Carolina, left a wide gap open, which the enemy began at once to take advantage of in order to re-enter the woods, though a galling fire was kept up by that regiment on their advancing line until I deemed it unsafe for that one regiment, unsupported, to remain in position while the enemy was massing upon its right and rear. The Forty-sixth, therefore, fell back, by my instruction, in good order and without the loss of a single straggler."[76]

VII

The Federal troops advancing on the right and rear of the 48th North Carolina were five regiments from Greene's division (Map 2.13: Situation 1030). Greene reported that as the enemy fell back, "the division advanced, driving the enemy from the woods near the church and occupying the woods." Some of the regimental commanders reported pushing clear through the woods in pursuit of the withdrawing Confederates. Major John Collins of the 5th Ohio claimed, "We followed them, driving them through the field into the woods in rear, and out of the woods into the corn still farther beyond," while Lieutenant Colonel Joseph M. Sudsburg of the 3rd Maryland remembered charging through the woods and driving the enemy out.[77]

If indeed some of Greene's regiments did make their way completely through the woods, it was only to be quickly recalled to take position approximately in the center of the lower section of the woods about two hundred yards west of the Dunker Church. Greene had Tyndale form three of his regiments in line facing west, while two regiments from Stainrook's brigade went into line on their right at a right angle facing south. These two regiments were along the very southern edge of the woods, their line extending back to the Hagerstown Pike. Greene realized that the "position of the division in the advanced wood was very critical. We were in advance of our line on the right and left of us." What Greene did not realize, however, was that his five regiments were alone in the West Woods. He had seen Sedgwick's division enter the woods about an

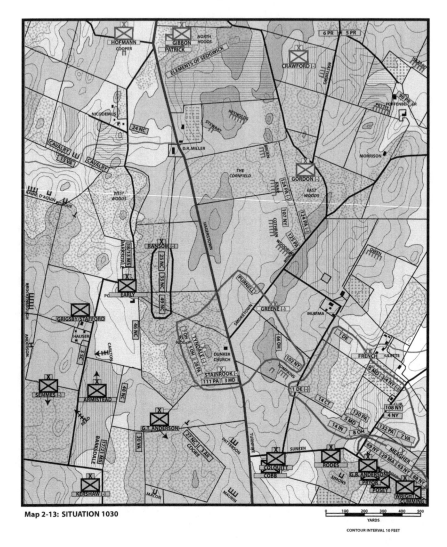

Map 2-13: SITUATION 1030

0 100 200 300 400 500
YARDS

CONTOUR INTERVAL 10 FEET

hour and a half earlier, but because of his occupation with the engagement on the ridge opposite the Dunker Church that began about thirty minutes after that, he had not seen Sedgwick's division leave the woods. At this point he still believed Sedgwick was in the woods to his right.

The entry of Greene's division into the West Woods did not reverse the success achieved by McLaws's division and the brigades of Early and G. T. Anderson in driving Sedgwick's division from the woods, but it did, temporarily at least, remove from Lee's hands the initiative and momentum that the success of the attack promised to restore. Greene entered the woods with just five regiments that had already been involved in several hours of intensive combat and that were again running low on ammunition. Even if Greene had completely understood his situation and the position of Confederate forces in and around the woods, he did not have sufficient strength to effectively clear and secure the woods.

To be sure, despite the losses suffered in driving Sedgwick from the West Woods, the Confederate left had sufficient force to at least drive Greene out and secure the woods. Ransom with three fresh regiments was only two hundred yards from Greene's right flank, although apparently Ransom was no more aware of Greene than Greene was of Ransom. Along the western edge of the woods were two regiments of Barksdale's brigade, Early's brigade, the 46th North Carolina, and G. T. Anderson's brigade. South of the woods Colonel Cooke still held a cornfield with two regiments of Manning's otherwise scattered brigade. In addition, the brigade of Brigadier General Lewis A. Armistead of Major General Richard H. Anderson's division was just arriving in the plowed field southwest of the woods as reinforcement for the left. Backing up all of this infantry were the batteries of artillery that had been assembled by Jackson and Stuart on Hauser's Ridge and the two batteries from Walker's division on Nicodemus Heights.[78]

Indeed, the problem of regaining the initiative and maintaining momentum no longer rested with the situation on the left in the vicinity of the West Woods; the problem was now the center of the Confederate line, a thousand yards to the south and east of the woods. Here, positioned in a sunken farm lane that formed a naturally entrenched position, some eight brigades primarily from D. H. Hill's and R. H. Anderson's divisions were being hard-pressed by the remaining two divisions of the Second Army Corps.

3

The Sunken Road

I

THE SUNKEN FARM LANE ON ANTIETAM Battlefield, known now as the Bloody Lane, was at the time a simple country pathway that had served area farmers for years as a byway connecting the Boonsboro Pike east of Sharpsburg with the Hagerstown Pike north of town. Using it allowed heavily laden farm wagons and their teams of draft horses to avoid going through the eastern end of the town. An unimproved dirt road, the lane had a surface that was constantly being cut and churned by wagon wheels and horse hooves, the dirt being washed away by rains, until in many places the lane was as much a trench as it was a pathway. Although the farm lane was made up of a number of sections that changed its direction, sometimes radically, sometimes only slightly, it consisted of two basic segments. The easternmost segment started at the Boonsboro Pike about a thousand yards from the edge of town and ran north and northwest, with several sharp angle turns for a distance of eight hundred yards. At that point, the northern segment began with a right angle turn that set the course of the lane generally west for a thousand yards to the point where it connected with the Hagerstown Pike about six hundred yards south of the Dunker Church.

The road had figured in Confederate deployments ever since the brigades of D. H. Hill's division began arriving at the Middle Bridge on Boonsboro Pike on the morning of the 15th. The first two of his brigades, Colquitt's and Rodes's, crossed the bridge before daylight that morning and marched on through Sharpsburg. Colquitt's continued on toward Blackford's Ford on the Potomac, while Rodes's brigade halted just west of the town "long enough to get a scanty meal and to gather stragglers." The remaining three brigades, McRae's, Ripley's, and G. B. Anderson's, had stopped during the night at Keedysville for a few hours rest, and did not cross the bridge until just past daybreak. When they reached the junction of the Sunken Road and Boonsboro Pike, General Longstreet ordered them into position. McRae's brigade was sent north along the Sunken Road to the northern segment, where it went into position facing north between the point where the road turned west and its junction with the Roulette farm lane. Ripley's brigade was halted along the Boonsboro Pike a few hundred yards beyond the entrance to the Sunken Road and took position on the high ground just north of the pike. Hill's last brigade, G. B. Anderson's, took position at the junction of the Sunken Road and Boonsboro Pike. At that point, Rodes and Colquitt were recalled. Rodes marched back through the town and went into position on McRae's right facing east on a plateau of high ground in front of the northernmost part of the eastern section of the Sunken Road. Colquitt, however, on reaching the town center, turned north on the Hagerstown Pike to take position on McRae's left facing north along the westernmost extension of the Sunken Road from Roulette's farm lane to the Hagerstown Pike. The guns of the King William Virginia Artillery under Captain Thomas H. Carter were then posted on the high ground at the point where the Sunken Road made its right angle turn to the west, covering the front of both McRae's and Rodes's brigades. At this point, Hill's division constituted the left of the Army of Northern Virginia.[1]

At about 8:00 A.M., Stephen D. Lee's artillery battalion arrived from the vicinity of Keedysville and five of his six batteries were placed on the high ground east of the Sunken Road in front of Rodes's and G. B. Anderson's brigades in what Lee later called "the best artillery position over-looking the ground across Antietam creek." As the infantry of Richardson's division of the Second Corps began to appear on the hills east of Antietam Creek at about 1:00 P.M., Lee opened on them with his long-range guns, two 3-inch Ordnance rifles from Captain William W. Parker's Richmond Battery, two 10-pounder Parrott rifles from Lieutenant William Elliott's Brooks South Carolina Battery, and one 3-inch Ordnance rifle from Captain Tyler C. Jordan's Bedford Virginia Artillery. The effect, Lee noted in his official report, was to cause "them to move back," but it also caused the Federals to bring up their long-range guns "which they opened on our guns whenever they fired on their infantry." The artillery duel, as Rodes remembered it, brought the brigades of D. H. Hill "under an occasional artillery fire."[2]

Late in the afternoon, as more and more of the Army of the Potomac arrived on the opposite side of Antietam Creek, General Lee determined to further strengthen his left. He ordered General Hood to take his two brigades, his own Texas Brigade under Colonel William Wofford of the 18th Georgia and the brigade under Colonel Evander M. Law of the 4th Alabama, which had been positioned on the right near the Rohrbach Bridge, and reposition them north of Colquitt's brigade in the vicinity of the Dunker Church. The march of Hood's brigades from the south to the north was visible to the Federal guns east of the creek, and caused them to intensify the fire directed toward the Confederate left, including the positions occupied by Hill's brigades. Colonel Wofford reported, "While we were moving to this position, the enemy opened a heavy fire upon us from their long-range guns, which was continued after we were in position." Hood's movement and the extension of the Confederate left as well as the concentration of Federal long-range artillery fire caused S. D. Lee during the night to move his batteries, except for Captain George V. Moody's, Madison (Louisiana) Light Artillery, from their positions on the high ground east of the Sunken Road to "a sheltered position on the Sharpsburg and Hagerstown pike, in front of [the Dunker] Church."[3]

On the 16th, fire from the Federal batteries east of Antietam Creek continued to be directed at Hill's brigades. Hill reported "a great deal of artillery firing during the forenoon," while Ripley remembered that "from about 9 o'clock until nightfall we were subjected to an annoying artillery fire." As Lee's strength continued to grow with the arrival southwest of Sharpsburg of Jackson's divisions, Hill's brigades remained in position along the lane and, together with Hood's two brigades in the West Woods, continued to constitute the left of the army. During the late afternoon, however, the left flank was suddenly threatened by the corps of Joseph Hooker, which had crossed the creek at about 2 P.M. in the vicinity of the upper bridge and advanced north and west to gain Smoketown Road just south of the George Line farm. Concerned that this might signal an advance by the Federals along the Hagerstown Pike, Hood sent companies from the 2nd Mississippi, 6th North Carolina, and 4th Texas to form a skirmish line along the southern edge of a plowed field just north of the D. R. Miller farm stretching from the Hagerstown Pike to the northernmost extension of the East Woods. Hill supported Hood's move by sending forward the four guns of Captain John Lane's Irwin (Georgia) Artillery from Lieutenant Colonel Allen S. Cutts's Artillery Battalion, which went into position along with two other guns on the knoll just to the east of the Hagerstown Pike and south of Miller's cornfield. Hill also sent forward to the East Woods several companies from Colquitt's brigade to act as a battalion of skirmishers. They extended Hood's skirmish line by taking position in the woods along its northern face just to the east of Smoketown Road. To the northeast of this line in the vicinity of the Samuel Poffenberger Woods was the 9th Virginia Cavalry with a section from Captain John Pelham's Virginia Battery, which had detected and was parrying Hooker's movement.[4]

Learning of the threat to the north, Lee ordered to the vicinity of the Dunker Church the divisions of J. R. Jones and Lawton of Jackson's command and Jackson himself to take command of the now extended left. As the Federal force continued to advance and the 9th Virginia Cavalry along with Pelham's section of artillery fell back south of the East Woods, Hood moved all of Wofford's and Law's brigades to the support of his skirmishers. As Hooker's leading brigade, Brigadier General Truman Seymour's, advanced down Smoketown Road, it was able to push back the line of skirmishers and gain a lodgment in the East Woods. Hood responded by shifting his brigades to the right with Law entering the woods to confront and stop Seymour's advance. Heavy skirmishing continued in the woods until darkness settled in at about 6:30 P.M.[5]

At about 8:00 P.M. Hood went to Lee to request that his brigades be relieved, at least temporarily, so that he might bring up his supply wagons and issue rations, which Hood's men had been without for three days. Lee demurred in Hood's request because he knew of no brigades with which he could relieve Hood, but told Hood to take his request to Jackson. With some difficulty, Hood finally found Jackson sleeping under a tree. Jackson acquiesced to Hood's request and about 10:00 P.M. the brigades under Colonels Marcellus Douglass and James Walker of Lawton's division replaced Hood's two brigades with Douglass's regiments covering the open area west of the southern extreme of the East Woods and Walker's extending the line to the southeast across the plowed field just in front of the lane to the Mumma farm from Smoketown Road. As Walker was putting his regiments in line, he found that he was supported in his rear by Ripley's brigade, which a little earlier in the evening had been ordered forward by Lee from its position along the Boonsboro Pike to one just south of the Mumma farmstead. Ripley reported that it was here that "the troops rested on their arms during the night of the 16th." The remainder of D. H. Hill's brigades did the same in their positions along the Sunken Road.[6]

II

As the battle opened on the morning of the 17th, it would be Ripley's brigade in its advanced position on the Mumma farm that would be the first of Hill's

division to become engaged. At first light, Ripley reported, the Federal batteries "on the eastern bank of the Antietam opened a severe enfilading fire on
the troops of my command, the position which we had been ordered to occupy being in full view of nearly all of his batteries. This fire inflicted serious
loss before the troops were called into positive action, the men lying under it,
without flinching, for over an hour, while the enemy plied his guns unceasingly."
Colonel William L. DeRosset, commanding the 3rd North Carolina, recalled
that "one of the first guns, from a point near which McClellan made his headquarters, fired a shell which fell just in front of the brigade, wounding some 16
men and officers of the 3rd." Ripley went on to note that it was during this period that the Mumma farm buildings "were set on fire to prevent them being
made use of by the enemy."[7]

As Ripley's men suffered under the fire of Federal artillery, Hooker's First
Army Corps began its attack on the Confederate left (Map 3.1: Situation 0620).
Walker's skirmishers were forced from the East Woods and formed with the
brigade's defensive line of battle in the plowed field just north of the Mumma
farm lane, approximately two hundred yards ahead of Ripley's brigade. Walker's
line was extended west to the Hagerstown Pike by Douglass's brigade backed
up by Hays's, and then beyond the pike and into the West Woods by the brigades of J. R. Jones's division. The fighting for the cornfield quadrangle between
Hooker's corps and Jackson's command continued back and forth for more than
an hour before Jackson's brigades became used up and gradually began a withdrawal into and beyond the West Woods. At about 7:00 A.M., to fill the void,
Jackson called on Hood, whose two brigades were still in the woods behind the
Dunker Church and were just beginning to cook their recently arrived rations.
Hood formed these brigades in line across the lower end of the quadrangle to
Ripley's left, and charged north, driving Hooker's brigades to the northern end
of Miller's cornfield.

Just as Hood's division was beginning its charge, D. H. Hill sent orders to
Ripley to advance and support Hood on his right. Ripley wrote, "The troops
sprung to their arms with alacrity and moved forward through the burning
buildings in our front." The reality, however, was that the brigade became divided by the conflagration at the Mumma farmstead. Because of the intense
heat generated by the burning buildings and haystacks, the 3rd North Carolina on the right of the brigade and at least several companies of the 1st North
Carolina to its left had to pass well to the east of the farmstead, while the re-

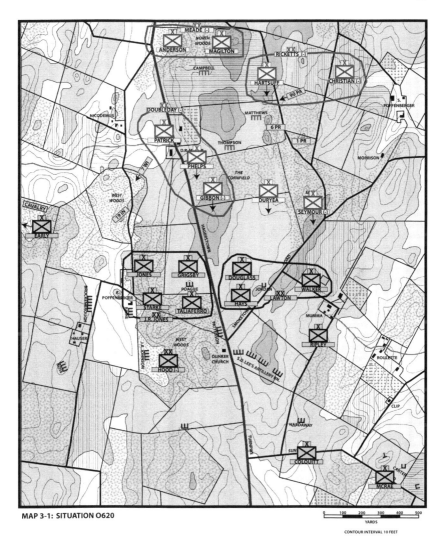

MAP 3-1: SITUATION 0620

0 100 200 300 400 500
YARDS

CONTOUR INTERVAL 10 FEET

mainder of the brigade rounded the west side. Major Stephen D. Thruston of the 3rd North Carolina remembered that the regiment had to climb "a high rail fence into and out of an apple orchard," and then continue to "a third high fence on the outside and northeast of Mumma's, to get out of his farm." At this third fence, Colonel DeRosset halted the regiment to await orders. He recalled that while in this position "there was a group of officers[,] evidently a Gen'l. and his staff, who rode out of the East Woods some 500 yards distant."

DeRosset immediately seized a rifle from one of his men and, resting it on the top rail of the fence, took careful aim at an officer on a white horse "being the most conspicuous object in the group." He remembered that "upon firing the group disappeared at once, going whence they came."[8]

While the 3rd North Carolina was halted at this fence line, Ripley, who had accompanied the regiment around the east side of the Mumma farm, was wounded. He reported, "While engaged in reforming the brigade, I received a shot in the neck, which disabled me, and the troops moved forward under command of Col. Doles, of the Fourth Georgia Regiment." As Colonel George Doles worked to gain control of the brigade, its advance toward the East Woods continued with the 3rd North Carolina obliquing to the left to reconnect with the rest of the brigade. When the brigade had covered about half of the distance to the woods, Hill appeared in person and, ordering it to change direction by the left flank, led the brigade in this column of fours formation around the southernmost point of the woods, across Smoketown Road, and then west across the quadrangle toward the Hagerstown Pike. When the last regiment, the 3rd North Carolina, crossed Smoketown Road, Hill had the brigade face front and advance across the pasture land toward D. R. Miller's now infamous cornfield, just as most of the regiments of Hood's division were withdrawing to the West Woods. That left only three regiments behind in the East Woods, the 4th Alabama and 5th Texas of Hood's division, and the 21st Georgia of Lawton's division, all under the command of Captain W. M. Robbins of the 4th Alabama (Map 3.2: Situation 0730).[9]

In this advance, the left regiments of the brigade, the 4th and 44th Georgia and a part of the 1st North Carolina, wheeled left toward the Hagerstown Pike, driving off the 19th Indiana of Gibbon's brigade and three regiments of Patrick's brigade, which had taken a flanking position there against Hood's advance. This segment of Ripley's brigade then wheeled back to the right to engage the 9th Pennsylvania Reserves of Lieutenant Colonel Robert Anderson's brigade on the high ground just south of the cornfield. The 9th Reserves, however, stubbornly held its ground and halted the forward movement of this segment of Ripley's brigade. In the meantime, the right of the brigade—the rest of the 1st North Carolina and the 3rd North Carolina—continued on toward the cornfield to engage two more of Anderson's regiments, the 11th and 12th Pennsylvania Reserves, which were arrayed in echelon deep inside the cornfield to the right and rear of the 9th. Of this engagement, Colonel DeRosset remem-

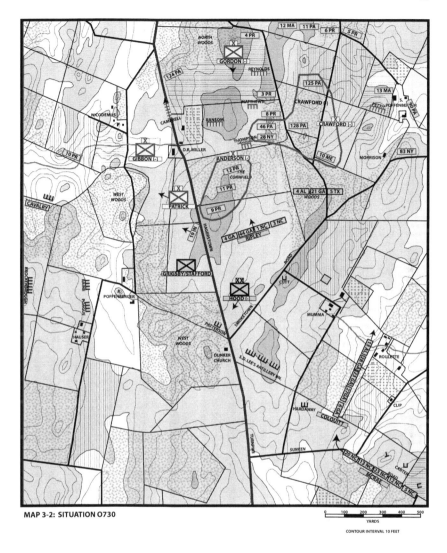

MAP 3-2: SITUATION 0730

0 100 200 300 400 500
YARDS

CONTOUR INTERVAL 10 FEET

bered that his regiment's "smooth bore muskets with the buck and ball cartridge did most excellent service being at very close quarters not over 100 yards from the first line of Yankees." The fire from the 1st and 3rd North Carolina drove the 11th and 12th Reserves from the cornfield and, according to Major Thruston of the 3rd, silenced a battery of six howitzers in the open field just north of the cornfield, about 100 yards west of the woods. These regiments then made a quarter wheel to the left and joined the 4th and 44th Georgia in attacking the

9th Reserves, which abandoned the high ground and withdrew to just beyond the northern end of the cornfield to take position on the right of the 12th Reserves. The 4th and 44th Georgia then occupied the high ground.[10]

As the 3rd North Carolina, which was arrayed in line from northeast to southwest with its right flank at the southern edge of the cornfield, participated in the attack on the 9th Reserves, Colonel DeRosset suddenly saw what he believed was a "brigade in column of battalion" come out "from the East Woods, on my right, in the cornfield" and halt "within 75 yards of my right and rear" (Map 3.3: Situation 0745). The column threatening the 3rd North Carolina was not a brigade, but the very new and very large 128th Pennsylvania of Crawford's brigade of the Twelfth Corps. DeRosset wrote, "Immediately upon discovering the flanking column I applied to Doles for orders, but found him so much interested in his command and ups [*sic*] set by the death of his Major, that declining to give me orders, instructed me to do as I thought best." What DeRosset thought best was to meet this flanking threat by changing "front to rear on [the] 10th Co." He chose this maneuver "to avoid the possibility of anything like a stampede on being faced to the rear to execute the order." Upon completion of the change of front, the regimental line of battle would be facing the threatening column. While carrying out this maneuver, however, the regiment "lost most heavily in officers," was thrown into some confusion and began to give ground. Among those wounded was DeRosset himself, and command of the regiment devolved on Major Thruston, who rushed to DeRosset's side, retrieving the pistol that he dropped as he fell. Thruston remembered that he then "looked to the colors, and saw the Corporal of the State Colors, facing to the rear." Thruston ordered the soldier "to face about, in which he was instantly killed, I caught the colors and called upon the Officers to assist in steadying the men."[11]

Seeing reinforcements coming up on the right rear, Thruston decided to order a charge against the 128th Pennsylvania, with the intent of driving it off and possibly capturing the silent guns in the pasture field (Map 3.4: Situation 0800). In this charge, the 3rd North Carolina was joined by a part of the 1st North Carolina that had become entangled with the ranks of the 3rd. Though wounded and in the process of being carried from the field, Colonel DeRosset remembered having the "satisfaction of seeing as grand a charge, by my regiment, under Lt. Col. S.D. Thruston, as brave and intelligent an officer as any in the Army—as any made upon an enemy anywhere." He believed that it "formed

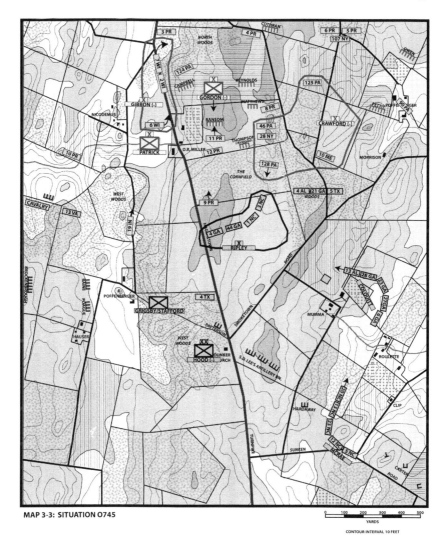

MAP 3-3: SITUATION 0745

0 100 200 300 400 500
YARDS

CONTOUR INTERVAL 10 FEET

a picture in which any soldier would feel proud to have a place." Thruston re-membered that "this charge of the 3rd N. C. went entirely through the corn-field," driving back the 128th Pennsylvania in the process, "and passed beyond the battery, until its right rested on the west edge of the East Woods, where it was arrested by the troops in the woods." The regiment then fell back to its previous position about a hundred yards south of the cornfield.[12]

The reinforcements that Thruston had seen coming up on his right before

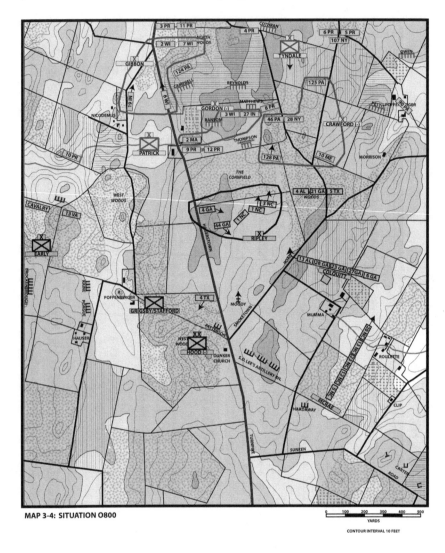

MAP 3-4: SITUATION 0800

0 100 200 300 400 500
YARDS

CONTOUR INTERVAL 10 FEET

making the charge against the 128th Pennsylvania were the regiments of Colquitt's brigade. At the same time that D. H. Hill ordered Ripley forward in
support of Hood, he also called up Colquitt's, McRae's and Rodes's brigades.
Colquitt, who had been in position along the western extension of the Sunken
Road since arriving on the 15th, marched his brigade by the left flank north between the Mumma and Roulette farmsteads, west past the burning Mumma
buildings, and then north along the western edge of the East Woods. After
passing the right of the 3rd North Carolina, then just returning from its charge

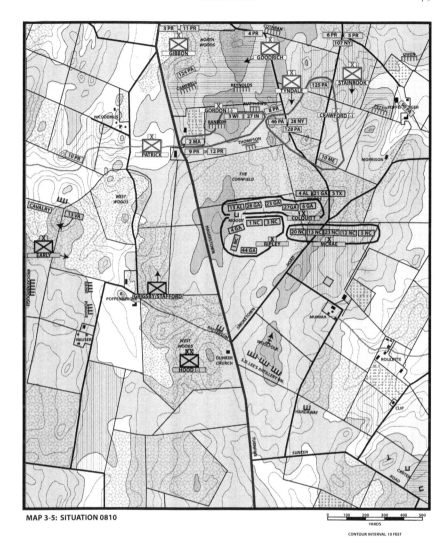

MAP 3-5: SITUATION 0810

0   100   200   300   400   500
YARDS

CONTOUR INTERVAL 10 FEET

through the cornfield, the brigade column turned left and filed across the front of Ripley's brigade. When the lead regiment, the 13th Alabama, was a sufficient distance west of the woodline, Colquitt ordered a halt, formed a brigade line of battle facing north, and opened fire on the enemy formations on the opposite side of the cornfield (Map 3.5: Situation 0810). In this exchange of fire, many of the soldiers were able to use the rock outcroppings just south of the cornfield as natural breastworks. Not all of the brigade, however, was in the open. A part of the 27th Georgia and all of the 6th Georgia, which unlike the rest of the brigade had entered the woods on crossing Smoketown Road, were still inside the woods just behind Robbins's command.[13]

For some few minutes, Colquitt allowed his regiments to exchange fire with the Federal troops north of the cornfield. His line was supported by a section of Moody's battery from S. D. Lee's battalion commanded by Moody and Lieutenant John B. Gorey that came up and took position behind the 13th Alabama. Colquitt reported, "After a few rounds had been discharged, I ordered an advance, and at the same time sent word to the regiments on my left to advance simultaneously. The order was responded to with spirit by my men, and, with a shout, they moved through the corn-field in front, 200 yards wide." In this advance the 27th Georgia and the 6th Georgia in the East Woods pushed around the left of Robbins's command, came out of the woods, and moved forward along the eastern edge of the cornfield. The regiments that Colquitt called on to advance with his brigade were Ripley's, but the only ones to respond were the 3rd North Carolina and a portion of the 1st North Carolina, which followed behind the center of Colquitt's line.[14]

In his report, Colquitt went on say that as his regiments advanced through the cornfield the "enemy was near and in full view. In a moment or two his ranks began to break before our fire, and the line soon disappeared under the crest of the hill upon which it had been established. It was soon replaced by another, and the fire opened with renewed vigor." This Federal line included the newly arrived 2nd Massachusetts, 27th Indiana, and 3rd Wisconsin of Brigadier General George H. Gordon's brigade of the Twelfth Corps. Adding to the weight of metal being thrown at Colquitt's advancing line was canister from the six 12-pounder Napoleons of Captain Dunbar R. Ransom's Battery C, 5th U.S. Artillery. Under this concentration of fire, Colquitt's regiments were able to advance no more than halfway across the cornfield before halting to return fire.[15]

Just as Colquitt was beginning his advance into the cornfield, McRae was forming his regiments in line of battle south of the East Woods. McRae had followed Colquitt north from the Sunken Road, passing around the east side of the Mumma farm as Colquitt had done, and continuing northwest "until we reached a point near the woods, when line of battle was formed and the advance begun." Before entering the woods, however, McRae was "cautioned by Gen'l Hill not to fire upon Colquitt who might be in our front." The brigade then moved forward. It crossed the fence at the southern edge of the woods, where it "was halted and formed and again advanced." Captain Thomas M. Garrett, commanding the 5th North Carolina on the right of the brigade line, reported that as the brigade advanced, "a state of confusion ensued which it is difficult to portray. Various conflicting orders . . . were passed down the line, the men in ranks being allowed by the officers to join in repeating them, so that it became utterly impossible to understand which emanated from the proper authority. The regiment, following the movements of the brigade, which were vacillating and unsteady, obliquing to the right and left, came upon a ledge of rock and earth, forming a fine natural breastwork. Under the cover of this the regiment, following the example of those on the left, fell down and sought shelter."[16]

McRae reported that when the brigade reached the rock outcropping, the enemy was sighted and "the firing was commenced steadily and with good will, and from an excellent position" (Map 3.6: Situation 0820). Almost immediately, however, "a cry went through the line that those were Colquitt's troops, and I gave the order for my men to desist firing until I could reconnoitre. At this time the brigade [was] in secure position[,] a ledge of rock stretching in front along a large portion of the line. I mounted a rock and looking over the slope for about a hundred yards I saw a line of what I suppose to be about a regiment with the flag of the U.S. flying and I ordered the brigade to fire and charge." At the same time, Captain Garrett also spotted what he believed to be an enemy regiment "coming up in the open field in our front and somewhat on the flank." Because of a turn in the rock outcropping, several files on the right of the line were exposed, and he ordered them "to deploy as flankers to the right and take shelter behind the trees." While Garrett was directing this movement, Captain T. P. Thomson of Company G came to him "and in a very excited manner and tone cried out to me, 'They are flanking us! See, yonder's a whole brigade!' I ordered him to keep silence and return to his place. The men before this were far from being cool, but, when this act of indiscretion occurred, a panic ensued, and, despite the efforts of file-closers and officers, they began to break and run."[17]

As the soldiers of the brigade began fleeing to the rear in a panic, Captain Garrett ordered "the few men who remained—not more than 10 in number—to retire, and called upon the few officers who were around me to rally behind the fence in our rear. A few rallied by the example of Lieut. Isaac E. Pearce, commanding Company B, who acted with great spirit, and all of the men belonging to my company present in the regiment rallied to my side. With them I made a stand at the fence, and ordered the men to fire upon the advancing

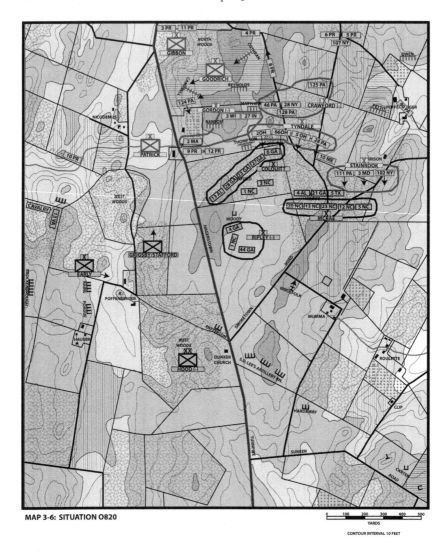

MAP 3-6: SITUATION 0820

0   100   200   300   400   500
YARDS

CONTOUR INTERVAL 10 FEET

enemy. This they did with coolness and deliberation. I observed, however, immediately, that all the brigade on the left were retreating in disorder, and had already passed the fence without halting. I retired with the few men behind the fence, toward the town."[18]

From McRae's prospective it was the sudden appearance of an enemy force on the right that caused the brigade "to break, and a general panic ensued. It was in vain that the field and most of the company officers exerted themselves to rally it. The troops left the field in confusion, the field officers, company officers, and myself bringing up the rear." McRae was dismayed that the "whole line vanished and a brigade famed [*sic*] for previous and subsequent conduct of each of its Regts. fled in panic from the field leaving me with one or two officers to get off the field as well as I could." He recalled that the two officers of Garland's staff who were serving as his staff that day, Captains D. P. Halsay and Charles Wood, were captured, although they were exchanged a few days later. McRae himself, seeing the line of the enemy advancing "made haste to escape. Being on foot my horse having been left beyond the fence I was subject to a very hot fire for about three hundred yards until I got into the woods from which Hood's troops had emerged early in the morn." As McRae crossed the lower end of the quadrangle toward the West Woods he was able to observe enemy regiments "in lines at least double" advancing south through the cornfield.[19]

Seeing McRae's brigade entering the East Woods, Colquitt believed that he was now supported on the right—he remained unaware of the presence of Robbins's command in the woods—and renewed his efforts to move his brigade forward across the cornfield. Most of the brigade, however, made little headway against the Federal fire, although the 6th Georgia on the right was able to reach the fence at the north end of the cornfield. This put the brigade line at a diagonal across the cornfield from northeast to southwest. Ripley's regiments had not advanced on Colquitt's left as he had asked. As McRae's brigade fled the East Woods, Colquitt found himself "exposed to a fire from all sides and nearly surrounded." He asked Hill for reinforcements, believing that with "steady supports upon the right we could yet maintain our position. The support was not at hand and could not reach us in time. The enemy closed in upon the right so near that our ranks were scarcely distinguishable. At the same time his line in front advanced. My men stood firm until every field officer but one had fallen, and then made the best of their way out."[20]

Ripley's brigade by this time was well on its way to the rear, retiring toward the West Woods (Map 3.7: Situation 0830). Even as the 3rd North Carolina was making its initial charge into the cornfield, Doles was pulling back his 4th Georgia from the acme of its advance to the high ground just south of the cornfield where the 9th Pennsylvania Reserves had been. The regiment was low on ammunition and retired to the low ground at the center of the lower quadrangle. The 44th Georgia also left the high ground, moving east along the lower cornfield fence in an attempt to connect with the 3rd North Carolina. Failing

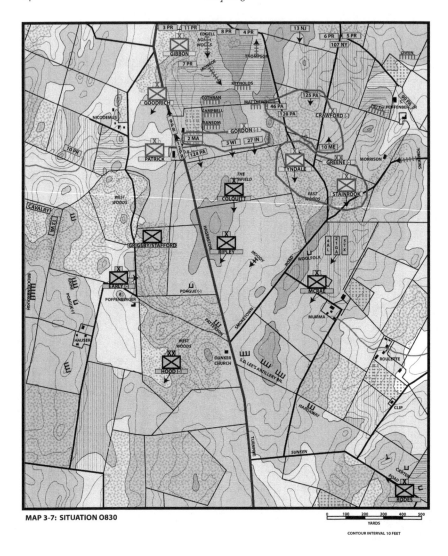

MAP 3-7: SITUATION 0830

0 100 200 300 400 500
YARDS

CONTOUR INTERVAL 10 FEET

this, the regiment moved south into the center of the lower quadrangle. The 1st North Carolina just south of the 4th Georgia formed a right angle line with its two left companies, B and K, being thrown back in an attempt to maintain a connection with the 44th Georgia. As McRae's brigade began to collapse in the East Woods, Hill, who was on Smoketown Road near the most southern point of the woods, hastened to order both Colquitt and Ripley to withdraw. Lieutenant Colonel H. A. Brown, commanding the 1st North Carolina, remembered, "General Hill came to this brigade alone without even a courier, and ordered a retreat . . . . The manner of this retreat was slow and in order, and under General Hill's personal supervision. Seeing an abandoned caisson he [Hill] ordered the soldiers to remove it from the field, which was done after replacing a broken wheel with the extra one usually carried by caissons for that purpose. As many of our wounded were placed upon the caisson as it would carry. The retreat was continued to the Dunker Church, where portions of many commands were in considerable confusion."[21]

Once in the West Woods, Doles managed to reassemble most of Ripley's brigade. Being out of ammunition, he led the regiments south to a woodlot on the S. D. Piper farm where the brigade ordnance train was located. Here Captain John C. Key, commanding the 44th Georgia, remembered his regiment "got a supply of cartridges and a lunch to eat—the first we had had for about forty hours."[22]

The withdrawal of Colquitt's brigade was not as orderly as that of Ripley's. Hill reported, "Colquitt had gone in with 10 field officers; 4 were killed, 5 badly wounded, and the tenth had been stunned by a shell. The men were beginning to fall back, and efforts were made to rally them in the bed of an old road, nearly at right angles to the Hagerstown Pike, and which had been their position previous to the advance. These efforts, however, were only partially successful."[23]

All of McRae's brigade, except for one regiment, had fled the East Woods and would not be rallied to fight as a brigade again that day. The one regiment that did not break was the 23rd North Carolina, which Hill said "was brought off by the gallant Lieutenant-Col. [Robert D.] Johnston, and posted, by my order, in the old road already described." Hill believed that it was Captain Thomson's cry, "they are flanking us," that caused the brigade to break "bringing up vivid recollections of the flank fire at South Mountain." McRae later explained it by saying, "Happily they thoroughly redeemed their good name on many a hard fought field afterwards, and their stampede that day was such an accident as sometimes happens to the best troops."[24]

The withdrawal of Ripley's, Colquitt's, and McRae's brigades from the cornfield quadrangle and the East Woods signaled the Confederate abandonment of the field east of the Hagerstown Pike and north of the Sunken Road. The section of Moody's battery that had advanced to support Colquitt, being "exposed to a most galling infantry fire," was ordered to fall back by S. D. Lee to his line of batteries opposite the Dunker Church. As Moody withdrew, he stopped several times to fire on the pursuing Federals. During one of these stands Lieutenant Gorey was killed instantly, "being shot in the head by a Minie-ball as he was sighting his piece for its last discharge." Robbins's two-regiment remnant of Hood's division and the 21st Georgia were compelled to abandon their position in the East Woods as they were flanked on the right and McRae's brigade collapsed behind them. A section of Pichegru Woolfolk's Ashland (Virginia) Artillery belatedly sent forward by S. D. Lee, which had just gone into Mumma's plowed field south of the East Woods, only had time to fire two rounds of canister before the gunners were forced to abandon the guns to the rapidly advancing Federal line. Captain George M. Patterson's Georgia Battery, which had been in position in the West Woods just north of the junction of the Hagerstown Pike and Smoketown Road, was ordered to the rear by Hill. Withdrawing to the southeast, Patterson took position in the southwest corner of Mumma's cornfield and opened fire on the advancing Federal line. After only a few shots, however, he was forced to withdraw to the west to a position just across the Hagerstown Pike from its junction with the Sunken Road where Colquitt was attempting to rally what was left of his brigade. D. H. Hill also ordered S. D. Lee, whose battalion was in a "wrecked condition," having lost some thirty-five men and sixty horses, to abandon his position on the plateau opposite the Dunker Church and move to the next ridge of hills to the southwest on the opposite side of the pike. In his official report, Hill commented, "We had now lost all the ground wrested from the enemy, and were occupying the position held in the morning."[25]

The Federal force that had flanked McRae and Robbins in the East Woods was Tyndale's and Stainrook's brigades of Greene's division. Supported by Tompkins's, Monroe's, and Edgell's batteries and the 125th Pennsylvania, these brigades continued their advance south of the Mumma farmstead, but they halted below the crest of the height of land for lack of ammunition and did not pursue the withdrawing Confederate forces into the West Woods. It was at this point that General Sumner arrived with Sedgwick's and Brigadier General William H. French's divisions. With three of his brigades "broken and much demoralized," there was nothing that Hill could do about the situation in the West Woods—that was Jackson's responsibility. Hill's responsibility was the center of the Confederate line east of the Hagerstown Pike, a line that he would form in the Sunken Road.[26]

III

The first thing that D. H. Hill did to shore up the Confederate center was to halt the advance of Rodes's brigade. That brigade, it will be recalled, had been called up at the same time that Hill ordered Colquitt and McRae to support Ripley. Rodes's brigade, though, was farther to the southeast, positioned along the northeastern section of the Sunken Road, facing east toward the Antietam. Rodes's march followed the course of the road, but as the head of his column passed the Roulette farm lane it became evident to him that Ripley, Colquitt, and McRae "had met with a reverse, and that the best service I could render them and the field generally would be to form a line in rear of them and endeavor to rally them before attacking or being attacked. Major-General Hill held the same view, for at this moment I received an order from him to halt and form line of battle in the hollow of an old and narrow road just beyond the [Piper's] orchard, and with my left about 150 yards from and east of the Hagerstown road. In a short time a small portion of Colquitt's brigade formed on my left, and I assumed the command of it. This brought my left to the Hagerstown road."[27]

After positioning Rodes's brigade, Hill went to find G. B. Anderson's brigade. When the other four brigades were called up, Anderson, who was at the junction of Sunken Road and Boonsboro Pike, was ordered to extend his line to cover the area vacated by Rodes. To that end he moved his regiments farther up the ravine toward the Piper farm. In this position, the soldiers were alerted to the deteriorating situation on their left as the wounded came limping back. Colonel Risden Tyler Bennett, commanding the 14th North Carolina, remembered, "Very soon streams of men came back from that direction in great disorder[,] these were broken Confederate troops and they belonged to Garland's [McRae's] brigade." When Hill arrived, he led the brigade to the head of the ravine, through Piper's cornfield, and placed them in the Sunken Road east of Rodes's brigade (Map 3.8: Situation 0910).[28]

As Hill was desperately trying to assemble this new defensive line in the Sunken Road with Rodes's and G. B. Anderson's brigades, Robert E. Lee himself, with only an orderly in attendance, was observing the situation from the base of Reel Ridge, just across the Hagerstown Pike and a couple of hundred yards south of the Sunken Road. Here he was suddenly confronted by a very ex-

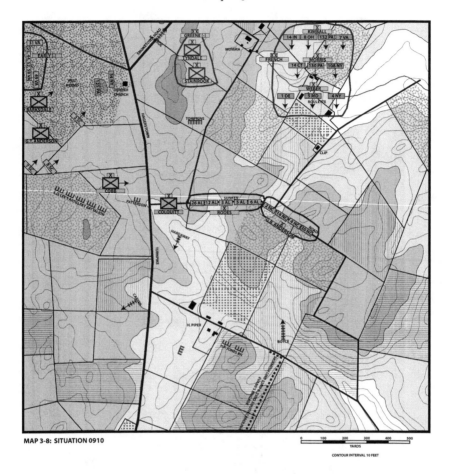

MAP 3-8: SITUATION 0910

0   100   200   300   400   500
YARDS

CONTOUR INTERVAL 10 FEET

cited S. D. Lee, who had been ordered by Hood "to turn over my artillery to the next officer in command, and go personally to find General R. E. Lee, and tell him the condition of affairs, and to say to him that unless reinforcements were sent at once, the day was lost." According to S. D. Lee, General Lee told him, "Don't be excited about it, Colonel, go tell General Hood to hold his ground, reinforcements are now rapidly approaching between Sharpsburg and the ford; tell him that I am now coming to his support." S. D. Lee protested, "General, your presence will do good, but nothing but infantry can save the day on the left." The artillery commander recalled, "I started to return, and had not gone over 100 yards when Lee called me and pointed to McLaw's division, then in sight, and approaching at a double quick."[29]

After talking with S. D. Lee, General Lee had his orderly lead his horse across the Hagerstown Pike to the Sunken Road, where D. H. Hill was positioning Rodes's and Anderson's brigades. Together with Hill, he rode behind the line encouraging the soldiers to prepare to hold their position to the last extremity. When they came to the 6th Alabama on the right of Rodes's brigade, Hill told the men, "Soldiers, you fought well on Sunday, but to-day you must fight harder," to which Lieutenant John D. Perry, commanding Company G, replied, "General, Company G will do their duty, and I am determined to *die* with them." The regimental commander, Colonel John B. Gordon, added, "These men are going to stay here, General, till the sun goes down or victory is won." No doubt encouraged by the enthusiasm he found in the Sunken Road, Lee returned to Reel Ridge to observe the continuing fight on the left of his line.[30]

Once Rodes's and G. B. Anderson's regiments were in position along the Sunken Road, they had little time to prepare before the enemy was upon them. Colonel Gordon noted that "General Lee had scarcely reached his left before the predicted assault came." In Anderson's brigade, Colonel Bennett of the 14th North Carolina thought that his regiment "did not occupy the road from choice but to meet the sudden and rapid deployment of the govt. forces." Captain John C. Gorman, commanding Company B in the 2nd North Carolina, remembered that after only a few moments in the lane "I could see the advancing line of Yankees. Three heavy columns are approaching us, extending to the right and left as far as we can see, each column about 100 yards behind the other, and the nearest scarce 400 yards distant. To oppose this, was Hill's weak little division, scarce one-fourth as large, and my very heart sunk within me, as I heard Gen. Anderson say to one of his aids [sic] to hurry to the rear and tell Gen. Hill for God's sake to send us reinforcement, as it was hopeless to contend against the approaching columns." Colonel Charles C. Tew, the regimental commander, ordered skirmishers out to a distance of just fifty yards. The main body of the regiment was "to lie down in the lane, and hold their fire till the enemy was close." Captain Gorman at this point was standing with Colonel Tew "on the crest of a hill, in front of our position, and gazed with tumultuous emotion over the fast approaching line. Our little corps seemed doomed to destruction, but not an eye flinched, nor a nerve quivered, and you could observe the battle-light of determination on every countenance, and I then felt sure we would do honor to our noble old state that day, though we would not live to see it again."[31]

The situation was the same in front of Rodes's brigade. He reported, "A short time after my brigade assumed its new position, and while the men were busy improving their position by piling rails along their front, the enemy deployed in our front in three beautiful lines, all vastly out stretching ours, and commenced to advance steadily." Like Tew and Gorman, Colonel Gordon climbed to the crest of the ridge in front of his regiment to observe the Federal advance. He recalled that "the men in blue filed down the opposite slope, crossed the little stream . . ., and formed in my front, an assaulting column four lines deep. The front line came to a 'charge bayonets,' the others to a 'right shoulder shift.' The brave Union commander, superbly mounted, placed himself in front, while his band cheered them with martial music."[32]

The Confederate side had no artillery to oppose the Federal advance. In his official report, Rodes noted that "Carter's battery had been sent to take position in rear, by me, when I abandoned my first position, because he was left without support, and because my own position had not then been fully determined. Three pieces, which occupied a fine position immediately on my front, abandoned it immediately after the enemy's skirmishers opened on them." The three pieces of artillery that Rodes referred to were from Captain Robert A. Hardaway's Alabama Battery, commanded this day by Lieutenant John W. Tullis. The battery consisted of two 3-inch Ordnance rifles and one breech loading Whitworth rifle. Normally the battery was a part of Jackson's command. But as Jackson crossed South Mountain during his march to capture Harpers Ferry, it had been detached and placed with Hill's division, according to Tullis, "to help hold McClellan back, because we had the best rifle guns in the Army." Tullis did not consider his position below the crest just south of Mumma's cornfield and east of the Mumma farm lane to be a "fine position" at all. Normally, because he had rifled guns, he preferred to take "position on a ridge" where their greater range and accuracy could be used to advantage. This was the one time during the campaign, he recalled, when an "infantry general forced me to take the position mentioned below the brow of the hill," where his range was short. Because of the rapid Federal advance, they "came near capturing us." Tullis did not say who the infantry general was.[33]

As the Federal columns passed the Roulette farm, skirmishers sent out from the Sunken Road opened fire. But they failed to slow the Federal advance. Captain Gorman in the 2nd North Carolina, still on the ridge in front of his regiment with Colonel Tew, remembered, "On moved the columns, until I could distinguish the stars on their flaunting banners, see the mounted officers, and hear their words of command. Just then a Yankee horseman waved his hat at us, and Col. Tew returned the compliment. It was the last I saw of the Colonel. Our skirmishers began to fire on the advancing line, and we returned to ours. Slowly they approach up the hill, and slowly our skirmishers retire before them, firing as they come. Our skirmishers are ordered to come into the line." Colonel Gordon of the 6th Alabama also found the continuing advance an inspiring sight. "Their gleaming bayonets flashed like burnished silver in the sunlight. With the precision of step and perfect alignment of a holiday parade, this magnificent array moved to the charge, every step keeping time to the tap of the deep-sounding drum."[34]

Watching the Federal columns, Rodes, Anderson, and the regimental commanders in the lane quickly grasped the objective of this Federal advance. Gordon spoke for all of them when he wrote in his memoirs, "Every act and movement of the Union commander in my front clearly indicated his purpose to discard bullets, and depend upon bayonets. He essayed to break through Lee's center by the crushing weight and momentum of his solid column." In the Sunken Road, both brigades were in a reverse slope position. There was no time now to move the regiments forward to the military crest of the forward slope. Their only hope of stopping the Federal advance would be to reserve their fire to the last second, releasing it in one devastating volley as the leading Federal line arrived on the crest above them. To this end, Gordon remembered, "all the horses were sent to the rear, and my men were at once directed to lie down upon the grass and clover. They were quickly made to understand, through my aides and line officers, that the Federals were coming upon them with unloaded guns; that not a shot would be fired at them, and that not one of our rifles was to be discharged until my voice should be heard from the centre commanding 'Fire.'"[35]

Rodes reported that as the "enemy came to the crest of the hill overlooking my position," the entire brigade rose and delivered its volley at a distance of no more than eighty yards (Map 3.9: Situation 0920). According to Gordon, "The effect was appalling. The entire front line, with few exceptions, went down in the consuming blast. The gallant commander and his horse fell in a heap near where I stood—the horse dead, the rider unhurt. Before his rear lines could

MAP 3-9: SITUATION 0920

0 100 200 300 400 500
YARDS

CONTOUR INTERVAL 10 FEET

recover from the terrific shock, my exultant men were on their feet, devouring them with successive volleys. Even then these stubborn lines retreated in fairly good order."[36]

In Anderson's brigade, Colonel Bennett of the 14th North Carolina reported that the Federals advanced "until a space not exceeding 50 yards separated the combatants. Then it was that a well-directed fire sent them in disorder some 50 paces rearward." In the 2nd North Carolina, Captain Gorman remembered that when the Federal line reached the crest of the ridge it was "scarce fifty yards off, but as if with one feeling, our whole line pour a deadly volley into their ranks—they drop, reel, stagger, and back their first line go beyond the crest of the hill." Edwin A. Osborne, a captain with the 4th North Carolina and later its historian, wrote that "the enemy's line of battle appeared, moving in magnificent style, with mounted officers in full uniform, swords gleaming, banners, plumes and sashes waving, and bayonets glistening in the sun. On they came with steady tramp and confident mien. They did not see our single line of hungry jaded and dusty men, who were lying down, until within good musket shot, when we rose and delivered our fire with terrible effect. Instantly the air was filled with the cries of wounded and dying and shouts of brave officers, trying to hold and encourage their men, who recoiled at the awful and stunning shock so unexpectedly received."[37]

The Federal lines coming against D. H. Hill's brigades in the Sunken Road were the brigades of Brigadier General French's division of Sumner's Second Army Corps, a new division formed on the march in Maryland. Along with Sedgwick's division, French had arrived in the East Woods only minutes after the withdrawal of Ripley, Colquitt, and McRae from the quadrangle and the woods. As Sedgwick was ordered across the quadrangle to the West Woods, Sumner ordered French to move south toward the Sunken Road to deal with Rodes and G. B. Anderson just then being positioned there by D. H. Hill. In accordance with Sumner's instructions, French had arranged his division in three consecutive brigade lines of battle with the brigades being between seventy and two hundred yards apart during their advance against the Sunken Road. In the first line were the three regiments of Brigadier General Max Weber's brigade, regiments not new to the service but experiencing their first taste of battle. The second line consisted of three new regiments that had been mustered into service during the previous month and assigned to the Second Corps only after it had begun its march into Maryland. For the time being, they were brigaded together by Sumner under the senior colonel, Dwight Morris of the 14th Connecticut. The last brigade line was that of Brigadier General Nathan Kimball, consisting of three battle-experienced regiments, plus one newly mustered regiment, the 132nd Pennsylvania.[38]

The concentrated volleys of Anderson's and Rodes's brigades stopped the advance of Weber's brigade, and even forced his regiments to withdraw from the crest of the ridge, especially the 1st Delaware on Weber's right, which being on more level ground, withdrew some one hundred and fifty yards to the southern edge of Mumma's cornfield. As the 5th Maryland reeled backward, a small group of Confederates, probably from the 6th Alabama, made a spontaneous rush for the regiment's colors. As one member of the 5th remembered

MAP 3-10: SITUATION 0930

it, the color guard saw them coming and quickly withdrew "while the boys in line met the venturesome rebels and sent them back quicker than they came."[39]

At that point, French's second line, Morris's brigade, pushed forward and also attempted a charge against the Sunken Road (Map 3.10: Situation 0930). As Gordon of the 6th Alabama saw it, the "first effort to penetrate the Confederate centre, did not satisfy the intrepid Union commander. Beyond the range of my rifles, he reformed his men into three lines, and on foot led them to the second charge, still with unloaded guns. This advance was also repulsed; but again and again did he advance in four successive charges in the fruitless effort to break through my lines with the bayonets." In Anderson's brigade, Captain Gorman of the 2nd North Carolina remembered, "Our men reload, and await for them to again approach, while the first column of the enemy meet the second, rally and move forward again. They meet with the same reception, and back they go." Colonel Bennett, 14th North Carolina, reported that after the first charge the enemy recovered, re-formed, and "charged our position with same result as aforesaid, with the addendum of wild confusion. The bravery of a field officer apparently checked the spreading symptoms of panic, and once more their courage was brought to the test. Poor return, indeed, they made for the gallantry of their leader. Confusion that seemed remediless followed." According to Captain Osborne in the 4th North Carolina, "Soon they rallied and advanced again; this time more cautiously than before. Our men held their fire until they were within good range again, and again they rose to their feet and mowed them down, so that they were compelled to retire a second time; but they rallied and came again."[40]

Osborne also remembered that at this point, the battle "became general all along the line." According to Rodes, the Federal line, now a combination of the regiments of Weber's and Morris's brigades, had been driven back several times by volleys from the regiments in the lane, but they "finally lay down just back of the crest, keeping up a steady fire." Captain Gorman also noted the change in tactics: the Federals, after being driven back a final time, "then approach the top of the hill, cautiously, and lying down, we pour into each other one continuous shower of leaden hail." Gorman initially thought that in this exchange of fire his side had an advantage. "Our men are protected by about 6 or 8 inches of the wear of the road, but that is great protection; they fire cautiously, and are apparently as cool as if shooting squirrels, taking sure aim every fire." Quickly enough, though, he realized "the protection, however, is not sufficient. The air is full of lead, and many are shot as they are aiming at the enemy, and the groans of the wounded are heard amid the roar of the musketry."[41]

In turning back the initial assaults of Weber's and Morris's brigades, the Confederates found the reverse slope position of the Sunken Road to be advantageous. It permitted Rodes's and Anderson's regiments to reserve their firepower and release it suddenly at a devastatingly short range. Once the initial assault had been stopped, however, the advantage of the terrain turned against the Confederate troops in the Sunken Road. Below the crest of the forward slope of the ridge, Weber's and Morris's men were protected from the fire coming from the Sunken Road by the intervening ridge line. There they loaded and reloaded their weapons in relative safety, and then moved up cautiously to the top of the ridge to a point where they could fire down into the mass of Confederate soldiers in the lane, exposing themselves only momentarily to the fire from the lane. In the lane, D. H. Hill's soldiers would have only a fleeting glimpse of partial enemy figures to fire back at. The Sunken Road position thus was becoming a virtual death trap for the regiments of Rodes's and Anderson's brigades. Gordon of the 6th Alabama remembered that "the fire from these hostile American lines at close quarters now became furious and deadly. The list of the slain was lengthened with each passing moment."[42]

As the battle degenerated into a disadvantageous contest of firepower for the Confederates, D. H. Hill began working to get batteries into position to support his infantry line in the Sunken Road. As he did, a section of Napoleon guns from Captain William K. Bachman's German Artillery (South Carolina) of Hood's division under Lieutenant James Simons reported to him near the Piper barn. Along with two rifled guns of the battery, this section had been in position on the high ground south of the Boonsboro Pike at the eastern edge of the town. At about 8:00 A.M., however, Lieutenant Simons was ordered to report to General Longstreet. When he found Longstreet, who was with Lee, he was ordered to continue on and report to General Hill. Simons recalled, "I asked Gen. Hill to show me just what he wanted done, and I remember vividly our conversation." Simons "left the two pieces and two caissons with the men, behind a rise in the ground or sort of hill, for protection, and went with Gen. Hill, to look at the place where he wished us to take position. My recollection is that he dismounted and gave the reins of his horse to one of our drivers." The position that Hill wanted Simons to take was some high ground in Piper's cornfield; Simons remembered it as "a very exposed position, not more than a hundred and fifty yards from the enemy's line of battle." Simons called Hill's "attention to some trees, as I remember it a sort of grove to the left of us, into which I thought sharpshooters would be sent." But Hill "told me that he had decided to have us take position there and fire canister on the people in its front." Simons wrote later that after taking position, "we promptly opened on them with canister plowing up their lines all around their flags. A hailstorm of minie balls soon commenced to rain on us[,] not to speak of shell."[43]

As Hill was positioning Simons's section, one of his aides, Lieutenant James A. Reid, found a battery moving west through Piper's cornfield. This battery was from Brigadier General Nathan Evans's brigade, the Macbeth (South Carolina) Light Artillery, commanded by Captain Robert Boyce. Like Bachman's, the battery had been in position on the high ground just east of the village and south of the Boonsboro Pike until it was ordered to the left by Colonel James B. Walton of the Washington Artillery. Boyce reported that "[I] proceed with my battery beyond the road north [Boonsboro Pike] of the town of Sharpsburg, to occupy a position to meet the enemy. On reaching the vicinity of the position I supposed I should occupy, I found no person to point it out to me." Colonel Peter F. Stevens of the Holcombe Legion, however, "placed me on the slope of the second hill from the road; but, finding my battery could be of no service in this position, I was posted farther down, in front of another battery. Here, discovering that I was still where I could not see the enemy, I moved my battery through a corn-field immediately in front, and, on reaching the farther side of this field, I found the whole line of battle, for at least a mile, extended before me." It was here that Boyce was picked up by Reid, and despite Reid receiving a painful wound, Boyce finally managed to get his battery into position on the side of the ridge in the rear of the Sunken Road just west of Piper's orchard. Boyce reported that in this position, "I placed my guns in battery in easy range of a portion of the line, but had to wait for an opportunity to fire, as our own troops, engaging the enemy, intervened."[44]

The intervening troops that kept Boyce from firing were from Rodes's brigade. In an attempt to regain the advantage of the ground, Longstreet sent orders to Rodes to make a charge against the Federal line in front (Map 3.11: Situation 0940). Rodes wrote in his official report, "I endeavored to charge them with my brigade and that portion of Colquitt's which was on my immediate left. The charge failed, mainly because the Sixth Alabama Regiment, not hearing the command, did not move forward with the others, and because Colquitt's men did not advance far enough. That part of the brigade which moved forward found themselves in an exposed position, and, being outnumbered and unsustained, fell back before I could, by personal effort, which was duly made, get the Sixth Alabama to move." Even as disjointed as this charge was, it did, at least momentarily, force Weber's regiments to back away from the crest of the ridge. But it also put Rodes's brigade in jeopardy of losing its position in the Sunken Road because his regiments on the left withdrew from the ridge in some disorder. Rodes wrote, "Hastening back to the left, I arrived just in time to prevent the men from falling back to the rear of the road we had just occupied. It became evident to me then that an attack by us must, to be successful, be made by the whole of Anderson's brigade, mine, Colquitt's, and any troops

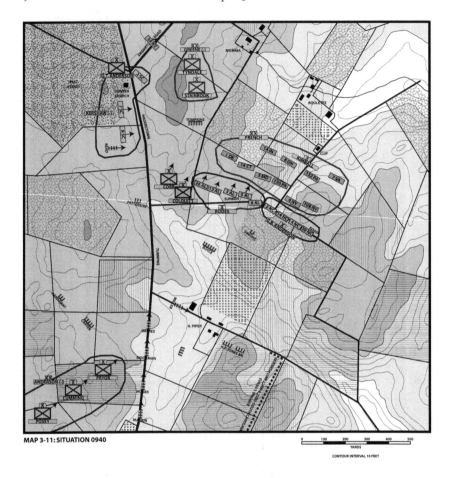

MAP 3-11: SITUATION 0940

0   100   200   300   400   500
YARDS

CONTOUR INTERVAL 10 FEET

that had arrived on Anderson's right. My whole force at this moment did not amount to over 700 men—most probably not to that number."[45]

What Rodes did not note in his report was the participation of Cobb's brigade in the charge. This brigade, a part of McLaws's division, under the command of Lieutenant Colonel C. C. Sanders, was ordered forward by Longstreet. As discussed in the previous chapter, McLaws had sent Cobb's brigade to the east to be the right of the division in its advance into the West Woods. But Sanders had missed the signal to turn the brigade north, and consequently it continued east across the Hagerstown Pike, finally taking position in the Sunken Road on the left of Colquitt's brigade with the left of the brigade at the pike. Lieutenant Colonel William MacRae of the 15th North Carolina, who wrote the brigade report, said "[we] took position behind a fence, covered from the enemy's musketry by a hill in front, but not protecting us from the heavy shelling of his several batteries planted on the side of the mountain on our right. For an hour we remained here inactive, suffering considerably." Then came Longstreet's order to charge. MacRae reported, "The men, eager to meet the foe upon a more equal footing, gallantly pressed forward with a cheer, the top of the hill gained amid a galling and destructive shower of balls. There we remained, unfaltering, until Colonel Sanders, finding himself unsupported, ordered us to fall back behind the fence. The command was executed in admirable order."[46]

Playing a large role in disrupting the charge of Rodes's brigade on the left was the presence of a battery of six 10-pound Parrotts, Battery A, 1st Rhode Island Light Artillery, under the command of Captain John A. Tompkins. This battery had arrived with Greene's brigades and took position ahead of them just below the crest and opposite Mumma's cornfield. The battery was in an ideal position to partially enfilade the left of Rodes's brigade as he attempted to make the charge from the Sunken Road. Lee, who was still observing the fighting from Reel Ridge, noticed Tompkins's battery and ordered Boyce to take it under fire. Boyce reported, "Shortly after taking . . . position, General Lee sent me an order to open fire on a battery which had formed on my left almost beyond the range of my pieces. I fired on the battery, and, having it enfiladed, soon forced it to slacken its fire and change position. I then turned my guns upon a column of the enemy moving through a corn-field, just to the left of the enemy's battery. The range, however, was too great to do much execution. I received an order at this time to cease firing in that direction."[47]

The column of troops that Boyce fired on was the 14th Indiana, which was moving through Mumma's cornfield and was the right flank of Kimball's brigade (Map 3.12: Situation 0950). As his first two brigades became intermingled and stationary in front of the Sunken Road, French received orders from General Sumner via his son and aide, Captain Samuel A. Sumner, "to make a vigorous attack in order to aid the advance" of Sedgwick's division in the West Woods. French responded by ordering Kimball, whose brigade had thus far been held in reserve, "to charge to the front." As Weber and Morris had done before him, Kimball first attempted to break the Confederate line in the Sunken Road with the bayonet, but he met with the same result. He reported, "As my line advanced to the crest of the hill, a murderous fire was opened upon

MAP 3-12: SITUATION 0950

0   100   200   300   400   500
                YARDS

CONTOUR INTERVAL 10 FEET

it from the entire force in front. My advance farther was checked." As Weber's and Morris's regiments had done after their initial repulse, Kimball's regiments now took up position just below the crest of the ridge and continued to pour fire down into Rodes's and Anderson's regiments in the Sunken Road.[48]

A third battery now coming into action south of the Sunken Road was the 3rd Company, Washington (Louisiana) Artillery, under the command of Captain Merritt B. Miller. As with Bachman and Boyce, Miller's four Napolean's had been positioned on the high ground south of the Boonsboro Pike until about 9:15 A.M., when the battery was ordered to move to the left. The battery went through Sharpsburg, then out the Hagerstown Pike as far as the Piper farm. There, Miller met Longstreet, who pointed out the position that he wanted the battery to take. This position was at the center of Piper's orchard about 100 yards south of its northern edge. According to Colonel James B. Walton, who as commander of the Washington Artillery reported on the employment of the battery, Miller "suffered considerably from the fire of the enemy's sharpshooters, losing two of his gunners and several of his cannoneers, wounded." Then "ascertaining that the enemy was beyond effective range, he was ordered by Gen. Longstreet to cease firing and go under cover" by moving the guns deeper into the orchard until they were effectively under the protection of the ridge.[49]

IV

As French was committing the last of his brigades to the fight for the Sunken Road, reinforcements were arriving on the Confederate side. The division of Major General Richard H. Anderson had been ordered to report to Longstreet in Sharpsburg as a reserve for the right. Even before visiting the Sunken Road, however, General Lee had realized that the position could not be held by the two small brigades of Hill's division and the remnant of Colquitt's brigade. Accordingly, he had sent orders recalling Anderson's division to reinforce the Sunken Road.[50]

Like McLaws, Anderson, whose division was second in the order of march from Harpers Ferry, had halted near Lee's headquarters and was still there when he received orders to go to the Sunken Road. The division marched through the open fields west and north of the town, stopping to pile knapsacks, then continuing in a northeasterly direction toward Piper's farm. As it did Anderson rode forward to the vicinity of the Sunken Road to find Hill. In his official report Hill recalled that "Gen. R.H. Anderson reported to me with some 3,000 or 4,000 men as re-inforcements to my command. I directed him to form immediately behind my men."[51]

Anderson's division consisted of six infantry brigades and an artillery battalion. The brigade of Brigadier General Roger A. Pryor led the way, followed by the brigade of Brigadier General Cadmus M. Wilcox under the command of Colonel Alfred Cumming. Next came the brigade of Brigadier General Winfield S. Featherston commanded by Colonel Carnot Posey, and then the brigade of Brigadier General Ambrose R. Wright. Brigadier General Lewis Armistead's brigade was detached early in the march and sent north to support

McLaws. Anderson's last brigade, that of Brigadier General William Mahone, was no brigade at all on the 17th. The fighting on South Mountain on the 14th had reduced it to no more than eighty-two effectives. Accordingly, it was consolidated as a single regiment under the command of Colonel William A. Parham, and it marched with Pryor's brigade.[52]

The artillery battalion counted four batteries and was normally commanded by Major John S. Saunders. But Saunders was sick as the division deployed on the morning of the 17th, so the battalion was under the command of Captain Cary F. Grimes, the senior battery commander. The battalion did not follow the route of the division's march, but rather kept on the Shepherdstown Pike into Sharpsburg, and then the Hagerstown Pike north out of town. Consequently, it reached the vicinity of Piper's farm not long after Miller's battery did, and ahead of Anderson's infantry brigades.[53]

Grimes placed all four batteries on the high ground north and west of the Piper farmstead. He put his own battery just to the right of the Hagerstown Pike about 150 yards north of the Piper farm lane. Captain Marcellus N. Moorman's battery was positioned about 200 yards to Grimes's right and 100 yards north of Piper's large stone barn. The remaining two batteries, Captain Frank Huger's and Captain Victor Maurin's, went into position just across the Hagerstown Pike from Grimes with Huger closest to the pike and Maurin on his left.[54]

First Lieutenant John H. Thompson, who commanded the right section of Grimes's battery, recalled that "we opened fire on the Federal lines immediately." The cost of such an action was to draw the rifled musket fire of the Federal infantry on the high ground above the Sunken Road and, even more damaging, the fire of Tompkins's battery opposite Mumma's cornfield, as well the fire of the heavy Federal batteries across Antietam Creek. Thompson remembered that "Captain Grimes, while directing the fire of the guns on the left, was shot from his horse, and while being carried from the field received two more wounds, and two of the men who were bearing him were killed before they got under cover."[55]

At this point, the infantry of Anderson's division was just beginning to arrive (Map 3.13: Situation 1000). Pryor's brigade in the lead reached the Hagerstown Pike about three hundred and fifty yards south of Piper's farm lane, turned north and marched on the pike as far as the lane, then turned down the lane and passed Piper's barn before filing to the left into Piper's orchard, where it

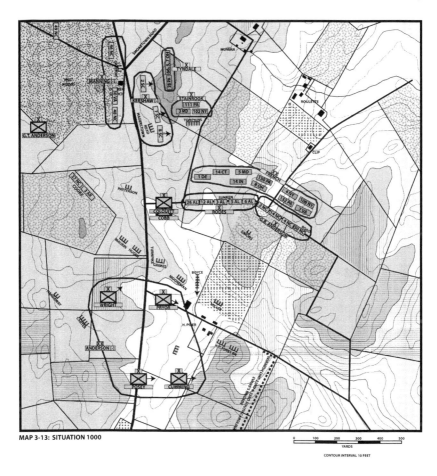

MAP 3-13: SITUATION 1000

0 100 200 300 400 500
YARDS
CONTOUR INTERVAL 10 FEET

halted and formed a line of battle with the 2nd Florida on the left and the 8th Florida, 5th Florida, 3rd Virginia, 14th Alabama, and Parham's command to its right in that order.[56]

Cumming's brigade followed Pryor's as far as the Hagerstown Pike. As the brigade reached the pike, Major Hilary A. Herbert of the 8th Alabama recalled "we passed by General Lee, who was standing on a rock. We cheered him as we passed. He stood with his hat off, the light of battle in his eyes, his gray hair glittering in the sunling [*sic*]; and I have always remembered him as he stood then, as the noblest figure that is imprinted in my memory." Rather than turning north along the pike as Pryor had done, Cumming crossed it and kept on east for another 400 yards to take position just below the crest of the ridge south and east of Piper's house. Posey, leading Featherston's brigade, followed Cumming and took position near that brigade.[57]

The last of Anderson's brigades in the line of march, Wright's, took a more northerly route than the other brigades and finally reached and crossed the Hagerstown Pike a little north of Piper's lane. Continuing on to the east, the brigade passed north of Piper's barn and entered the southern end of Piper's orchard, having some difficulty in making openings in the strong oak picket fence that surrounded the orchard. While tearing at the fence, the brigade came under severe fire from the Federal guns east of the Antietam, which continued to plague it as it marched in rear of Pryor's line. Wright finally formed an oblique line of battle on Pryor's right with the 22nd Georgia on the left and the 44th Alabama, 48th Georgia, and 3rd Georgia in that order extending to the right.[58]

After forming his line of battle, Wright immediately moved the brigade forward in a northeasterly direction toward the crest of the ridge behind which was the Sunken Road (Map 3.14: Situation 1010). As Colonel William Gibson of the 48th Georgia remembered it, while still "under a severe cannonading of the enemy's guns . . . the brigade moved steadily forward under its gallant commander . . . though many of his comrades were falling on the right and left, killed and wounded." As the brigade left the orchard it started across a plowed field toward a cornfield. It had not gone a hundred yards when an artillery shell killed Wright's horse. Wright managed to extract himself from under the mangled animal and continued on foot with the brigade. Passing into the cornfield to the north and reaching the crest of the ridge, the brigade came under musketry fire from the Federal regiments on the high ground on the far side of the Sunken Road. Here Wright was wounded by a ball that passed through the calf muscle of one of his legs. Colonel Robert Jones of the 22nd Georgia took command of the brigade, but Jones was immediately disabled by a shot through his chest, and Colonel William Gibson of the 48th Georgia took over. Also wounded during the brigade's advance to the Sunken Road was the division commander, R. H. Anderson, who was following behind the brigade.[59]

As Wright's regiments emerged from the cornfield at the edge of the Sunken Road, Federal fire became severe enough that they were driven back into the corn. Gibson and the remaining regimental officers, however, managed to rally the men and move the brigade forward into the lane on the right of G. B. Anderson's brigade. Though somewhat protected from the Federal fire coming

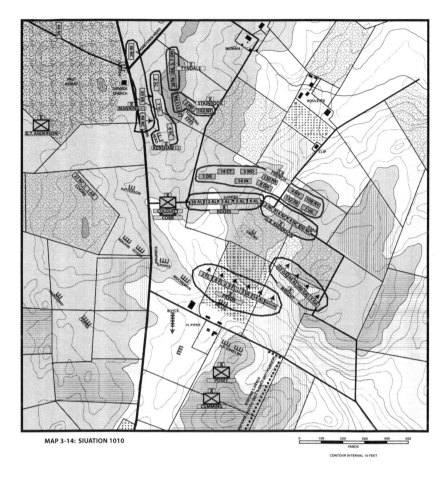

MAP 3-14: SIUATION 1010

from the front by the depression of the road, the brigade was still under an enfilading artillery fire from across the Antietam, and the nearest Federal regiments, the 7th West Virginia and 132nd Pennsylvania of Kimball's brigade, were beginning to gain ground on the brigade's left. Wright, although wounded a second time, managed to stay with the brigade by having himself carried forward on a litter. He had expected Pryor's brigade to move up on his left as reinforcement. When Pryor did not advance beyond the orchard, however, and as Wright's brigade grew more and more unsteady, he directed Gibson to "advance the brigade nearer the enemy at a charge bayonet."[60]

The brigade's charge out of the road was anemic at best (Map 3.15: Situation 1020). The regiments of the left and center made little progress and were

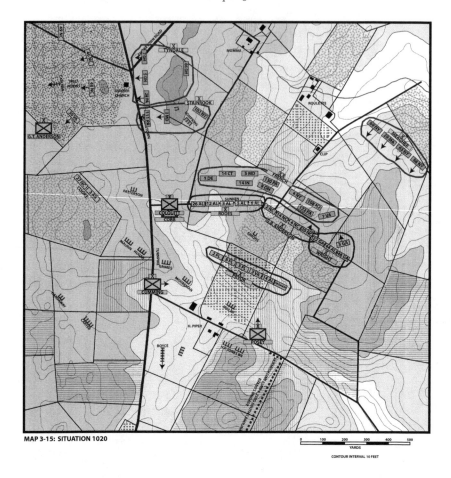

MAP 3-15: SITUATION 1020

0   100   200   300   400   500
YARDS

CONTOUR INTERVAL 10 FEET

almost immediately driven back into the lane. Only the 3rd Georgia on the right of the brigade made any headway. That regiment, under the command of Colonel R. B. Nisbit, left the road and, executing a left wheel, succeeded in gaining the flank of the 7th West Virginia. The 3rd Georgia's success, however, like that of the other regiments of the brigade, was short-lived and it was soon driven back into the lane. Colonel Nisbit was wounded and had to be left on the field. He was subsequently taken prisoner. Brigadier General Kimball described the charge of Wright's brigade and his response to it in his official report. "The enemy, having been reinforced, made an attempt to turn my left flank by throwing three regiments forward entirely to the left of my line, which I met and repulsed, with loss, by extending my left wing, Seventh Virginia and One hundred and thirty-second Pennsylvania, in that direction." With his brigade back in position in the Sunken Road, Colonel Gibson decided that the best he could do was to hold his position: "the brigade numbering under 200, with every field officer its General and one of his aids [*sic*] wounded and lying on the field, I contented myself with holding our advanced position."[61]

Wright's staff or other officers in his brigade attempted to get G. B. Anderson's brigade on their left to join the charge. Colonel Bennett of the 14th North Carolina gave "orders for bayonets to be fixed, preparatory to an advance of the line." Had Wright's and Anderson's brigades been able to make a concerted effort against the regiments of Kimball's brigade in their front, they might have been able to regain and hold the advantage of the ridge, but the response of G. B. Anderson's regiments was disconnected at best. Major William W. Sillers, of the 30th North Carolina, just to the left of Wright's brigade, reported that his regiment "was ordered to advance" and did advance as far as the crest of the ridge in his front, where "a hot fire was kept for a few minutes." But soon the regiment "was ordered to take its first position, and did so." To the left of the 30th, the story was different. The soldiers were reluctant to leave what they thought was the security of the lane. Lieutenant James W. Shinn of the 4th North Carolina wrote in his diary, "Gen Wrights [*sic*] Brigade came in, Wright was drunk & tried to order our Brigade forward, but the commanders choose to await Anderson's orders as we were under cover & preferred to let the enemy come up."[62]

V

One of the reasons the 14th North Carolina did not advance, Colonel Bennett said, was that "two fresh columns of the enemy were seen double-quicking to the relief of the shattered ranks of the foe, and stern necessity bade us be satisfied with [the] simple holding of our ground." The two fresh columns that Bennett referred to came from the Second Corps division of Major General Israel B. Richardson. This division had been held back by McClellan when Sumner was ordered to march to the front with Sedgwick's and French's divisions. McClellan wanted to ensure that the division of Major General George W. Morrell, Fifth Army Corps, was in place before releasing Richardson, so Richardson was not able to begin his march until about 9:00 A.M. Crossing the creek at Pry's Ford as the other divisions of the Second Corps had done,

Richardson marched southwest across the Neikirk farm toward the sound of the fighting at the Sunken Road. In a deep ravine approximately eight hundred yards northeast of the Sunken Road, he deployed the division with Brigadier General Thomas F. Meagher's brigade on the right, Brigadier General John C. Caldwell's on the left, and Colonel John R. Brooke's in the rear behind Meagher. As the division started forward, the right of Meagher's brigade guided on the Roulette farm lane bringing it directly in front of the section of the Sunken Road occupied by Anderson and Wright, just as the 132nd Pennsylvania and 7th West Virginia were withdrawing after repulsing Wright's brigade and the 30th North Carolina.[63]

On the left of D. H. Hill's line beyond the Roulette lane, the arrival of R. H. Anderson's brigades was noted by Rodes. In his official report he stated, "About this time I noticed troops going in to the support of Anderson, or to his right, and that one regiment and a portion of another, instead of passing on to the front, stopped in the hollow immediately in my rear and near the orchard." The troops that Rodes saw near the orchard were those of Pryor's brigade, which, as already noted, remained stationary in and about the orchard and did not advance toward the Sunken Road as Wright's brigade did. Rodes then took it upon himself to see what the problem was. He wrote, "As the fire on both sides was, at my position at least, now desultory and slack, I went to the troops referred to, and found that they belonged to Gen. Pryor's brigade. Their officers stated that they had been ordered to halt there by somebody, not Gen. Pryor." One of the officers that Rodes spoke with at this point was Captain William D. Ballantine commanding the 2nd Florida on the left of Pryor's line. Rodes asked Ballantine why his regiment was not engaged, and Ballantine replied that he had no orders. Rodes told Ballantine that there was a desperate need for additional troops at the front, pointed out to him where his regiment was most needed, and ordered him to go in. Rodes then went in search of Pryor, who with the wounding of Anderson now commanded the division. Pryor, however, did not know what deployment orders had been given to Anderson. When Rodes found him after "a few moments" and informed him of the situation, Pryor responded by giving Colonel John C. Hately of the 5th Florida, who now commanded Pryor's brigade, orders to move forward immediately.[64]

While Rodes was searching for Pryor, Ballantine moved the 2nd Florida forward to the northern edge of the orchard and re-formed the line so that it was oriented to the northeast with the right of the regiment in the orchard and the left in the open field. When Colonel Hatley ordered the rest of the brigade forward the regiments dressed on the line of the 2nd Florida, and then the entire brigade charged through the cornfields toward the portion of the Sunken Road occupied by G. B. Anderson's and Wright's brigades. As Pryor's brigade entered the cornfields it came under heavy musketry fire from Meagher's soldiers now on the ridge above the Sunken Road. Colonel George A. Coppens of the 8th Florida was killed, as was his successor, Captain Richard A. Waller, who fell with the regimental colors draped over his shoulders. Once the brigade reached the lane a portion of it was stopped by Federal fire. Another portion, however, passed around the right of the 14th North Carolina and continued to the top of the ridge, but it was almost immediately forced to withdraw to the lane, where it mixed in with G. B. Anderson's troops.[65]

Coming on right behind Pryor's brigade were the remaining two brigades of R. H. Anderson's division, Posey's and Cumming's. As noted, these two brigades had initially taken position on the ridge southeast of the Piper farmstead, but they were soon ordered to follow Wright and Pryor. Posey's brigade, moving due north, came into the orchard just as Pryor's was moving forward and followed it in the charge toward the Sunken Road. The order of the regiments from left to right was the 16th Mississippi, the 12th Mississippi, 19th Mississippi, and 2nd Mississippi Battalion. On reaching the lane Posey's brigade did not stop but passed through Anderson's and Pryor's men, advancing some thirty to forty yards toward the top of the ridge in the face of fire from Meagher's regiments. Colonel Bennett of the 14th North Carolina commented that Posey's men "flowed over and out of the road and many of them were killed in this overflow. The 16th Mississippi disappeared as if it had gone into the earth." Lieutenant Shinn in the 4th North Carolina understatedly remembered that the blending of Posey's and Anderson's men in the confines of the Sunken Road "created some confusion."[66]

In moving to the Sunken Road, Cumming's brigade followed a more circuitous route. It first went back to and recrossed the Hagerstown Pike to the west, then marched several hundred yards north to again turn east crossing the pike once again north of Piper's lane. Lieutenant Alexander C. Chisholm of Company I, 9th Alabama, recalled that just before recrossing the pike "we met some of the 4th Alabama [Hood's division] from our town coming out of the fight as we were going in."[67]

After crossing the pike, the brigade marched east through Piper's orchard, discovering that it was at least partially enclosed by an unusually stout fence. Lt. Chisholm remembered, "The east fence of Piper's orchard was made of wide boards with ends up with top ends sawed like saw teeth." The fence was so strong that "we knocked off only a few pickets so we could get through at our leasure [sic]." Once through the orchard, the brigade partially crossed the plowed field beyond, before turning north toward the Sunken Road. The left of the brigade, consisting of the 10th and 11th Alabama, continued straight on and entered the cornfield, finally taking position on the right of Pryor's brigade and behind Wright's, where it formed a second line. Sawler Darby of the 10th Alabama remembered that "we went very near, if not to the lane" (Map 3.16: Situation 1030). The right of the brigade, however, the 8th and 9th Alabama, crossed over the southern extension of the sunken lane, moved north across the pasture field on the east side of the lane, and according to Lt. Chisholm "took an advanced position along an old rail fence the field open in our front and sloping gradually down to some woods some 2 or 300 yards distance between which and our position we could plainly see 2 or 3 blue lines of battle, on our left was a cornfield." Once in position, the brigade suffered heavily from Federal musketry fire and artillery fire from the batteries beyond the Antietam. Chisholm remembered that "one of our regiment named Smith got his head taken off with a shell or solid shot, his brains spattered upon several of us who were close to him, I saw parts of his skull with hair attached go high into the the air." Chisholm thought that the Federal soldiers would also remember this ghastly incident, because "such a thing seldom happened in either army."[68]

After Rodes got Pryor's brigade moving toward the Sunken Road, he turned back to tend to the needs of his own brigade. As he was walking between the orchard and the lane, however, he met Lieutenant Colonel James N. Lightfoot. Lightfoot had succeeded to command of the 6th Alabama, replacing Gordon who by now had been wounded five times, was unconscious, and was being borne to the rear on a litter. Lightfoot told Rodes "that the right wing of his regiment was being subjected to a terrible enfilading fire, which the enemy were enabled to deliver by reason of their gaining somewhat on Anderson, and that he had but few men left in that wing." Rodes told Lightfoot that he should pull the right wing of the regiment out of the lane and reset it at an acute angle to the left wing on the high ground just to the rear of the lane. Lightfoot turned and dashed off at once, but instead of executing the order as it had been given him, he "moved briskly to the rear of the regiment and gave the command,

MAP 3-16: SITUATION 1030

0 100 200 300 400 500
YARDS

CONTOUR INTERVAL 10 FEET

'Sixth Alabama, about face; forward march.'" The movement of the 6th Alabama to the rear was observed by Major E. Lafayette Hobson commanding the 5th Alabama to the left of the 6th. Hobson called to Lightfoot, asking if the order to move to the rear "was intended for the whole brigade." Lightfoot for some unexplained reason replied yes. According to Rodes, "The Fifth, and immediately the other troops on their left, retreated."[69]

Rodes, however, did not see what was going on in the lane. "Just as I was moving on after Lightfoot," he reported, "I heard a shot strike Lieut. [John] Birney, who was immediately behind me. Wheeling, I found him falling, and found that he had been struck in the face. He found that he could walk after I raised him, though he thought a shot or piece of shell had penetrated his head

II2   Chapter 3

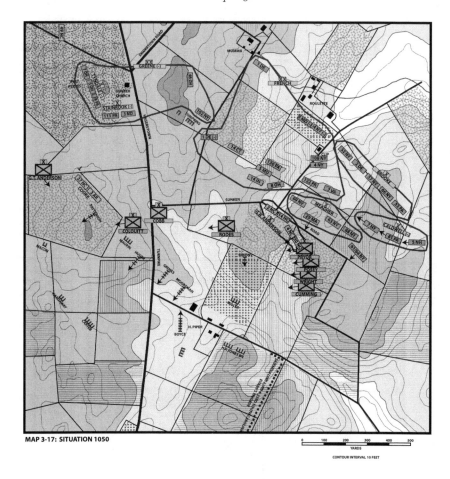

MAP 3-17: SITUATION 1050

0   100   200   300   400   500
YARDS

CONTOUR INTERVAL 10 FEET

just under the eye. I followed him a few paces, and watched him until he had
reached a barn, a short distance to the rear, where he first encountered some
one to help him in case he needed it." Rodes turned back toward his brigade,
but "was struck heavily by a piece of shell on my thigh. At first I thought the
wound was serious, but finding, upon examination, that it was slight, I again
turned toward the brigade, when I discovered it, without visible cause to me,
retreating in confusion. I hastened to intercept it at the Hagerstown road. I
found, though, that, with the exception of a few men from the Twenty-sixth,
Twelfth, and Third, and a few under Major Hobson, not more than 40 in all,
the brigade had completely disappeared from this portion of the field." One
soldier who did not withdraw from the road with the brigade was Lieutenant

Perry of Company G, 6th Alabama, who had promised Lee that he would do his duty and die with his company. And such was the case. The *Selma Morning Reporter* commented on 18 December 1862, "During the hotly contested battle no one was more conspicuous for gallantry and daring than he, and though wounded early in the action, being the only officer with his company, he remained until a fatal shot laid him low."[70]

As Rodes's brigade withdrew from the Sunken Lane, so also did the rallied elements of Colquitt's and McRae's brigades and Cobb's brigade still under the command of Lieutenant Colonel C. C. Sanders (Map 3.17: Situation 1050). Sanders, however, did not pull back very far, only realigning the brigade along the Hagerstown Pike south of the Sunken Road with his left at the junction of the two. Lieutenant Colonel William MacRae, commanding the 15th North Carolina, one of the brigade's regiments, reported that the brigade was still in position along the Sunken Lane when "the force on our right gave way. To prevent flanking, we changed front to the rear on the Fourth Battalion, and took position behind a stone fence, our extreme left remaining unchanged."[71]

VI

To the right of Rodes's brigade the situation was also growing desperate. The regiments of G. B. Anderson's, Wright's, Pryor's, and Posey's brigades were all massed together in the lane or just behind it, with the 10th and 11th Alabama of Cumming's brigade just to the rear of lane on the right. Cumming's 8th and 9th Alabama extended the line to the east beyond the right angle turn of the lane. To add to the confusion, no one officer was exercising command over the troops in this section of the road. D. H. Hill was preoccupied with the collapse of Rodes on the left, and R. H. Anderson was wounded and being carried to the rear. Command of his division had passed to Pryor, but not knowing what orders Anderson had received, Pryor was unable to exercise effective control over the division's brigades. The only other general officer present was G. B. Anderson, but at this point he was wounded in the foot (a wound that would prove fatal) and was out of action.[72]

Command of Anderson's brigade passed to Colonel Tew of the 2nd North Carolina. However, as he was being informed of Anderson's wounding and his elevation to command of the brigade, Tew himself was struck by a Minie ball. John Finn, a member of the regiment, later remembered "the bullet striking him on the left temple passing through the head, and coming out at the right temple dislodging the eyes from the sockets. He was sitting up with his back against the embankment, as this was a deep cut road or lane. I think that he was unconscious of what was going on around him, and knew that it was impossible for him to live more than an hour or so at best. He was sensible enough to hold a tight grasp to his sword, of which we were very anxious to secure, and which was taken from him by the Company, as also his waist belt and scabbard."[73]

Command of Anderson's brigade now devolved upon Colonel Bennett of the 14th North Carolina. His initial observation was that the brigade was "perfectly self-possessed" and holding its own, but he was immediately informed that he needed "to keep lookout on the extreme right." When he did look to the right he saw the troops of R. H. Anderson's division "in great confusion" and as he continued to watch, they "broke beyond the power of rallying after five minutes' stay." In an instant, the entire line in the Sunken Road to the right of the 14th North Carolina was gone.[74]

What caused the line east of the 14th to break so suddenly was the nearly simultaneous, though uncoordinated, advance of two Federal regiments. The first was by a regiment of Meagher's brigade, the 29th Massachusetts. This regiment had advanced in line toward the Sunken Road with the rest of Meagher's brigade, but had not been included in the initial charge of the brigade against the road because Meagher had sent the regimental commander, Lieutenant Colonel Joseph Barnes, no orders. Rather, the 29th took position behind a small hilltop one hundred yards in front of the 4th and 30th North Carolina. This position had given the 29th a unique advantage in the battle for the Sunken Road by shielding it from direct fire coming from the road, while still permitting the soldiers to use their Enfields to fire into the cornfield beyond the Sunken Road; their fire was heavy enough that it was like "cutting off the stalks of green corn as would a scythe, and having their effect upon the enemy who were hiding there." After a time, however, Barnes became worried about the condition of the other regiments of the brigade that were more exposed. Going to his right, he found that the 69th New York, "though holding on bravely, had lost nearly half their number." On the left, he found the 63rd New York "had fared equally as hard, and the officers and men of both regiments were striving to keep up their formations." To maintain the brigade line and gain time until reinforcements could arrive, Barnes determined to lead his regiment in a sudden charge toward the road. Calling for three cheers, he gave the order "Forward." As the 29th surged toward the road, some men in the other regiments of Meagher's brigade followed suit. According to the regimental historian, a member of the regiment, "The shouts of our men, and their sudden dash toward the sunken road, so startled the enemy that their fire visibly slackened, their line wavered, and squads of two and three began leaving the road and running into the corn."[75]

A regiment of Caldwell's brigade, the combined 61st/64th New York under the command of Colonel Francis Barlow, made the second thrust at the Sunken Road. Caldwell's brigade had advanced on the left of Meagher with his regiments thrown back in echelon so that they were well below the ridge where the Sunken Road turned sharply south, and thus unseen from the Confederate position in the road. As the condition of Meagher's brigade deteriorated, Richardson decided to have Caldwell come across to replace it. To that end, he sent a staff officer to bring the 61st/64th New York, Caldwell's right regiment, up on the left of Meagher's line, while Richardson himself sought out Caldwell to order him to bring the rest of his regiments in behind Meagher. When the 61st/64th New York formed on Meagher's left, Barlow immediately ordered it forward toward the Sunken Road. Lieutenant Charles A. Fuller, an officer in the 61st New York, remembered, "Instead of halting his men where Meagher had, [Barlow] rushed forward half the distance to the rebel line, halted, and at once opened fire. We were so near to the enemy, that when they showed their heads to fire, they were liable to be knocked over." According to the 29th's historian, these combined advances were "altogether too much of a shock for the enemy; they broke, and fled for the corn-field."[76]

In the 9th Alabama in Cumming's brigade, which together with the 8th Alabama formed the extended Sunken Road line, Lieutenant Chisholm recalled that after "fighting hard for some time that old familiar sound Hip Hip Huzzah told us that some thing had to be done, and that quickly for the Federals were on their feet their colors up and they were coming fast. All of us that could got away from there, every man looking out for himself. I am sorry to say that in our rapid backward movement our color bearer [received] a shot that broke his arm, and lost our flag." To the right of the 9th was Major Herbert's 8th Alabama. He remembered that he "ordered the regiment back when our left was observed to be giving away. I tried very hard to keep the regiment in line as we went back, but I was behind the line towards the enemy and we were much exposed in falling back, and consequently did so in much confusion. When we got down under the brow of the hill over which we retreated I had only eight men around my colors."[77]

To the left of Cumming's brigade, Colonel Gibson decided it was time for him to withdraw Wright's brigade. He reported, "The support on our right and left having withdrawn and none being in our rear that I knew of, with our cartridges exhausted[,] upon seeing a new formation of the enemy in our front of a very large force, and a movement by our right flank, from which a brigade had long before retired[,] I withdrew the brigade in order to a stone fence in the rear." That stone fence was some seven hundred yards to the southwest along the Hagerstown Pike. Colonel Posey, observing the withdrawal of both Cumming's and Wright's regiments, as well as the great confusion and loss caused by the overcrowding in the lane, decided that it was time for him to withdraw his brigade, and Pryor did likewise with his. Even the regiments of G. B. Anderson's brigade were affected by the sudden collapse of the Confederate line to their right. Bennett reported, "In this stampede, if we may so term it, the Fourth North Carolina State Troops and Thirtieth North Carolina Troops participated." Lieutenant Shinn in the 4th North Carolina remembered his regiment being ordered to the rear. "The minnie balls[,] shot & shell rained upon us from every direction except the rear. We were ordered to fall back & many men took this as a chance (from all Regt's) to leave the field entirely. We fell back something over a quarter of a mile." But not all members of the 4th got the order to withdraw. Captain Osborne, who by this time had replaced the mortally wounded Captain William T. Marsh as regimental commander and had himself been wounded and carried from the field, later wrote that "the Fourth Regiment lost a number of men from companies I and K, on the left, who were taken prisoners: being separated from the right by a little hillock, they did not know the retreat had taken place until they were in the hands of the enemy."[78]

As the entire Confederate line in the Sunken Road to the right of the 14th North Carolina began to withdraw, Colonel Barlow realized that his position opposite the most eastern extension of the Sunken Lane gave him a particular advantage "for attacking in flank this part of the enemy's line." Accordingly, he advanced the 61st/64th New York all the way to the lane, then wheeled the line to the right to obtain "an enfilading fire upon the enemy" remaining in the road. William A. Smith in Company C of the 14th North Carolina recalled that once the enemy "obtained a position from which he could enfilade our position . . . the slaughter was awful." Colonel Bennett, now finding himself alone with only the 2nd and 14th North Carolina, watched as the "dark lines of the enemy . . . swept around our right." Realizing that "to contend against front and rear attacks we were totally inadequate, and the bare alternative of retreat was presented. The command was ordered to make the retreat by the right-oblique, with frightful loss." In the 2nd North Carolina, Captain Gorman noted, "Our left has given away, and the enemy has already crossed the lane in our rear. At last, the order is given to fall back, and the few that remain uninjured fall suddenly back."[79]

As in the 4th North Carolina, not all of the 14th North Carolina got the order to withdraw from the lane. Sergeant Newsom E. Jenkins was on the extreme right of the 14th's line as a member of Company A. Up to this point, he had considered the company fortunate to be located "in an old road, washed out on a hill slope, which gave us some protection over our less fortunate comrades of the 4th & 30th. They suffered more as they were on top of the hill, and had no protection. In consequence of this exposure and large odds against them, they gave away . . . and that left our right exposed, so the enemy came down on us and forced us to surrender. Col. Bennett had gotten out and Capt. Freeman was acting as major and surrendered about 80 men, whilst we thought the whole regiment was there, and we were still keeping [the] line at bay in front." Jenkins remembered that "when the flanking line came over the hill, I was not more than 30 yards from them." Barlow reported that "seeing the uselessness of further resistance, the enemy, in accordance with our demands, threw down their arms, came in in larger numbers, and surrendered. Upward of 300 prisoners thus taken by my regiments were sent to the rear with a guard of my regiment."[80]

As the infantry withdrew from the lane, so too did much of the artillery that had been positioned to support the troops there. As previously noted, Miller's battery had already withdrawn to a secure position within Piper's orchard below the ridge, and Boyce's battery had also pulled back toward the Piper farmstead. Major Saunders, who commanded the artillery battalion supporting R. H. Anderson's division and who had earlier been absent sick, now returned to duty only to find his battalion in desperate straits. He remembered "finding as I arrived its commander Grimes had been mortally wounded, and the command so crippled that it was ordered to the rear." He resumed command of the battalion and immediately started three of its four batteries to the rear. The one battery to remain in position was Maurin's. Eugene H. Levy, who was with that battery, recalled, "We covered the advance of our division to the relief of D.H. Hill's demoralized troops until the pressure was relieved on the left wing of our army." Perhaps the battery remained in position because it was farthest from the fighting, or perhaps because it was inspired by the presence of General Lee who, Levy wrote, "was near our guns for some time looking anxiously in the direction of the heavy infantry fighting about the centre of line of battle."[81]

With some difficulty, Lieutenant Simons was able to withdraw the section of Bachman's battery that he had brought forward to the cornfield north of Piper's orchard. His problem was that six of the twelve horses that had brought the guns forward were now disabled, so his gunners had to drag the pieces by hand to the more secure place below the ridge in the lower part of the orchard where he had left the caissons. Then he "went back with some men and brought out the men who had been shot." Simons recalled that once back with the caissons, he "staid [*sic*] here a considerable time trying to put things in shape for further service." He then withdrew the section to Sharpsburg.[82]

VII

Although the collapse of the Confederate line in the Sunken Road east of the Roulette lane had been complete, its suddenness caught the Federals unprepared for immediate pursuit. Captain Gorman in the 2nd North Carolina thought that the enemy had "been so badly punished, they were not able to follow us immediately." More to the point, however, it took time for Barlow and his 61st/64th New York to sweep down the length of the Sunken Road from its eastern apex to its junction with the Roulette farm lane. As he was doing this, the rest of Caldwell's brigade was moving in behind what was left of Meagher's line. Caldwell only then began his forward movement toward the lane, his regiments passing through Meagher's as they withdrew to the rear. On reaching the edge of the lane, Caldwell's regiments halted to fire on the Confederates withdrawing through the cornfields south of the lane. Lieutenant Thomas Livermore of the 5th New Hampshire recalled that "we fired by file a little before we advanced across the road." This maneuvering and Caldwell's brief halt to fire gave Confederate leaders some small time to begin rallying what troops they could to resist the Federal advance. Caldwell reported that once across the road and into the cornfield beyond, "the enemy opened upon us a terrific fire

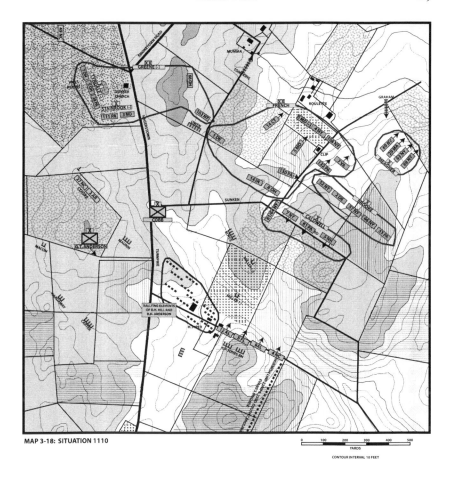

MAP 3-18: SITUATION 1110

from a fresh line of infantry, and also poured upon us a fire of grape and canister from two batteries, one in the orchard just beyond the corn-field, and the other farther over to the right" (Map 3.18: Situation 1110).[83]

The batteries that challenged Caldwell's brigade were a section of Miller's in the northern edge of Piper's orchard and Boyce's to its left in the open field immediately to the northwest of the orchard. Both of these batteries had been in action supporting the Sunken Road position but had been ordered back and had taken secure positions in defilade below the ridge line, Miller in the orchard and Boyce to the west of the Piper farmstead. Colonel Walton in his report wrote that when the enemy advanced, Miller "ordered his battery again into position. Lieut. [Andrew] Hero having been wounded and Lieut. [Frank]

McElroy having been left to watch the movements of the enemy on the right, Capt. Miller found himself the only officer with his company, and, having barely men enough left to work a section effectively, he opened upon the enemy with two pieces with splendid effect." Boyce's battery was ordered into position by D. H. Hill, who was in the vicinity of the Piper farm attempting to rally whatever forces he could to resist a continued Federal advance. He reported, "I found a battery concealed in a cornfield, and ordered it to move out and open upon the Yankee columns. This proved to be Boyce's South Carolina battery. It moved out most gallantly, although exposed to a terrible direct and reverse fire from the long-range Yankee artillery across the Antietam. A caisson exploded, but the battery unlimbered, and with grape and canister drove the Yankees back." Boyce in his report recalled that "my battery was at this time thrown forward . . . into an open field 200 or 300 yards in advance of its original position. The enemy then advanced through a corn-field to the field in which my battery had taken its position, showing a front of several hundred yards in extent, plainly on the right and center, but partly concealed by the corn on the left. The whole line of the enemy here was within canister range, and I opened upon him a destructive fire, cutting down two of his flags at the second or third discharge of the guns."[84]

The fresh line of infantry that Caldwell encountered as he entered the cornfield was not a fresh line at all but an ad hoc collection of troops that after leaving the lane rallied in the vicinity of the Piper house and along Piper's lane to the east. They included what was left of the 4th North Carolina, 9th and 12th Alabama, and the 5th Florida. Lieutenant Chisholm of the 9th remembered that on reaching the vicinity of Piper's house, "we immediately reformed[,] advanced and this time met the Federals in the cornfield this side of and to the left of the line they had driven us from." Chisholm went on to say that during the fighting in the cornfield "1st Lt Taylor commanding our company was wounded in the knee, I as 2nd Lt took command. Two men started back with Taylor."[85]

This initial counterattack against Caldwell's advancing line fell heaviest on the 5th New Hampshire on the left of the brigade line (Map 3.19: Situation 1130). After advancing across the lane and into the cornfield under "a heavy fire of shell and canister-shot, which killed and wounded quite a number of officers and men, a single shell wounding 8 men and passing through the State colors of my regiment," the 5th's commander, Colonel Edward E. Cross, reported, "I had scarcely reached my position on the left of the first line of battle and opened

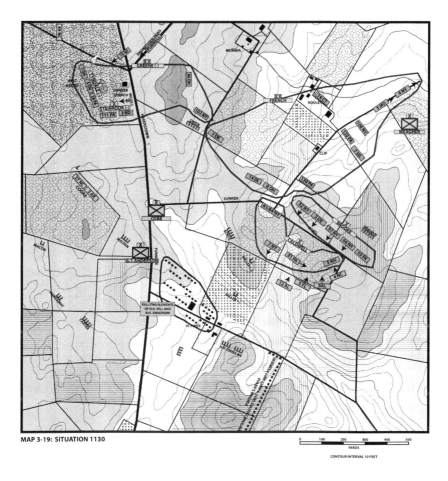

MAP 3-19: SITUATION 1130

CONTOUR INTERVAL 10 FEET

fire, when it was reported that the enemy were cautiously attempting to out-flank the entire division with a strong force concealed behind a ridge, and in the same corn-field in which I was posted. They had, in fact, advanced within 200 yards of the left of our lines, and were preparing to charge. I instantly ordered a change of front to the rear, which was executed in time to confront the advancing line of the enemy in their center with a volley at very short range, which staggered and hurled them back. They rallied and attempted to gain my left, but were again confronted and held, until, assistance being received, they were driven back with dreadful loss."[86]

The assistance that Cross spoke of came from the 81st Pennsylvania that had advanced across the Sunken Lane and into the cornfield on the right of the 5th New Hampshire "under a heavy fire of grape." However, as the 5th maneuvered to the left and rear to meet the counterattack, it opened a gap between itself and the 81st, which the 81st's regimental commander, Major H. Boyd McKeen, moved immediately to close. He reported, "At this time I noticed the enemy's flags approaching from the orchard, and engaging the Fifth New Hampshire. The Fifth having taken up their position on the edge of the corn-field, and in the old road, I immediately changed the position of my regiment, taking position on their right, opening fire on the enemy with terrible execution. The Fifth New Hampshire and Eighty-first Pennsylvania thus completely frustrated an attempt to flank the division."[87]

The movement of the 5th New Hampshire and the 81st Pennsylvania opened a large gap between them and the right regiments of Caldwell's brigade, the 7th New York, advancing directly toward the orchard and Miller's battery, and Barlow's 61st/64th New York, just beginning to advance into the cornfield from the vicinity of the junction of the Roulette farm lane and the Sunken Road. In an attempt to fill this gap and to support Caldwell, Colonel John R. Brooke brought forward the last of Richardson's brigades, crossed the Sunken Road, and advanced south into the cornfields toward Piper's orchard and farmstead.[88]

In remembering the fight with the 5th New Hampshire and the 81st Pennsylvania, Lieutenant Chisholm wrote that "after exchanging shots with them for some time they again advanced, we saw we couldn't stop them, we had either to run or surrender[;] we ran rapidly back through a large orchard." The orchard was, of course, Piper's, which the 9th had gone through earlier as Cumming's brigade advanced toward the Sunken Road. Chisholm commented that "the holes we made in the fence on our advance, were not enough for us in our rapid retreat with the Federals upon our heels, shooting with all their might, so that many of our men were either killed or forced to surrender at the fence." In going through the orchard, Chisholm and the other members of the 9th who managed to get through the fence caught up with the men carrying the wounded Lieutenant Taylor to the rear and "we carried him to Piper[']s barn from which place he was carried in an ambulance to the rear." They then joined with "a small body of many commands" that rallied on the ridge northwest of Piper's barn with their left resting on the Hagerstown Pike and their right at Piper's barn.[89]

VIII

Another movement slowing the Federal pursuit of the Confederates was a desperate counterattack being made against French's right flank. Shortly before the withdrawal from the Sunken Lane, Longstreet had been arranging for an attack by all available units to turn that flank of French's division at the Sunken Road. The units included Rhodes's, Colquitt's, and Cobb's brigades in the Sunken Road left of the Roulette farm lane. They also included two regiments from Manning's brigade, the 27th North Carolina and 3rd Arkansas, under the command of Colonel J. R. Cooke of the 27th, which were positioned in a cornfield on a high ridge some 250 yards west of the junction of the Hagerstown Pike and the Sunken Road. Cooperating in the attack by moving against Richardson's front would be the regiments of G. B. Anderson's brigade and R. H. Anderson's division west of the Roulette farm lane. However, before orders could be issued to begin the attack, the precipitious withdrawal from the Sunken Road took place. Nevertheless, with the situation even more desperate than before, orders were now sent to Cooke and Cobb to advance against French's right.[90]

As has already been discussed, Manning on arriving in the vicinity of the West Woods had sent Cooke with his own 27th North Carolina and the 3rd Arkansas to the right "to hold the open space between the woods and Longstreet's left." In that position, Cooke skirmished with elements of Greene's division as they moved into the West Woods. Lieutenant James A. Graham in Company G of the 27th later wrote that shortly before receiving the order to move against French's flank, Cooke had ordered the two regiments "to fall back some twenty steps in the cornfield and lie down, so as to draw them [the enemy] on; he in the meantime, regardless of personal danger from sharpshooters, remained at the fence beside a small hickory tree. After remaining there some twenty minutes the enemy attempted to sneak up a section of artillery to the little woods on our left. Colonel Cooke, watching the movement, ordered the four left companies of the Twenty-seventh North Carolina up to the fence and directed them to fire upon this artillery. At the first fire, before they had gotten into position, nearly every horse and more than half the men fell, and the infantry line which had moved up to support them showed evident signs of wavering." The section of artillery that Cooke observed was from Captain Joseph M. Knap's Battery E, Pennsylvania Light Artillery, under the command of Lieutenant James D. McGill. McGill remembered that in the process of attempting to position one of his guns in the woods "two horses were shot (one killed) and the pintle hook so bent that it was impossible to unlimber the gun, although we had the assistance of dozens of men of the Infantry."[91]

It was at this point that Cooke received the order from Longstreet to move forward and, accordingly, he ordered the two regiments to charge the woods (Map 3.20: Situation 1150). Graham remembered that "without waiting [for] a second word of command both regiments leaped the fence and 'went at them.'" Graham also recalled that "soon after we started the charge, some drunken officer on horseback, (who or of what command I never learned), rode in front of the Twenty-seventh North Carolina, then commanded by Lieutenant-Colonel R.W. Singletary, and pulling off and waving his hat, yelled out, 'Come on, boys, I'm leading this charge.' Lieutenant-Colonel Singletary immediately ran up to him (the regiment being then at double-quick) and replied, 'You are a liar, sir, we lead our own charges.'"[92]

The 27th North Carolina and the 3rd Arkansas naturally went for the troops directly in their front, the two regiments of Stainrook's brigade, the 111th Pennsylvania and the 3rd Maryland, that were in position behind the rail fence at the very southern extent of the West Woods, their line extending all the way to the Hagerstown Pike. The 3rd Maryland, which was on the right of the line and outside of the woods, had already been weakened by the skirmish fire of the 27th North Carolina. It began to withdraw, immediately followed by the 111th Pennsylvania. Major Thomas M. Walker, commanding the 111th, reported that his regiment withdrew because "a new regiment, formed at right angles to our right, receiving the fire of an advancing line, broke and ran through us, carrying us back over part of the ground we had fought so hard to gain."[93]

The advancing line that Major Walker referred to was not Cooke's line but a second advance being made against Greene's right flank by two more of Walker's regiments, the 35th and 49th North Carolina of Ransom's brigade. This attack on Greene's right was not coordinated with the attack being made by Cooke but was an entirely separate attack. Ransom's two regiments were in the center and upper southern section of the woods in the same position that they had been in since the arrival of the brigade in the woods behind McLaws's and Early's brigades, and from which they had repulsed the advance of two of Gordon's regiments. Ransom himself was not with the brigade at this time. He had gone to the left to find the 24th North Carolina, leaving his brother, Colonel

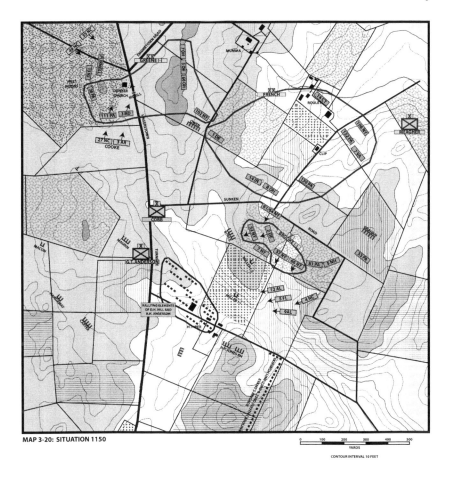

MAP 3-20: SITUATION 1150

Matthew W. Ransom of the 35th, in temporary command of the three remaining regiments. Colonel Ramsom observed McGill's section advance down Smoketown Road, turn south on the Hagerstown Pike and attempt to take position near the Dunker Church. Believing that no Federal infantry stood between him and McGill's guns, he determined to push forward through the southern section of the woods with the 35th and 49th North Carolina to capture them. Accordingly, he gave orders to Lieutenant Colonel Lee M. McAfee to pivot the 49th to the right and charge for the church, to be followed by the 35th. As the 49th North Carolina was making this maneuver and starting down deeper into the woods, Benjamin F. Dixon, a member of the regiment, recalled that "Union forces appeared in front across a ravine but we were undetermined whether they

were enemies or not. Colonel McAfee . . . sent Captain Cicero Dunham to reconnoiter and he was called on to surrender, upon which he wheeled his horse
and a hot fire was opened by both sides."[94]

The appearance of the 49th coming forward across the ravine was as much
of a surprise to the Federals as their presence on the opposite side of the ravine was to the 49th. Detecting some movement across the ravine, Colonel
Ezra A. Carman of the 13th New Jersey sent Major Charles A. Hopkins to
see what it was. Hopkins recalled, "The foliage of the trees prevented my getting a good view until they had nearly reached the extreme depression between
the two hills. As soon as I discovered they were Confederates, I started back,
shouting 'they are rebels.' Our men immediately began firing and the rebels,
deploying on their first division, opened fire simultaneously. Being caught between the lines of fire, I dropped to the earth and remained there, until hearing the rebels charging and yelling behind me, I looked back and saw them
coming." As it made its way out of the ravine the 49th overlapped the right of
the 13th New Jersey, which caused Carman to pull back the three right companies of the regiment until they were nearly at a right angle with the remaining companies. Passing the flank of the 13th New Jersey, the 49th North Carolina came up against an equally surprised Purnell Legion, whose commander,
Lieutenant Colonel Benjamin L. Simpson, reported that "the enemy appeared
in overwhelming numbers and compelled it to retire." With the right and rear
exposed by the attack of the 49th and 35th North Carolina and the left under
attack by the 27th North Carolina and 3rd Arkansas, Greene stated that "the
enemy advancing in large force, threatening to envelop the small command,
they were forced to retire." Lieutenant McGill also had to hurriedly start his
section to the rear, abandoning for lack of horses the gun and limber that he
had tried to position in the woods near the church.[95]

Continuing their charge through the woods, the 49th and 35th North Carolina approached the Hagerstown Pike and came close to capturing McGill's
retiring section as it turned onto Smoketown Road (Map 3.21: Situation 1200).
As McGill remembered it, "The enemy made a charge, as I had looked for, and
we were compelled to fall back with the four horses, but leaving the gun which
could not be extricated, having lost four men wounded and one killed in our
retreat. All the detachment would have been killed or taken prisoners had not
the other gun, which was fortunately loaded and halted on the road, been fired
on the pursuing enemy without being unlimbered, which checked his advance

MAP 3-21: SITUATION 1200

CONTOUR INTERVAL 10 FEET

long enough to save the one gun and the two Caissons." Lieutenant Walter Clark, adjutant of the 35th, remembered that his regiment "charged a piece of artillery (Knap's) which had been put in position near the Dunker Church. We killed the men and horses, but did not bring off the artillery, as we were ourselves swept by artillery on our left, posted in the 'old corn field.'" The artillery that Clark referred to was a line of Federal batteries at the western edge of the East Woods, beginning at Smoketown Road. It was to the rear of these batteries and the perceived safety of the East Woods that the Federal regiments were withdrawing. Only a few men of the 49th and 35th crossed the pike; the rest took shelter behind a barricade of rails, the same barricade that the 46th North Carolina had sheltered behind earlier, to fire on the retreating Federals.

The Federal artillery fire proved to be so heavy, however, that both regiments were forced to withdraw deeper into the woods and slightly to the left.[96]

South of the woods, the 27th North Carolina and 3rd Arkansas did cross the pike in pursuit of the Federal regiments withdrawing from the woods. Lieutenant Graham of the 27th remembered McGill's section being near the Dunker Church. He wrote, "A battery posted near a little brick church upon a hill (the Dunkard church …), was playing sad havoc with us, but thinking that [it] would be taken by the troops upon our left, who we supposed were charging with us, we still pursued the flying foe. Numbers of them surrendered to us and they were ordered to the rear." R. D. Patterson, also in the 27th, remembered that the regiment "crossed through the gap to the right of the church, and on the hill beyond there we turned to the right." As the two regiments raced toward the crest of the ridge, Colonel Cooke told the color bearer of the 27th, Private William H. Campbell of Company G, that he needed to go slower "as the regiment could not keep up with him." Private Campbell replied, "Colonel, I can't let that Arkansas fellow get ahead of me."[97]

Just beyond the crest of the ridge and directly in the path of these two regiments was the Second Corps battery of Captain Charles D. Owen, Battery G, 1st Rhode Island Light Artillery, supported by the 102nd New York from Stainrook's brigade. Owen had been sent forward to replace Tompkins's battery when it became low on ammunition, and had only been in position about twenty minutes when Owen reported "a noise from my right attracted my attention, and I saw our infantry retreating in disorder toward me, and then about 150 yards off, closely followed by the rebels. I limbered up quickly and started on the trot into the road leading direct from the [Mumma farm] ruins, and when the last caisson left the ground the enemy were close upon us." The 102nd New York, also without ammunition and otherwise unsupported, joined the other regiments of its brigade in withdrawing to the East Woods.[98]

Crossing the crest of the ridge, the 27th North Carolina and the 3rd Arkansas continued down toward the Roulette farm and the flank of French's division and the rear of Richardson's. Just before crossing the lane leading to the Mumma farmstead, however, Captain Adams and Lieutenant Graham, commanding the two left companies of the 27th, noticed what Graham remembered as two or three hundred Federal soldiers taking "shelter behind a lot of haystacks, and fastening white handkerchiefs to their muskets and bayonets, held them out offering to surrender." These two officers double-quicked with their companies to the haystacks, accepted the surrender of the Federals, ordered them to the rear, and then hastened back to their regiment, which was now midway through the Mumma cornfield.[99]

Years later Graham recalled that in the charge through Mumma's cornfield, Cooke's two regiments were able to deliver an enfilade fire against a Yankee line, "breaking six regiments, which fled in confusion. Only one Federal regiment, that I saw, left the field in anything like good order." In this, however, Graham was mistaken. The Federal regiments in front of Cooke were not fleeing in confusion; rather, Kimball was repositioning them to meet the charge head-on. Kimball reported that the enemy "succeeded in gaining a corn-field directly on my right. To repulse them, a change of front was made by the Fourteenth Indiana and Eighth Ohio Volunteers." The change of front made by these two regiments was to the right rear, which may have given Graham the impression that they were withdrawing in disorder. The new line of battle they formed was with their backs along the Roulette farm lane (Map 3.22: Situation 1215). Joining them on this line was the 130th Pennsylvania of Colonel Dwight Morris's brigade. Graham remembered these three regiments as "a body of the enemy behind a stone wall in a corn field," even though the line was largely in a plowed field and the stone wall to the rear. Graham went on to say that "Stopping to contend with these we found that we were almost out of ammunition; the cartridges which we had captured on the field, and of these there was a large quantity, not fitting our guns."[100]

As Cooke's regiments halted in the Mumma cornfield, their situation was growing ever more desperate. To Cooke's right on a ridge just south of the Sunken Road another Federal line was being formed by no less than four regiments coming from Caldwell's and Brooke's brigades. These regiments had been pushing toward Piper's orchard, but had turned back to meet the threat posed by Cooke. Yet another Federal regiment, the 53rd Pennsylvania, was maneuvering through the Roulette orchard toward Cooke's left front, and two brigades, those of Colonel William H. Irwin and Brigadier General William T. H. Brooks of Major General William F. Smith's division of the Sixth Army Corps, were moving toward his left from the vicinity of the East Woods. Cooke's two regiments were also under a heavy fire of spherical case shot and shell from two batteries, Lieutenant Evan Thomas's Consolidated Batteries A and C, 4th U.S. Artillery with six 12-pounder Napoleons positioned just north of Smoketown Road near its junction with the Mumma farm lane, and Captain William

MAP 3-22: SITUATION 1215

0   100   200   300   400   500
YARDS

CONTOUR INTERVAL 10 FEET

M. Graham's Battery K, 1st U.S. Artillery, six 12-pounder Napoleons located on the high ground just north of the Sunken Road at its easternmost point. Lieutenant Graham of the 27th North Carolina wrote that Cooke, "seeing that we were not supported in our charge, ordered us to fall back to our original position. This, of course, was done at double-quick."[101]

Graham continued: "As we returned we experienced the perfidy of those who had previously surrendered to us and whom we had not taken time to disarm. They, seeing that we were not supported, attempted to form a line in our rear and in a few minutes would have done so. As it was, we had to pass between two fires, a part of the troops having been thrown back to oppose our movement on their flank and these supposed prisoners having formed on the other side. A bloody lane indeed it proved to us. Many a brave man lost his life in that retreat. At some points the lines were not sixty yards distant on either side of us. Arriving at our original position both regiments halted and were soon reformed."[102]

Although Graham twice mentioned that in the charge toward the Roulette farm Cooke was unsupported, he did acknowledge that at least in the withdrawal "we were very materially aided and protected by Cobb's Brigade, then commanded by Colonel William MacRae, of the Fifteenth North Carolina Regiment." MacRae reported that shortly after his brigade had pulled back behind the stone fence along the Hagerstown Pike when the Sunken Road was abandoned, "Gen. D. H. Hill rode up and ordered us forward to check the advance of the enemy. Col. Sanders, though very unwell, had gallantly remained on the field, cheering his men by words and example until this moment, when he was too much exhausted to remain any longer. Being next in rank, the command devolved upon me."[103]

MacRae lead the brigade, "numbering now about 250 men," from its position at the junction of the Sunken Road and Hagerstown Pike, northeast up the hill toward the Mumma farm lane, just as Cooke was leading his two regiments across the ridge and toward Mumma's cornfield. Instead of continuing on Cooke's right, however, MacRae stopped the brigade when he reached the lane, some 150 yards south of the cornfield. In this position, MacRae had to face the fire of the four Federal regiments on the ridge south of the Sunken Road, as well as the spherical case shot and shell of Graham's battery. MacRae claimed that three times these regiments attempted to advance against him, but they were held back "by the galling fire of our gallant little band. We held them in check (momentarily expecting re-enforcements) until our ammunition was expended." With the withdrawal of Cooke's regiments from the Mumma cornfield and "seeing no sign of support, I was constrained to give the command to fall back. We left the field with not more than 50 of the 250 men. We fell back about 300 yards and joined Col. Cooke, of the Twenty-seventh North Carolina, remaining with his shattered regiment until he was relieved about 3 P.M."[104]

As Cooke and Cobb were withdrawing across the Hagerstown Pike to Reel Ridge, the position from which Cooke had originally advanced, General Smith sent two of Irwin's regiments, the 33rd and 77th New York, down either side of Smoketown Road toward the Dunker Church "for the purpose of cutting off the flying enemy." On approaching the West Woods, however, Lieutenant

Colonel Joseph W. Corning, commanding the 33rd, reported that "the enemy suddenly and unexpectedly opened on the regiment a heavy fire from their infantry, who were in the woods." The two regiments returned fire, but were quickly ordered by Smith to rejoin Irwin's other regiments, which had taken cover under the height of land. The fire that drove the New York regiments back came from the 35th and 49th North Carolina. Although these regiments had withdrawn deeper into the woods to avoid Federal artillery fire, they were still able to observe the advance of Irwin's regiments down Smoketown Road, and they advanced once again to the rail barricade along the Hagerstown Pike and opened fire.[105]

IX

Just after giving MacRae orders to advance against French's flank, D. H. Hill rode back to the Piper farm to try to rally the regiments that had abandoned the Sunken Road. Despite the limited success and small amount of time that had been gained by the counterattacks of Manning's, Cooke's, and Cobb's regiments, the situation south of the Sunken Road and at the Piper farm remained grim. Boyce's battery, which along with Miller's two guns in the Piper orchard had the held the Yankee advance back for a time, was now gone. Longstreet remembered that as the Federal advance continued through the cornfields south of the Sunken Road, Boyce's battery was cut off "so that it was obliged to retire to save itself." Boyce himself reported that "having no support of infantry, and no other battery assisting me in resisting this large body of the enemy, and being exposed the whole time to a galling fire from the enemy's sharpshooters, after firing 70 rounds of canister and some solid shot I was forced to retire from this hazardous position."[106]

After making a desperate fight of it, Miller's battery was also being pressed to the point where it would have to retire. One problem was that his two guns were without cannoneers. Major G. Moxley Sorrel, an assistant adjutant general on Longstreet's staff, remembered:

The gunners had fallen by their pieces, which were temporarily without cannoneers. Longstreet was with us. [Major John W.] Fairfax, [Captain Thomas J.] Goree, [Lieutenant Colonel Payton T.] Manning, [Major Thomas] Walton, myself, and perhaps some others took our horses' bridles as we leaped from them to the guns. The position was important and it would never do for these "barkers" to be dumb, even for a minute; so at it we went, the improvised gunners. . . . I had the rammer, number 1, I think it is in the drill. Our fire was really strong and effictive, until some reliefs from the Washington Artillery came up "ventre a terre," and with hearty shouts took their guns in hand. The enemy opened a severe fire on us, but fortunately none of our party was hurt. We mounted again with cheerful grins at our sudden adventure, and Longstreet, much pleased, turned his attention to other imperiled points.

Colonel Walton in his report noted that the relief for Longstreet's staff was brought by Sergeant William H. Ellis of Miller's battery "who had succeeded in rallying some infantry to his assistance, brought one of the guns of his section into action on Miller's left, and gave them canister, with terrible effect. The three guns succeeded in checking the enemy's advance, and remained in action until the ammunition was exhausted, when they were retired to be refilled."[107]

The Federal regiments that had repelled Cooke's and Cobb's attack toward the Roulette farm had by this time turned back again to the cornfield and were advancing toward the orchard. Barlow, commanding the combined 61st/64th New York, said that "on retiring from this position, the enemy renewed their attack on our old front. My regiments again changed front, and advanced into the corn-field which we had left, to assist in repelling the flank attack of the enemy just mentioned. Beyond this corn-field was an orchard, in which the enemy had artillery (two pieces to the best of my knowledge). From these pieces, and from others still farther to our right, they had been pouring a destructive fire of shell, grape, and spherical-case shot during the above-mentioned engagement of our infantry." On moving toward the orchard Barlow was wounded "in the groin by a ball from a spherical-case shot," probably one of the last shots fired by Miller's guns before the battery withdrew. Barlow was succeeded in command by Lieutenant Colonel Nelson A. Miles, who also noted in his report that "about this time a sharp musketry firing commenced on our left, or old front, it being evident they were advancing another line through the corn-field."[108]

The Confederate attack that was coming from the southwest was being led by D. H. Hill himself (Map 3.23: Situation 1230). Rodes in his official report mentioned that after the collapse and withdrawal of his brigade from the Sunken Road, he managed to rally some one hundred and fifty of the brigade, along with some Mississippians and North Carolinians. He stationed them "behind a small ridge leading from the Hagerstown road eastward toward the orchard

MAP 3-23: SITUATION 1230

YARDS

CONTOUR INTERVAL 10 FEET

before spoken of, and about 150 yards in rear of my last position." Rodes went on to say that "this force, with some slight additions, was afterward led through the orchard against the enemy by General D. H. Hill, and did good service, the general himself handling a musket in the fight." On returning to the vicinity of the Piper farm after giving orders to Cobb, Hill discovered this force, and reported, "I was now satisfied that the Yankees were so demoralized that a single regiment of fresh men could drive the whole of them in our front across the Antietam. I got up about 200 men, who said they were willing to advance to the attack if I would lead them. We met, however, with a warm reception, and the little command was broken and dispersed. Maj. [E. Lafayette] Hobson and Lieutenant [J. M.] Goff, of the Fifth Alabama, acquitted themselves handsomely in this charge."[109]

One of the soldiers who was a part of this small command was Lieutenant Chisholm of the 9th Alabama, who, it will be recalled, had reached the hill just west of the Piper barn after making his way back through Piper's orchard after participating in the counterattack against the 5th New Hampshire and 81st Pennsylvania. He remembered, "At this point Genl. D.H. Hill was with us in person walking up and down our lines and speaking words of encouragement to his already twice beaten regts, soon our skirmishers were driven in. Genl. Hill in a clear loud voice gave the order—*Attention—Charge*. We went at the Federals with such a vim that they fell back in confusion. We followed them to the edge of the field of corn that lay along the pike. I remember well seeing a large new U.S. flag as it was borne over the top of the corn in retreat." Once the charge reached the cornfield, however, Chisholm wrote, "the Artillery fire was so severe at this place that we couldn't stay there and we were not strong enough to follow the Federals into the corn, so we fell back, ... [returning] to the brow of the hill we had charged from."[110]

Hill's attack was not the only Confederate counterattack at this time in the vicinity of the Piper farm. Hill also reported that "Col. [Alfred] Iverson, Twentieth North Carolina; Col. [D. H.] Christie, Twenty-third North Carolina; Capt. Garrett, Fifth North Carolina; Adjutant [J. M.] Taylor and Lieutenant [Isaac E.] Pearce, of the same regiment, had gathered up about 200 men, and I sent them to the right to attack the Yankees in flank. They drove them back a short distance, but in turn were repulsed." This attack, which came slightly after Hill's attack toward the cornfield, was made against three Federal regiments, the 7th New York of Caldwell's brigade and the 57th and 66th New York of Brooke's brigade, which were advancing south through Piper's orchard and the plowed field to the east of it. Henry Gerrish of the 7th New York remembered that "as we got out of the corn field we soon found we were outflanked. We had fire on our front and also our right flank. We had to move at once by our left flank for a different position, and by bad luck we landed in front of a very large farm."[111]

The "very large farm" that Gerrish referred to was the Piper farmstead. He further remembered that "there was probably a whole regiment in and around the outbuildings, stationed there with a number of cannons" (Map 3.24: Situation 1245). While there can be no doubt that the Confederates had infantry in and around the Piper farmstead at this time, they were not organized to resist the Federal advance and were probably withdrawing toward the Hagerstown Pike to join the remnants of D. H. Hill's and R. H. Anderson's divisions that were attempting to rally there. The only organized bodies of Confederate in-

MAP 3-24: SITUATION 1245

0   100   200   300   400   500
YARDS

CONTOUR INTERVAL 10 FEET

fantry in the vicinity of the Piper farm were a detachment of three small regi-
ments from Brigadier General Nathan Evans's brigade and the brigade of G. T.
Anderson. The three regiments of Evans's brigade were the 18th, 22nd, and 23rd
South Carolina under the command of Colonel Stevens. The 22nd and 23rd
South Carolina were deployed as a thin skirmish line that extended from the
Piper farm lane three hundred yards east of the farmstead south to the Boonsboro Pike, while the 18th South Carolina was laying down in a swale between
two hills that formed a ridge to their rear. The brigade of G. T. Anderson was in
line along the Hagerstown Pike at its junction with the Piper farm lane. After
withdrawing from the vicinity of the Dunker Church, Anderson had for a time
remained in position along the southwest face of the West Woods. In his of-

ficial report Anderson said that "from this point I was ordered to the Hagers-town road by a staff officer of Gen. Longstreet, and moved to that place, tak-ing position behind the stone fence—a large number of the enemy in front of us in a corn-field. In a short time the enemy opened an enfilade fire on my po-sition with long-range artillery, and I was forced to change, moving down the road toward Sharpsburg under the crest of the hill."[112]

What force the Confederates did have at the Piper farm to resist the ad-vance of the three Federal regiments was the artillery that Gerrish referred to. Just a hundred yards east of Piper's house on the point of a ridge was a sec-tion of the Jefferson Davis (Alabama) Artillery under Captain James William Bondurant. This battery, one of D. H. Hill's, had bivouacked the previous night west of Sharpsburg along the Shepherdstown Pike near the Stephen Grove farm, and was brought forward as the fight for the Sunken Road was devel-oping. The battery consisted of four guns, three 3-inch Ordnance rifles, and one 12-pounder Napoleon, but because of a lack of men and ammunition, Bon-durant could only put two guns in position. Corporal John Purifoy, a member of the battery, recalled, "Upon reaching our position we immediately began fir-ing on the enemy lines which resulted in drawing his fire from right and left as well as front. One of the two pieces was dismounted, and several men were killed and wounded." The enemy lines that Purifoy wrote of were the Federal regiments of Caldwell's and Brooke's brigades assembled in the cornfields south of the Sunken Road. The Federal batteries engaging Bondurant were Graham's just north of the Sunken Road and the long-range guns east of the Antietam. Purifoy went on to say that "immediately succeeding this artillery duel, the enemy made a charge at the battery, through the cornfield . . . which was met and repulsed by Evans' South Carolina Brigade, passing through the Jeff Davis Battery, in its counter movement." This charge was probably made by the 66th New York, which was on the left flank of the three Federal regiments that had reached the Piper farmstead and lane.[113]

The infantry that came up in support of Bondurant's battery was not all of Evans's brigade but only the 18th South Carolina under the command of Colonel William H. Wallace. In his official report Wallace wrote: "Col. Stevens (acting brigadier-general), being under the impression that a charge was be-ing attempted by the enemy upon a battery in position on the second hill, im-mediately in our front, ordered the regiment forward to repel the charge. The regiment moved rapidly by the left flank around the hill upon which they had been lying, and, while ascending the hill upon which the battery was placed that was being charged, formed in line of battle and advanced to the battery, when it was discovered that the battery had succeeded in defending itself and had driven off the enemy. The regiment then took position close to and immediately upon the left flank of the battery in the edge of a corn-field."[114]

A second artillery piece being used against the Federal regiments at the Piper farm was an abandoned gun discovered by G. T. Anderson. He wrote, "At this point I found a 6-pounder gun, and, getting a few men to assist in placing it in position, a lieutenant of infantry, whose name or regiment I do not know, served it most beautifully until the ammunition was exhausted." The infantry lieutenant that Anderson referred to was William W. Chamberlaine, 6th Virginia, Mahone's brigade. Chamberlaine, who was in the vicinity of Piper's lane helping to rally the remnants of his brigade after its repulse from the Sunken Road, noticed the abandoned gun and, with the help of men from Anderson's brigade and the 6th Virginia, moved it a hundred yards up the Hagerstown Pike to the crest of the ridge. Here he fired several rounds at the Federal troops moving through the cornfield toward the Piper farmstead. But finding himself in an exposed position, Chamberlaine moved the gun back to the mouth of Piper's lane and engaged the Federal infantry (which included Private Gerrish and the 7th New York) assembled around Piper's barn and house. Gerrish recalled, "I happened to be the fifth man from our flag in the front rank, and as they began I saw a cannonier [*sic*] loading a gun, saw it pushed in position to fire. It was undoubtedly loaded with grape and canister, for it killed six and wounded nine." The gunner who fired this first shot down Piper's lane was Major John W. Fairfax of Longstreet's staff. As the Federal infantry withdrew from the farmstead and back through the cornfield toward the Sunken Road, Chamberlaine moved the gun again some fifty yards north along the Hagerstown Pike; from that position he continued to fire on the retreating Federals.[115]

X

It was about 1:00 P.M. when the Federal regiments withdrew from the vicinity of the Piper farmstead. For the first time in three and a half hours, since 9:30 A.M. when French had first engaged Rodes's and G. B. Anderson's brigades in the Sunken Road, the Confederate center faced no active threat, even though Richardson's and French's divisions were reassembling north of the Sunken

MAP 3-25: SITUATION 1300

YARDS

CONTOUR INTERVAL 10 FEET

Road and two fresh brigades from Smith's division of the Sixth Army Corps were taking up position on their right south of the Mumma farmstead. This pause, however short it might be, would give Confederate leaders time to shore up the center against a continuation of the Federal attack. But they had little infantry left they could count on (Map 3.25: Situation 1300). D. H. Hill and other officers managed to rally some of what was left of Hill's and R. H. Anderson's divisions in the Piper farmstead area, on the ridge running northwest from Piper's barn to the Hagerstown Pike and along the pike itself. G. T. Anderson's brigade also remained in position along the pike. Cooke with the 27th North Carolina, 3rd Arkansas, and the remnant of Cobb's brigade extended the line along the pike to the northwest. Because the available infantry was largely disorganized, very nearly demoralized, or out of ammunition, the primary task would have to be the assembling of artillery batteries to resist the advance that all believed was sure to come. To this end, some nineteen guns belonging to five batteries were being positioned on the Reel farm ridge west of the Hagerstown Pike across from the Piper farm.[116]

The focal point for the positioning of these guns was the four guns of Maurin's battery that had been in position on the ridge since its arrival ahead of R. H. Anderson's division. The reader will recall that Maurin's was the one battery that did not withdraw when Major Saunders, Anderson's chief of artillery, ordered the other three batteries of the division to the rear. To the right of Maurin's battery at a distance of 200 yards were the four guns of Hardaway's battery under Lieutenant Tullis. Tullis had taken his guns to Reel Ridge after withdrawing from his initial position just south of the Mumma farm, and for a time had been in position on the ridge farther to the north. He may have taken the guns out of action for a time, sheltering them below the ridge on the west side, but in the current emergency he brought them back into battery after receiving orders from Generals Lee and Longstreet. Tullis recalled, "Our infantry were in confusion and then it was that our artillery held the line and gave the infantry the chance to rally on us, Longstreet did it and was near to our Battery a little say 50 yards to our left, we repulsed the Federals and about the time [they] were forming to charge both Genl Lee an[d] Longstreet came by us, Genl Lee stopping with me pointing out [the Federal] lines and ordered me to begin firing."[117]

To the left of Maurin's battery at a distance of just 100 yards behind a rail fence was Captain Thomas Carter's battery of D. H. Hill's division. Carter, it will be recalled, had been in position at the beginning of the battle on the high ground north of the Sunken Road where it made the right angle turn to the south, but had been ordered to the rear by Rodes when that brigade was ordered to the north. In attempting to get to Reel Ridge, Carter had taken the battery south to the outskirts of Sharpsburg before finding a way to cross the stone wall that lined the east side of the Hagerstown Pike. There Lee ordered Carter back north to support McLaws's attack into the West Woods. As the crisis following the collapse of the Sunken Road line developed, Carter got orders from "Gen. Rodes to plant my battery on the left of the Hagerstown road, near the Donaldsonville Artillery [Maurin's battery]. With the consent of Gen. Lee, I at once moved my battery to this point. On reaching it, I found several batteries engaged in driving off a Yankee battery posted near the spot occupied in the morning by my two howitzers. My battery at once took part in this fire, and continued firing until the battery was withdrawn." Carter wrote his wife that he "protected the battery as far as possible by placing the guns just behind the crest so that they would fire over. In this way the balls of the enemy strike the crest in front[,] ricochet & pass over." Coming along with Carter and going into position to his left front at a distance of 200 yards were four guns from Captain Jefferson Peyton's Orange (Virginia) Artillery, and immediately to their left was a section from Captain Miles C. Macon's Richmond (Fayette) Artillery under the command of Lieutenant William I. Clopton. The Federal battery that Carter mentioned they were attempting to drive off was Graham's.[118]

In addition to the nineteen guns on Reel Ridge, Lieutenant Chamberlaine continued to man his gun on the Hagerstown Pike, and Bondurant's single gun remained in position east of the Piper farm. It was joined by two guns from Boyce's battery that went into position on lower ground just to the east. Boyce reported, "After resting and refreshing my men, and sending some disabled pieces to the rear and repacking my ammunition chests, I found I would only be able to manage two pieces on the field the remainder of the day."[119]

Once the batteries on Reel Ridge managed to force the retirement of Graham's battery, D. H. Hill was able to push a skirmish line north through Piper's orchard and out into the cornfields beyond. This skirmish line was supported by two guns of Miller's battery, which returned to its former position in Piper's orchard with a fresh supply of ammunition. Hill reported that in the effort to restore the Confederate center in the vicinity of Piper's farm, in particular the counterattacks that had been led by himself, Colonel Iverson, and others, "the yankees were completely deceived by [our] boldness, and induced to believe that there was a large force in our center. They made no further attempt to pierce our center, except on a small scale." Longstreet's assessment of the situation was that "though the Confederates had but fragments here and there, the enemy were kept busy and watchful lest they should come upon another surprise move." Thus ended the battle for the Sunken Road and the Confederate center.[120]

4

The Afternoon

I

THE FIGHTING FOR THE CONFEDERATE left and center, the West Woods and the Sunken Road, virtually ended with the abandonment of the Sunken Road and the limited counterattacks in the vicinity of the Mumma and Piper farms that discouraged any immediate Federal exploitation. Of course, at the time, this was unknown to the Confederate command structure, so efforts to prepare for a renewal of the battle on the left and in the center continued throughout the afternoon of 17 September.

As much as they could, commanders at all levels focused on rallying, consolidating, positioning, and repositioning the forces available behind the center and left (Map 4.1: Situation 1300). D. H. Hill's efforts to rally his own and R. H. Anderson's divisions along the Hagerstown Pike and in the vicinity of the Piper farm, as well as the positioning of batteries along Reel Ridge to support this effort, has already been discussed. These men would continue to hold their positions throughout the afternoon, but they were incapable of retaking the offensive. It was with a sense of pride that Colonel Bennett of the 14th North Carolina, commanding what was left of G. B. Anderson's brigade, reported that "the command was reformed at the road leading to Sharpsburg, and participated in all of the skirmishes of the afternoon." This sentiment was echoed by Captain Andrew Jackson Griffith, who now commanded the 14th in place of Bennett: "Having but few men, it rallied with other regiments and drove the enemy back, and remained in line in front of the enemy until late at night." Still, the situation was desperate at best. Lieutenant Chisholm of the 9th Alabama, who with his company participated in two counterattacks against the advancing Federal forces after abandoning the Sunken Road, thought that "had McClellan known our condition there he would have pushed us into the Po-

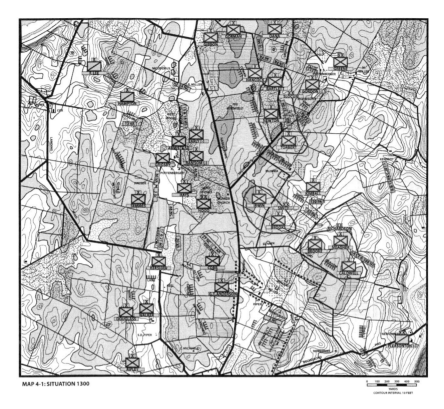

MAP 4-1: SITUATION 1300

tomac and we couldn't have prevented it, he had a good force, and we had a
small discouraged army."[1]

G. T. Anderson's brigade, in somewhat better condition than the remnants
of Hill's and R. H. Anderson's divisions, was still in line along the west side of
the pike supporting the rallied elements of the two divisions that Hill had positioned on the ridge to the northwest of Piper's stone barn. G. T. Anderson reported, "Parts of several brigades by this time had been collected at this point,
and, by direction of Gen. D. H. Hill, were formed in line perpendicularly to and
on the right of the road near the position occupied by Rodes' brigade early in
the morning." Across the pike, this line was extended along Reel Ridge to within
one hundred and fifty yards of the southernmost tip of the West Woods, by
what remained of Cobb's brigade and Cooke's 27th North Carolina and 3rd Arkansas. The latter command, however, was entirely "without a cartridge." Cooke
appealed to Longstreet for resupply, but Longstreet, unable to meet the request,

said that "Cooke stood with his empty guns, and waved his colors to show that his troops were in position."[2]

In the southernmost section of the West Woods, rallied elements of Hood's division and an ad hoc brigade made up of stragglers from other commands were in position, sheltering from the continuing artillery fire well below the height of land, some three hundred yards west of the Dunker Church. James S. Johnston, a courier on the staff of Colonel Evander M. Law, who commanded one of the brigades of Hood's division, recalled that after being forced from the cornfield quadrangle and the West Woods, "Hood marched the remnant of his division some distance to the rear, where it was deployed as skirmishers in the shape of a V, with orders to pass all stragglers, regardless of regiment or brigade or division down to the point of the V. In the course of two or three hours about 5,000 men had been collected at this point. They were then formed into companies, regiments, and a brigade. It was, perhaps, an anomolous [*sic*] organization in warfare. No man knew any officer over him, nor even his file leader, or the man to the right or left of him. And thus was taken away every influence which gives men confidence and conduces to their greatest efficiency as soldiers."[3]

Hood reported that about noon, after replenishing his ammunition, he was ordered by General Lee to return and take position in the West Woods, and he marched with the rallied elements of his own division and the ad hoc brigade of stragglers. Johnston says that "a little after they had begun marching in column of fours by the right flank, the men at the head of the column saw General Lee standing with bared head and calm but anxious expression under the shade of an apple tree close beside their line of march. As they passed he said, loud enough to be heard by several companies at a time, 'Men, I want you to go back on the line, and show that *the stragglers* of the Army of Northern Virginia, are *better than the best troops of the enemy.*' The effect as may be imagined was magnetic. 'The Stragglers' brigade,' as it was afterwards called, was thrilled with enthusiasm, and had they been called into action that day would have fully realized the expectations of their noble chief."[4]

A hundred yards behind Hood's left was the remnant of the brigade of Brigadier General Harry T. Hays of Lawton's division. After fighting in the cornfield quadrangle against the initial Federal attack and suffering 323 killed or wounded out of 550, Hays, like Hood after him, had withdrawn beyond the West Woods. Hays reported, "I then proceeded to gather together the remnant of my brigade. When this was accomplished, I moved again toward the front, but, on reaching the skirt of the woods above referred to, I found Gen. Hood's brigade, sheltered by the nature of the ground from a very severe artillery fire directed upon it. Upon consultation with Gen. Hood, I considered it best to remain there."[5]

Extending Hood's line to the north through the upper portion of the southern section of the West Woods and along the eastern edge of the center section were the 46th North Carolina of Manning's brigade and the three regiments of Ransom's brigade. Although nominally commanding Manning's brigade, Colonel Edward D. Hall of the 46th had been unable to assemble or even contact any of the other regiments of the brigade and so continued to command his regiment, which included a company of the 30th Virginia and one from the 3rd Arkansas. After he was forced to withdraw from the West Woods he had met Jackson, who ordered him to report to McLaws. McLaws "ordered me to endeavor to hold the woods at all hazards. I then advanced in line of battle to the edge of the woods, which by that time was filled with the enemy, and placed the regiment behind a ledge of rocks, throwing out Company A and the company from the Thirtieth Virginia, as skirmishers." The company from the 30th Virginia was Company F under the command of Captain John Hudgins. It was particularly well-suited to skirmisher duty being armed with Sharps rifles. Despite this firepower, Hall reported, "These were, shortly after, driven in. I then sent word to Gen. McLaws that if he would protect my left I would charge the woods. A few minutes after, a brigade, which proved to be Gen. Barksdale's, passed on to my left. As soon as it entered the woods, I moved forward and came upon the right of Gen. Ransom's brigade, which had been engaged and had succeeded in driving the enemy from the woods. Having only my own regiment with me, I informed Gen. R[ansom] that I would connect myself with his command, to which he readily consented. We then took up our position in line of battle, as much protected as the nature of the ground would allow."[6]

After finding that the 24th North Carolina was in position on the extreme left, 200 yards north of the woods between the Nicodemus and Miller farmsteads, too far away to call back, Brigadier General Ransom returned to the woods and resumed command of his remaining three regiments. The 49th and 35th North Carolina, which had made the sortie against the right flank of Greene's division, were now back in their original positions, and the 25th North Carolina was to their left along the eastern edge of the woods, the position that it had held since arriving there. These three regiments were under fire from the Federal batteries positioned across the quadrangle along the edge of the East Woods, and the 35th and 25th in particular were not sheltered as well as the regiments to their right.

To the left of Ransom's brigade was Early's, extending the line along the eastern edge of the woods to the northern end of the center section. After participating with McLaws's brigades in driving Sedgwick's division from the West Woods, Early had withdrawn his regiments behind the woods in order to re-form them. After accomplishing this, he wrote that "they were again posted in their former position on the small ridge." The drop-off from the height of land was more precipitous at this point than it was to Early's right. Early recalled in his memoirs that "the enemy continued to shell the woods in which we were for some time, doing, however, little or no damage, as we were under cover, and his shot and shells went over our heads." But Early also remembered that "some of our batteries, which had been brought up to the hills in our rear, opened fire on the woods where we were, on two occasions, under the impression that they were occupied by the enemy, and I had to send and have it stopped."[7]

Almost immediately behind Early, somewhat to the right and very nearly at the western edge of the woods, was the brigade of Brigadier General Lewis Armistead, which belonged to R. H. Anderson's division. As the rear guard, it had been the last in the division column as Anderson marched to the support of D. H. Hill. Rather than follow the division to the Sunken Road, Armistead had been detached and ordered to support McLaws in the West Woods. Passing Hauser's farmstead en route to the woods, it came under heavy artillery fire, which killed Captain William G. Pollard, commanding the 53rd Virginia, and wounded several others. On approaching the western edge of the woods, the brigade was met by Lieutenant Clark, adjutant of the 35th North Carolina, who had been sent to guide the brigade into position. Clark remembered that when he found Armistead "he was on foot, sword drawn, leading his Brigade. . . . I saluted, told him why I was there, [he] answered gruffly I thought & I stepped a little to his left." Just at that point, Armistead was wounded in the foot by a solid shot that came bounding along the ground. Clark said that Armistead "saw the ball as it came rolling down the hill, and could have moved out of its course with all care, but, probably thinking it a shell and likely to explode, stood as one transfixed and did not move his foot or a muscle." With the wounding of Armistead, command of the brigade devolved on Colonel James G. Hodges of the 14th Virginia. Although the brigade was in some confusion at this point due to the artillery fire, Hodges managed to gain control, and move it to the left. There he reported to Early, who placed it "in line on the edge of the plateau . . . and parallel to the Hagerstown road, but under cover."[8]

Extending Armistead's line into the northern section of the West Woods were two regiments of Barksdale's brigade, the 13th and 18th Mississippi. Barksdale's brigade, it will be recalled, had been divided as it withdrew after the attack on Sedgwick's division. The 13th and 18th Mississippi withdrew through the narrow center section of the woods and rallied just north of the Alfred Poffenberger farm. It was from this position that they moved back to the northern section of the woods and took position on the left of Armistead. The other two regiments of the brigade, the 17th and 21st Mississippi, withdrew well south of the woods, all the way back to the plowed field where the brigade had deployed initially, and at this point they were still there under the protection of their stone fence.[9]

Extending the line west from the West Woods 1,300 yards to Landing Road along the river were two of Stuart's cavalry brigades. Immediately to the west of the woods, in a draw created by a stream that had its source among the buildings of the Miller farmstead, was the brigade of Brigadier General Wade Hampton. Having been the rear guard for McLaws and R. H. Anderson on the march from Harpers Ferry, Hampton's brigade had spent the morning in the vicinity of Lee's headquarters and was just now moving into position on the left. On the high ground behind Hampton were the four guns of Captain Louis E. D'Aquin's battery supported by the 13th Virginia. Extending the line from there to the northwest all the way to the Landing Road, sheltered behind Nicodemus Heights, was the brigade of Brigadier General Fitzhugh Lee. In front of this brigade on Nicodemus Heights, but just below the crest, were the batteries of Poague and Raine.[10]

Behind this defensive line that extended from the Piper farm to the river were the rallying elements of many of the divisions, brigades, regiments, and batteries that fought for the center and left during the morning hours. Ripley's brigade under the command of Colonel George Doles was assembled in a woodlot on the S. D. Piper farm just north of Sharpsburg, drawing ammunition and its first rations in forty hours. The rallying point for the brigades under Colonel James A. Walker (Trimble's) and Colonel Marcellus Douglass (Lawton's) of Lawton's division was also on the Piper farm. Walker reported that he "ordered Captain [William C.] Hall, of General Trimble's staff, to direct the commandants of regiments to bring back what men were still left with them to a designated point in rear of the village of Sharpsburg, where they could be supplied with ammunition, and ordered the other staff officers of the brigade to gather up the stragglers from the different regiments of the command and carry them to the same point." Rallying with Walker's brigade were about one hundred men of Douglass's now under the command of Major John H. Lowe of the 31st Georgia, and nearby was Captain Basil C. Manly's North Carolina Battery of McLaws's division.[11]

Captain John Lane's Irwin Georgia Artillery was located along the west side of Landing Road across from the Reel farm, and most of Kershaw's brigade was in line along the road just to the north and on the right of Barksdale's 17th and 21st Mississippi. In the cornfield in front of Barksdale's two regiments was a part of one of Manning's regiments, the 30th Virginia, while 200 yards to the north was another of that brigade's regiments, the 48th North Carolina. Semmes's brigade was on a knoll just south of the Hauser farmstead, the point to which McLaws had ordered it "to be reassembled in reserve." Along the Hauser farm lane near the farmstead itself was the 3rd South Carolina of Kershaw's brigade and another part of the 30th Virginia. To their north at the point where the lane turns east toward Poffenberger's farm was what was left of Jackson's division still under the command of Colonel Grigsby. On the heights to the west of Hauser's were Brockenbrough's Maryland Battery, J. R. Jones's division, and two guns of Captain Edward S. McCarthy's, 1st Company, Richmond Howitzers, of McLaws's division.[12]

II

On examining the Confederate position in the vicinity of the West Woods, McLaws concluded that the best that he could hope for was for the army to remain on the defensive. He reported, "I could do nothing but defend the position my division occupied. The line was too weak to attempt an advance. There were not men enough to make a continuous single line. In some places for considerable distance there were no men at all, while just beyond us, across an open field, about 400 or 500 yards distant, were the lines of the enemy, apparently double and treble, supporting numerous batteries, which crossed fire over every portion of the ground." Stonewall Jackson seemed to be of similar mind, but he was unconcerned about the ability of the forces on the left to maintain their position. At about 1:00 o'clock, Dr. Hunter McGuire, Jackson's medical director, happened to have urgent business that took him to the front in search of Jackson. In looking for Jackson, McGuire discovered that the forces on the left were "reduced to a thin line." When he found Jackson, McGuire did not hesitate to express his "apprehension lest the surging mass of the enemy might get through," and probably requested Jackson's permission to begin moving the wounded across the Potomac into Virginia. Jackson, however, was indifferent to the request, telling McGuire "I think they have done their worst and there is now no danger of the line being broken."[13]

Not long after the meeting with Hunter McGuire, Jackson was visited by the army commander himself. Lee no doubt made Jackson aware of a new threat developing on the right as a result of the seizure of the Rohrbach Bridge at about 1:00 P.M. by the Ninth Army Corps under Brigadier General Jacob D. Cox, and its subsequent advance—albeit a slow one—toward the high ground south of Sharpsburg. Should the Federals seize the height of land there, they would effectively cut off the Army of Northern Virginia, still largely north of Sharpsburg, from its only crossing point on the Potomac, Boteler's Ford. Major General Ambrose Powell Hill's division coming up from Harpers Ferry was across the ford and marching toward the height of land but was still far enough away that it might not arrive in time to prevent a seizure of the heights by the Ninth Corps.[14]

However, rather than ordering Jackson to take forces from the left to meet the threat on the right, Lee ordered him to assemble a force to move "to the left with a view of turning the Federal right." Although some Confederate commanders on the left and in the center were convinced that the offensive power of the army had been spent, Lee was of a different mind. He believed he could regain the initiative, despite the new and serious Federal threat on the extreme right, or perhaps because of it. The effort to get around the Federal right, however, would not be for the purpose of destroying the Army of the Potomac or dealing a blow to McClellan that would mean winning the battle for the Confederate side. Lee was as aware as McLaws and others that this was not possible. McLaws reported, "The enemy having abandoned their attempt to advance, I had an opportunity to examine the relative positions of our troops and those of the enemy, and soon became convinced that we had nothing to gain by an advance of our troops. The strong position of the enemy was along the An-

tietam, the right bank of which (the side toward our army) was swept by numerous batteries of artillery posted along the left bank, which commanded the
right. Their position along the left bank was a very strong one, having the Antietam in their front and Maryland Heights [Red Hill] in their rear. For us to
force them back on the Antietam was to force them to [concentrate] on their
reserves, of which we had none, to weaken our lines, and scatter our troops, so
that, in the event of a reverse, no rally of any considerable body could be made,
and the final results would not probably have been such as to have entitled us
to claim, as we now can, the battle of Sharpsburg as one of the greatest suc-
cesses, if not the greatest success, of the war, when the enormous disparity between our forces and those of the Yankees are considered."[15]

Rather, Lee's purpose in ordering Jackson to "turn the Federal right" was to
create a gap between that flank and the Potomac large enough for the Army of
Northern Virginia to pass through and move in the direction of Hagerstown.
If successful, this would put Lee in a position where he could again freely maneuver his army. It would force McClellan to react, to follow. It would thus restore the initiative to Lee and allow him to continue his campaign in Maryland. It would be a risky operation. It almost certainly would mean leaving
behind much needed material, and it might put the troops south of Sharpsburg, including A. P. Hill's division, in the position of hastily withdrawing via
Boteler's Ford. There was also the danger that an uncharacteristically aggres-
sive McClellan with his larger force might suddenly move forward, catch the
Army of Northern Virginia strung out on the march, and destroy it piecemeal.[16]

For a force to carry out his commander's orders, Jackson turned to Stuart
and told him to prepare Hampton's and Fitz Lee's cavalry brigades for an expedition around the Federal right. In addition to being a highly mobile force
of seven regiments, these two brigades had not yet been engaged. Moreover,
the Federals had not spotted them because the brigades were positioned well
below the height of land. By moving toward the river, they could remain un-
detected under the cover of the river bluffs until they were well beyond the Federal right and would thus have the advantage of surprise. To add to their firepower, Stuart was assigned nine guns from the various batteries that he had
been supervising all morning. The guns would be under the command of his
own chief of artillery, Captain John Pelham.[17]

As Jackson was overseeing the assembling of this expeditionary force, Walker
arrived to report what he thought was the movement of a Federal force toward

the gap in the line south of the West Woods where Cooke's two regiments and Cobb's brigade were located. Walker recalled that "I found Jackson in rear of Barksdale's brigade, under an apple tree, sitting on his horse, with one leg thrown over the pommel of his saddle, plucking and eating the fruit. Without making any reply to my report, he asked me abruptly: 'Can you spare me a regiment and a battery?' I replied that Colonel [Robert C.] Hill's 48th North Carolina, a very strong regiment, was in reserve, and could be spared, and that I could also give him both [Captain Thomas B.] French's and [Captain James R.] Branch's batteries, but that they were without long-range ammunition, which had been exhausted at Harpers Ferry." Thus Jackson was able to add an infantry regiment and two more artillery batteries to Stuart's flanking force.[18]

Lee and Jackson were not the only senior commanders thinking in terms of renewing the offensive at this point. Longstreet was in the West Woods assessing the possibility of making an assault across the quadrangle toward the East Woods. He wrote, "At one or two points near our center were dead angles into which I rode from time to time for closer observation of the enemy when his active aggression was suspended. General Burnside was busy at his crossing, but no report of progress had been sent me. One of my rides towards the Dunker chapel revealed efforts of the enemy to renew his work on that part of the field. Our troops were ordered to be ready to receive it. Its non-aggression suggested an opportunity for the Confederates, and I ordered McLaws and Walker to prepare to assault. Hood was back in position with his brigades, and Jackson was reported on his way, all in full supply of ammunition. It seemed probable that by concealing our movements under cover of the wood from the massed batteries of Doubleday's artillery on the north, and the batteries of position on the east, we could draw our columns so near to the enemy in front before our move could be known that we would have but a few rods to march before we could mingle our ranks with those of the enemy; that our columns massed and in goodly numbers, pressing severely upon a single point, would give the enemy much trouble, and might cut him in two, and break up his battle arrangements at the lower bridge." Longstreet's plan for an attack across the quadrangle toward the East Woods was undertaken on his own initiative and without knowledge of Lee's and Jackson's plan for a movement against the Federal right.[19]

Jackson was also planning an attack across the quadrangle in coordination with and in support of Stuart's attack on the Federal flank. Lieutenant Walter Clark, the adjutant of the 35th North Carolina, recalled that it was about 2:00

o'clock "that Stonewall Jackson came along our lines. . . . Jackson remarked to Col. Ransom, as he did to other colonels along the line, that with Stuart's cavalry and some infantry he was going around the Federal right and get in their rear, and added 'when you hear the rattle of my small arms, this whole line must advance.' He wished to ascertain the force opposed, and a man of our regiment named Hood was sent up a tall tree which he climbed carefully to avoid observation by the enemy. Stonewall called out to know how many Yankees he could see over the hill and beyond the East Woods. Hood replied, 'Whew! There are oceans of them, General.' 'Count their flags' said Jackson. This Hood proceeded to do until he had counted 39, when the general told him that would do and to come down."[20]

After his meeting with Jackson, Walker returned to his command and "repeated Jackson's order to my brigade commanders and directed them to listen for the sound of Stuart's guns. We all confidently expected to hear the welcome sound by 2 o'clock, at least, and as that hour approached every ear was on the alert. Napoleon at Waterloo did not listen more intently for the sound of Grouchy's fire than did we for Stuart's. Two o'clock came, but nothing was heard of Stuart. Half-past two and then three, and still Stuart made no sign." Walker then went on to say that "about half-past three a staff-officer of General Longstreet brought me an order from that general to advance and attack the enemy in my front. As the execution of this order would materially interfere with Jackson's plans, I thought it my duty before beginning the movement to communicate with General Longstreet personally. I found him in rear of the position in which I had posted Cooke in the morning, and upon informing him of Jackson's intentions, he withdrew his order." Walker reported that while he was in conversation with Longstreet, "Gen. Jackson himself joined us, and informed us that Gen. Stuart had made the attempt spoken of but found it impracticable, as the enemy's right was securely posted on the Potomac and protected by heavy batteries of his reserve artillery."[21]

Stuart's column of cavalry had moved out along the River Road at about 3:00 P.M. with the 4th Virginia Cavalry of Fitz Lee's brigade leading the way. The head of the column advanced the better part of a mile until it was at New Industry. At that point, from the center of the column, Pelham took his nine guns to the east along the road leading to the toll gate at the Hagerstown Pike just across from the North Woods. When he reached the heights of the river bluffs, he ordered the guns into position to the right of the road and opened fire on the Federal left flank some 900 yards to his front. He was met by the concentrated fire of nearly thirty Federal guns positioned on the height of land just north of the Joseph Poffenberger farm. Captain William T. Poague, who was there commanding a single gun from his Rockbridge Virginia Artillery, remembered, "Late in the afternoon with the only gun for which I had enough horses I reported to General Stuart and under Major Pelham with some other guns we moved under the cover of the woods close up to the Federal batteries on their extreme right and opened on them; but they were too many for us and soon shut us up." Captain Charles J. Raine, commanding the Lee Virginia Battery, contributed two rifled pieces to this effort, and in the short exchange of fire lost five men.[22]

The super battery that Pelham encountered on the Federal right flank had been assembled by General Sumner as the commander on that part of the field, and it was under the direction of Brigadier General Abner Doubleday of the First Army Corps. Doubleday reported, "Thirty guns had been concentrated on the right flank of the general line of battle, and my division was directed to join the remains of Gen. Sumner's corps as a support to these guns. Gen. Sumner assumed command in person [on the right], and I was directed by Gen. Meade, who received the order from Gen. Sumner, to assume special command of these thirty guns in addition to the command of my division."[23]

When Pelham withdrew his guns from the heights above the river, Stuart abandoned his attempt at turning the Federal right flank with his cavalry. He recalled, "I found that the river made such an abrupt bend that the enemy's batteries were within 800 yards of the brink of the stream, which would have made it impossible to have succeeded in the movement proposed, and it was accordingly abandoned." It is curious that Stuart was not aware of the bend in the river and the narrowness of the gap—the actual distance was 1,300 yards—between the massed federal guns and the river before setting out on the expedition. Fitz Lee's brigade had been in the area screening the Army's left since the afternoon of the 15th, and Doubleday's guns could easily be seen from Nicodemus Heights.[24]

It also seems to have been a mistake to allow Pelham to engage the Federal battery before the column had passed completely around the Federal flank, which it could have done by continuing along the River Road to Mercersville and then taking that road back to the Hagerstown Pike north of Ground Squirrel Church. Pelham's officers objected to opening fire from the point that he did. In his memoir, Poague remembered that "we artillery captains didn't know the object of the movement, and were disposed to criticize Pelham for turning us loose within 500 yards upon an immense battery of some thirty pieces in plain view and easily counted. Fortunately we were concealed in a body of small trees and they could only mark our places by the smoke rising above them. We protested against attacking such an overwhelming force. Pelham replied with a laugh, 'Oh, we must stir them up a little and then slip away.' And so we did stir them up, and with a vengeance they soon stirred us out. Pelham skillfully led us to one side out of range of the murderous fire which was continued for some time on the place we opened from." Poague, however, at the time of the writing of his memoirs rethought Pelham's responsibility for the movement and realized its real purpose. "We battery commanders thought Pelham had gotten permission to look up a fight and were down on him for what we regarded as a most indiscreet proceeding. . . . But we did him injustice. We know now that General Stuart in compliance with instructions from General Lee through Jackson, took this method of determining whether McClellan's flank could be turned. I suppose Pelham knew what he was sent there for."[25]

Walker later recalled that he was surprised at "Stuart's failure to turn the Federal right, for the reason that he had found it securely *posted on the Potomac*." According to Walker, "Jackson replied that he also had been surprised, as he had supposed the Potomac much farther away; but he remarked that Stuart had an excellent eye for topography, and it must be as he represented." Walker stated, "it was then determined that the attempt to force the enemy's right with our fearfully thinned ranks and in the exhausted condition of our men was an effort above our strength."[26]

III

For the most part, the remainder of the afternoon on the left and center was spent in making minor adjustments along the line in the West Woods and south of it to the Piper farm as more and more regiments and some brigades recovered from the morning's fighting and were brought back on line (Map 4.2: Situation 1630). Armistead's brigade moved a little north of its previous position in the West Woods to be behind and to the left of Early's brigade, which continued in position on the east side of the northern part of the center section of the woods. Armistead's move to the right was facilitated by McLaws's

MAP 4-2: SITUATION 1630

0   100   200   300   400   500
YARDS
CONTOUR INTERVAL 10 FEET

decision to bring up Kershaw's brigade from the vicinity of the Reel farm to take position along the west side of the northern extension of the West Woods behind the left of Armistead. Barksdale was able to reunite all four of his regiments, and they took position on Armistead's right and behind Ransom's left.[27]

South of the West Woods, Ripley's brigade came back to take position on Reel Ridge behind Cooke's command. Brigadier General Ripley, recovering somewhat from his earlier neck wound, "returned to the field with such force as I could collect from detachments, and found my brigade relieved and in position to the west of Sharpsburg." This was the position in S. D. Piper's woods that the brigade had withdrawn to after leaving the quadrangle and where it had found its ordnance train and some lunch. Ripley remained with the brigade for some time, but finding himself "faint and exhausted," he was forced once again to turn over command of the brigade to Colonel George Doles. Captain John C. Key, commanding the 44th Georgia, recalled that "between 2 and 3 P.M. the Brigade then under the command of Col George Doles of the 4th Ga. was marched back to the front and formed line of Battle in a cornfield some distance to the west of the Pike road from Sharpsburg to Hagerstown and to the North or NW from Sharpsburg and faced to the North." This new position was directly behind Cooke's 27th North Carolina and 3rd Arkansas, and it allowed Cooke's command to come off the line, at least temporarily. James A. Graham of the 27th North Carolina recalled that "about 5 P.M. we were relieved by other troops and moved about a mile to our right and near a large well and got water and were supplied with ammunition—having been on the line of battle without a cartridge for two hours or more. We then moved back up the little plantation or country road to a position just in the rear of the one we had been holding all day and remained there till about dark, catching all the shells etc. that came over our front line. I well recollect that I thought the sun never would go down on that afternoon."[28]

At about 3:00 P.M., the same time that Stuart was setting off in search of the Federal right, D. H. Hill saw what he thought was a "heavy column" of Federal troops advancing up the Boonsboro Pike from the Middle Bridge. As already noted, the only troops on the north side of the pike at this time were three regiments of Evans's brigade under Colonel Peter F. Stevens of the Holcombe Legion, strung out as a thin skirmish line along the ridge running from the Piper farm lane to the Boonsboro Pike. To bolster this line, Hill quickly ordered G. T. Anderson to take some 200 to 300 men to the hills just behind Stevens's skirmish line. Anderson reported, "I moved to the position and sent forward skirmishers, but failed to find the enemy; and the enemy opening a cross-fire of artillery from the left on us, I moved back to the other position, which was approved by Gen. Hill." The other position mentioned by Anderson was the ridge line running from Piper's stone barn to the Hagerstown Pike.[29]

As Anderson was moving his command back to the Piper farm, Evans was also bringing up a small force to back up Stevens's line. He reported that "about 2 P.M. I was ordered to rally the troops then flocking to the town from our right [left] and bring them into action. After considerable exertion, with the assistance of my entire staff, I succeeded in collecting about 250 men and officers, whom I formed into two commands, and placed them, respectively, under the command of Cols. [Alfred H.] Colquitt and [Alfred] Iverson, of Maj. Gen. D. H. Hill's division."[30]

Another officer who was in the town of Sharpsburg at this time attempting to rally his men was Captain Thomas M. Garrett of the 5th North Carolina. He recalled, "I met Gen. Lee in the street, and reported to him the misfortune which had befallen me, and asked for directions. He ordered me to rally all the stragglers I could, without regard to what command they belonged, and report with them to Gen. Evans. Only about 50 of my regiment could be found; but, with the assistance of yourself [Lieutenant James M. Taylor, the regimental adjutant] and Lieut. [Isaac E.] Pearce, about 150 were rallied and carried up to Gen. Evans, on the hill, on the north edge of the town. These were formed in line, under my command, along with other stragglers, and all placed under the command of Col. Iverson, of the Twentieth North Carolina."[31]

In addition to the infantry, there was a considerable amount of artillery available. Captain Boyce with the remaining two pieces of his South Carolina Artillery was already in position on high ground just to the rear of Stevens. Colonel S. D. Lee, whose battalion had been off line since retiring from Reel Ridge earlier during the morning, reported that "about 3 P.M., the batteries having refitted and replenished with ammunition, I again moved to the front with twelve guns, all that could be manned, and received orders from one of Gen. Longstreet's aides to take position in front of the village of Sharpsburg, to the right and left of the turnpike, relieving Col. [James B.] Walton, of the Washington Artillery, of New Orleans. Four of [Captain George V.] Moody's guns were placed on the right of the village; two of [Captain William W.] Parker's and two of [Captain Tyler C.] Jordan's were placed at the left; Rhett's two pieces [Lieutenant William Elliott] were placed on a ridge to the left of the village, on the Sharpsburg and Hagerstown pike." Behind the ridge on the north side of the pike there were three batteries, twelve guns in all, from Major Hilary P. Jones's battalion. On the ridge south of the pike, Captain Charles W. Squires had four rifled pieces in position to the right of Moody, and at some distance to the right of Squires was Captain Hugh P. Garden's South Carolina Battery of six guns. These batteries were supported by two small brigades from D. R. Jones's division under the command of Colonel Joseph Walker and Brigadier General Richard B. Garnett. Garden's battery and Walker's brigade were at the extreme southern limit of the ridge, covering the flank of the line and the Rohrbach Bridge Road against the advance of the Ninth Corps.[32]

The Federal force moving up the Boonsboro Pike against this ad hoc collection of infantry and artillery was itself an ad hoc collection of regular U.S. Army infantry battalions from the division of Major General George Sykes of the Fifth Army Corps under the command of Captain Hiram Dryer of the 4th Infantry. It had initially consisted of one battalion made up from the 2nd and 10th Infantry under Captain John S. Poland sent across the Middle Bridge as support for three batteries of horse artillery from Major General Alfred Pleasonton's cavalry division. When two of those batteries used up their ammunition, Sykes, over his objection, was ordered to replace them with two of his own. At that point, Sykes ordered Dryer across the Middle Bridge with four additional battalions and directed him to take command of all of the regular infantry on that side of Antietam Creek. These four additional battalions were Dryer's 4th Infantry; the 1st Battalion, 12th Infantry under Captain Matthew M. Blunt; the 1st Battalion, 14th Infantry under Captain W. Harvey Brown; and the 2nd Battalion, 14th Infantry under Captain David B. McKibbin.[33]

On arriving at the batteries, which were on the first ridge coming up from the bridge and on either side of the pike, Dryer immediately ordered Poland, whose battalion was "deployed as skirmishers, with his right resting on the pike and near the crest of the hill that the batteries occupied, . . . to take possession of some hay-stacks situated in a field about 150 yards to the front and about 400 yards to the left of the pike. I at the same time directed Lieut. [Caleb] Carlton to deploy the three leading companies of the Fourth, G, I, and K, to the right of the pike, with his left resting on the pike and to advance near the crest of a hill, about 250 yards to the front, using the remaining five companies of the regiment as his support. I then ordered Capt. Brown to march his battalion of the Fourteenth in line of battle under cover of a hill, and [Captain] Poland's skirmishers to a fence near a lane running at right angles with the pike, where he halted and put his men under cover." The lane that Captain Poland's skirmishers advanced to was the Sherrick farm lane, which ran south from the pike.[34]

As the 4th Infantry under Carlton began moving up the hill toward Evans's line they came under the fire of Boyce's, Jordan's, and Parker's six guns, which, according to D. H. Hill, allowed the enemy to come within easy range and then unleashed a sudden storm of grape and canister, which drove the Federals back "in confusion." Seeing an opportunity, Evans ordered an advance with Stevens on the left and Colquitt and Iverson on the right. Captain Garrett, who was with Iverson, remembered that "we moved up in line on the right and engaged them with spirit, and forced them, for a moment, to give back." The line did not advance far, however, before Carlton's regulars made a stand and again began to advance. Major M. Hilton, commanding the 22nd South Carolina, deployed as skirmishers on the left of the line, reported "when the enemy again advanced with large brigades[,] I ordered the pickets to fire and fall back on the Eighteenth and Twenty-third South Carolina Regiments, which was done, and the engagement became general." The movement, however, caused the left to begin to waver and then the entire line to begin to fall back. Colonel William H. Wallace of the 18th South Carolina reported that "Col. Stevens, who was upon the left of our line, seeing the left was beginning to suffer severely, ordered the whole line to retreat to a stone fence some distance in our rear and upon the road running in a north westerly direction from Sharpsburg [the Hagerstown Pike]. This retreat was accomplished under a sharp fire of musketry and artillery, from which the regiment sustained some damage. Almost immediately the regiment was reduced to a handful of men." Garrett reported, "Very soon, . . . the left of the line of which my command formed part gave way, and being left with but the men from my regiment, I ordered them to retire, and form behind a large rock in the field, about 50 yards distant. This was done, and, by the determined conduct of these few men, the regiment of the enemy was held in check for twenty-five of thirty minutes. After feeling our strength, however, he began to advance and I ordered the men to retreat." Garrett's stand behind the large rock gave Boyce the opportunity to withdraw his two guns below the ridge. He reported, "I immediately ordered out my two pieces, crossed over to the slope of the hill lying in the direction of the town, and put my pieces in battery, commanding the crest of the two hills, to meet the enemy if he should compel our forces to retire."[35]

While what remained of Stevens's regiment, and no doubt some others, assembled behind the stone fence along the Hagerstown Pike, most of the rest of the line, including Colquitt's and Iverson's commands, withdrew into the streets of Sharpsburg. As they fell back, the regulars of the 4th Infantry under Lieutenant Carlton continued their advance, reaching the crest of the ridge just to the right of the Boonsboro Pike from which they could look down into the town. Just at this point, however, the Federal line came under a sharp flanking fire of canister and musketry from south of the Boonsboro Pike. This fire came from a section of Moody's battery and some infantry of the 56th Virginia of Garnett's brigade, which was in the cornfield just in front of the ridge. Up to this point Moody's battery and Garnett's brigade had been engaged with Poland's line sheltered along Sherrick lane. Both S. D. Lee and Garnett had been watching this engagement and had not noticed Carlton's advance until it was directly to their left. Lee then order the repositioning of Moody's left section, and Garnett turned back a few of the 56th Virginia to fire down Carlton's line. Lee reported, "Two guns of Moody's battery, with Garnett's brigade, drove the enemy from the ridge to the left of the village after they had taken the ridge from our troops." Garnett in turn wrote that "a large number of the enemy's skirmishers were seen to our left, as if to flank us. There were none of our forces in sight in that direction. A brisk fire from the left checked and finally caused them to retire."[36]

The flanking fire that Carlton endured no doubt caused him to consider a withdrawal from his advanced position, but it was also at this point that he received orders from Sykes through Dryer to pull back. The movement of Carlton's battalion up the Boonsboro Pike had been observed by Captain William H. Powell, adjutant of Lieutenant Colonel Robert C. Buchanan's First Brigade of Sykes's division. Powell recalled that "knowing it was not the intention, nor could we afford, at that particular time, to make any forward movement on the center, I reported this to Generals Sykes and Buchanan, who were together at the time, and I was directed by General Sykes to proceed at once to the advanced position which Captain Dryer had obtained . . . and direct him to withdraw his troops immediately to the original position at the head of the bridge, and then report in person to General Sykes." Accordingly, Carlton was ordered back down the hill as far as the Newcomer farmstead, taking up position there along the western edge of a small triangular cornfield on the left of McKibbin's 2nd Battalion, 14th Infantry, which was in line along the southernmost extension of the Sunken Road.[37]

As Carlton began his withdrawal, Stevens, Boyce, and Evans hastened to reestablish themselves on the crest of the ridge north of the Boonsboro Pike. Stevens reported, "Perceiving that my retreat had left unsupported a section of Boyce's artillery, which I had not before seen, I again resumed my position, and, bringing up Boyce's battery, opened fire with musketry and artillery upon a line of the enemy advancing on the right of the road." Boyce reported, "Col. Stevens advanced, at this juncture, with a few skirmishers to the crest of the hill, and, finding the ground not occupied by the enemy immediately beyond, signaled me to advance. I went forward and placed my guns on the hill within canister range of the enemy. A few shots soon drove him beyond the reach of canister. I afterward used solid shot, cutting down his flag and driving him back." Evans said simply, "My brigade then resumed its original position and bivouacked for the night, sleeping on their arms."[38]

At about 5:00 P.M., one final action in the vicinity of the Piper farm took place as the 7th Maine of Irwin's brigade attacked across the Sunken Road toward G. T. Anderson's position on the ridge northwest of the Piper barn. Anderson recalled that shortly after returning to the ridge, D. H. Hill "riding forward to the crest of the hill in our front, called my attention to a line of the enemy advancing apparently to attack us. Suffering them to come near us, I ordered my command to charge them, which they did in splendid style and good order, killing and wounding many of the enemy, taking several prisoners, and routing the remainder."[39]

According to Major Hilary A. Herbert, commanding the 8th Alabama, a regiment of Cumming's brigade rallied with Anderson; they formed a line below the crest of the ridge so that the Maine men could not see them as they approached. Herbert recalled that the Maine "regiment which was coming up the right flank towards us and had gotten close up when we rose up from behind the brow of the hill and fired into him and drove him back." Major Thomas W. Hyde, commanding the 7th Maine, said that as his regiment was charging up the hill "a rebel regiment rose suddenly from behind a stone wall on our right, poured in a volley, and at the same time I saw them double-quicking around to the left to cut off our retreat. . . . Looking back and seeing no support, to escape being surrounded I marched the regiment by the left flank, formed them on a crest in the orchard, poured a volley into those who were endeavoring to cut off our retreat, and faced those in front." When Lieutenant Alexander C. Chisholm of the 9th Alabama, another of Cumming's regiments now with Anderson, saw the direction that the Maine men were taking, he remembered the trouble that his regiment had had getting through the orchard's picket fence and was delighted. He wrote, "Now when the Maine right was repulsed near the barn and retreated through the orchard . . . we knew the trouble that awaited them at the fence. I heard such expressions from our boys as 'Ground them to the fence' 'we will get them at the fence' and we did get them there, fully fifty or more. I saw the brave fellows doing their best to get through, but we were upon them, and as they turned to face us and threw up their hands in token of surrender a 'rebel yell' went up that must have been heard by many of their retreating but more fortunate comrades."[40]

While withdrawing through the orchard, Major Hyde recalled that "we received a severe fire from three directions, and the enemy advanced in force. I saw four battle-flags. A battery opened on us with grape. Here we met a heavy loss, but were shielded some by the trees of the orchard. Having disposed of most of our cartridges, we retreated through the orchard, gave them another volley as they attempted to follow, which drove them back, and, closing up on the colors, I marched the regiment back in good order to their old position on the left of the Third Brigade." Anderson's collection of remnants pursued the 7th Maine as far as possible, but "we could not pursue them as far as I wished," according to Anderson, "because of the severe fire of artillery directed against us from long-range guns that we could not reach." Hyde reported, "The affair lasted perhaps thirty minutes. The color-sergeant was killed, and all the guard shot but one, who brought off our flag riddled with balls. Fifteen officers and 166 men went into the fight, and our loss was as follows: Enlisted men known to be killed, 12; wounded and brought off, 60; fate still unknown, 16. Lieuts. Brown and Goodwin and Sergeant-Maj. Parsons, killed; Capts. Jones, Cochrane, and Cook and Adjutant Haskell, wounded and missing; Lieuts. Shorey, Benson, and Emery, wounded. But one officer, Lieut. Nickerson, escaped untouched in clothes or person, and but very few men. Capt. Channing and Lieut. Webber had each three bullets through their clothes. The adjutant and myself both had our horses shot under us."[41]

Carlton's withdrawal from the high ground north of the Boonsboro Pike and the repulse of the 7th Maine from the vicinity of the Piper farm effectively ended the fighting for the Confederate left and center, although efforts at adjusting and reinforcing the line continued into the evening. Hood reported that "about 4 P.M., by order, the division moved to the right, near the center, and remained there until the night of the 18th instant, when orders were received to recross the Potomac." Hood took a position just west of the Hagerstown Pike, a few hundred yards south of Piper's lane. The remaining major action of the battle now shifted to the right, to the height of land south of Sharpsburg, as Major General Ambrose Powell Hill's Light Division arrived to successfully counter the advance of the Ninth Army Corps.[42]

IV

For Robert E. Lee, the battle had been more about maintaining the initiative than about defending the position at Sharpsburg. At the time of the Battle of Antietam, Edward Porter Alexander was a lieutenant colonel of ordnance with the Army of Northern Virginia. He later was a military critic of the Confederate conduct of the war, writing that Lee "gave battle unnecessarily at Sharps-

burg Sep. 17th, 1862. The odds against him were so immense that the utmost he
could have hoped to do was what he did do—to repel all assaults & finally to
withdraw safely across the Potomac. And he probably only succeeded in this because McClellan kept about 20,000 men, all of Fitz John Porter's corps, *entirely*
out of the fight so that they did not pull a trigger. And Lee's position was such,
with a great river at his back, without a bridge & with but one difficult ford,
that defeat would have meant the utter destruction of his army. So he fought
where he could have avoided it, & where he had nothing to make & everything to lose—which a general should not do." This critique of Lee at Sharpsburg is well taken if one is looking in hindsight at the campaign and the battle.
But it does not consider the campaign's objectives or the possibilities that Lee
saw for maintaining the initiative when he chose the position at Sharpsburg.[43]

Up to the 16th when Hooker crossed Antietam Creek and advanced toward
the height of land and the left of the Army of Northern Virginia, Lee held the
initiative. He lost that initiative, however, as a result of the attacks made by the
First and Twelfth Army Corps early on the morning of the 17th. Then with the
arrival of the Second Army Corps at about 9:00 A.M., Lee was forced into a
desperate defensive battle for the very life of his army. The counterattack into
the West Woods against Sedgwick's division of the Second Corps by McLaws's
division, as well as Early's and G. T. Anderson's brigades, once again turned the
tide of battle and restored the initiative to Lee. In the determined defense of
the center against two more divisions of the Second Corps, French's and Richardson's, at the Sunken Road and the Piper farm, the divisions of D. H. Hill
and R. H. Anderson prevented McClellan from once again wresting that initiative from Lee. This allowed Lee to continue to think in terms of restarting a
campaign of maneuver—not by withdrawing across the Potomac into Virginia
but by moving north to Hagerstown, which had been his original objective in
taking position at Sharpsburg. However, Stuart's unsuccessful attempt to turn
the Federal right and create a gap wide enough for the entire Army of Northern Virginia to slip through demonstrated that that was not a viable option,
despite the fact that A. P. Hill successfully countered the attack of the Ninth
Army Corps on the Confederate right.

On the evening of the 17th Lee still believed he held the initiative, and he
was determined to maintain and exercise it. As his senior and division commanders came to headquarters that night to report the dismal condition of the
Army of Northern Virginia and to recommend immediate withdrawal to Vir-

ginia, Lee told them, "Gentlemen, we will not cross the Potomac to-night. You will go to your respective commands, strengthen your forces; send two officers from each brigade towards the ford to collect your stragglers and get them up. I have had the proper steps taken to collect all the men who are in the rear. If McClellan wants to fight in the morning I will give him battle again. Go!"[44]

On the 18th, Lee again suggested to Jackson the possibility of opening a gap on the left wide enough to take the army through to Hagerstown by crushing the Federal right with fifty pieces of artillery. When Jackson demurred, Lee sent S. D. Lee to him to further assess the possibility of success. Only when S. D. Lee returned and told Lee that he did not think such a maneuver could be successful did Lee finally give up the idea of moving the army north to Hagerstown. S. D. Lee recalled that when he reported his grim assessment, "I saw a shade come over General Lee's face."[45]

Accordingly, Lee finally determined that the Army of Northern Virginia would withdraw into Virginia via Boteler's Ford under the cover of darkness on the night of the 18th. But even then, Lee did not give up the hope of a successful campaign north of the Potomac, for rather than withdrawing deep into Virginia, the army would march west to Martinsburg and then north to Williamsport to recross into Maryland only six miles from Hagerstown; there, the army would be on the flank and in the rear of the Army of the Potomac. Lee would again hold the initiative.[46]

The river crossing during the night of the 18th to 19th was successful, and during the day of the 19th the army marched for Martinsburg and Williamsport. The advance was led by Stuart, who by noon had occupied Williamsport with Hampton's brigade, the 12th Virginia Cavalry of Munford's brigade, and some small detachments of infantry and artillery. Then came Jackson's command, followed by Longstreet's. Left to guard Boteler's Ford and the army's rear was the Reserve Artillery—forty-four guns—under the command of Brigadier General William N. Pendleton, supported by 400 infantry from Douglass's brigade—now under the command of Colonel John H. Lamar—200 from Armistead's still under Hodges, and 200 cavalry from Colonel Thomas T. Munford's brigade.[47]

Late in the afternoon, Federal artillery opened across the river against Pendleton's rear guard. Lacking sufficient ammunition, Pendleton's guns failed to respond, and the Federals crossed the river with two regiments. They scattered the Confederate infantry and cavalry, threatening to capture nearly all of the guns.

Lacking any means of response, Pendleton rode to get help. He first found Brigadier General Pryor, still in command of R. H. Anderson's division, but Pryor thought the responsibility too much for him. Hood's staff next told Pendleton that Hood was unwell and could not respond, and no one knew where Longstreet could be found. Continuing on along the column to Jackson's command, Pendleton located D. H. Hill, but he offered no help. Finally, Pendleton reached Jackson, who alerted his command for a return but gave no orders. Jackson preferred that Pendleton first see Lee himself, which Pendleton was unable to do until nearly 1:00 A.M., some seven hours after starting out. Lee feared the capture of all of his reserve artillery, or worse that the entire Army of the Potomac may have crossed into Virginia and was now in his rear, so he immediately ordered Jackson back to the ford with all four of his divisions and sent orders to Longstreet to be prepared to support him. On the 19th and 20th, thirteen Federal regiments successfully crossed, but they were able to capture only four of the Reserve Artillery's guns and were easily driven back across the river with the arrival of the first of Jackson's divisions under A. P. Hill.[48]

The Battle of Shepherdstown was a minor affair that represented no real threat to the Army of Northern Virginia, but the confused and halting response to it gave Lee his first realization of the totally exhausted condition of his army. In addition, during the day three brigades of fresh Federal infantry and two of cavalry forced Stuart to abandon Williamsport, denying Lee his planned point of reentry into Maryland. It was under these conditions that Lee finally gave up any effort at maintaining the initiative. In his official report he wrote, "The condition of our troops now demanded repose, and the army marched to the Opequon, near Martinsburg, where it remained several days, and then moved to the vicinity of Bunker Hill and Winchester." Thus it was that Lee finally ended the Maryland Campaign.[49]

Notes

Chapter 1

1. Joseph L. Harsh, *Taken at the Flood: Robert E. Lee and Confederate Strategy in the Maryland Campaign of 1862* (Kent, OH: Kent State University Press, 1999), 300–1. Harsh's masterful study of Lee and his strategy in the Maryland Campaign will be the basic source of material on Lee in this study.

2. War Department, *War of the Rebellion: The Official Records of the Union and Confederate Armies* (Washington: Government Printing Office, 1881–1901), Series I, vol. 19, pt. 2, 590–91. Hereafter cited as OR. All references are to Series I unless otherwise noted.

3. Harsh, *Taken at the Flood*, 60, 492; Stephen W. Sears, *Landscape Turned Red: The Battle of Antietam* (New York: Ticknor & Fields, 1983), 69; and OR 19, pt. 1, 145; pt. 2, 600.

4. Harsh, *Taken at the Flood*, 303–6.

5. OR 19, pt. 1, 53–54.

6. Harsh, *Taken at the Flood*, 325–6; OR 19, pt. 1, 844, 922–23.

7. Harsh, *Taken at the Flood*, 334–35.

8. Ibid., 333.

9. Ibid., 343–44.

10. Ibid., 356–57.

11. OR 19, pt. 1, 30, 217.

12. Ibid., 55, 217.

13. Ibid., 217–18, 923, 937; Harsh, *Taken at the Flood*, 358.

14. Harsh, *Taken at the Flood*, 359–60, 363; OR 19, pt. 1, 845.

15. Harsh, *Taken at the Flood*, 363; OR 19, pt. 1, 923; and John Bell Hood, *Advance and Retreat: Personal Experiences in the United States and Confederate States Armies*, ed. Richard N. Current (Bloomington: Indiana University Press, 1959), 42.

16. Harsh, *Taken at the Flood*, 41.

17. OR 19, pt. 1, 857; Harsh, *Taken at the Flood*, 364–65.

18. Joseph L. Harsh, *Sounding the Shallows: A Confederate Companion for the Maryland Campaign of 1862* (Kent, OH: Kent State University Press, 2000), 19.

19. OR 19, pt. 1, 914; John G. Walker, "Sharpsburg," *North to Antietam*, vol. 2, *Battles*

and Leaders of the Civil War, eds. Robert U. Johnson and Clarence C. Buel (New York: Century, 1887–88; reprint, New York: Castle Books, 1956), 675; and Harsh, *Taken at the Flood*, 366.

20. OR 19, pt. 1, 857–58; Harsh, *Taken at the Flood*, 366–67, 368–69.

21. OR 19, pt. 1, 218.

22. Ibid., 956.

23. Ibid., 923, 937–38.

24. Ibid., 269.

25. William F. Fox, *Regimental Losses in the American Civil War, 1861–1865* (Albany, NY: Brandow Printing Co., 1898; reprint, Dayton, OH: Morningside House, 1985), 556; OR 19, pt. 1, 923, 938.

26. Congress, Senate, Joint Committee on the Conduct of the War, *Report of the Joint Committee on the Conduct of the War*, 3 pts., 37th Cong., 3rd sess., 1863, Rep. Com. 108, pt. 1, 368; OR 19, pt. 1, 475.

27. OR 19, pt. 1, 475, 1033, 1054.

28. Ibid., 495.

29. Ibid., 845, 1023.

30. Ibid., 1036–37.

31. Harsh, *Taken at the Flood*, 378–82.

Chapter 2

1. OR 19, pt. 1, 967; Heros Von Borcke, *Memoirs of the Confederate War for Independence* (Edinburgh: William Blackwood & Sons, 1866; reprint, Dayton, OH: Morningside, 1985), 1:231; and Robert L. Dabney, *Life and Campaigns of Lieutenant General Thomas J. Jackson* (New York: Blelock & Co., 1866; reprint, Harrisonburg, VA: Sprinkle Publications, 1977), 562–63.

2. OR 19, pt. 1, 244, 967, 968.

3. Ibid., 819, 968.

4. Ibid., 969.

5. Ibid.

6. Ibid., 969–70.

7. Ibid., 970.

8. Ibid.

9. Ibid., 228, 970.

10. Ibid., 970.

11. Ibid.

12. Jubal A. Early, *Lieutenant General Jubal A. Early, C.S.A., Narrative of the War between the States* (New York: Da Capo Press, 1989), 147; OR 19, pt. 1, 492, 971.

13. Jonathan C. Gibson to Ezra A. Carman, Sept. 6, 1899, and June 21, 1901, Antietam Studies [Microfilm], National Archives and Records Administration (Washington) reel 2, frames 578–84 and 327–29, respectively. Hereafter cited as NARA Antietam

Studies. The regimental history of the 125th Pennsylvania states that Early made four charges. See Regimental Committee, *History of the One Hundred and Twenty-Fifth Regiment Pennsylvania Volunteers, 1862–1863* (Philadelphia: J. B. Lippincott Co., 1906), 72.

14. OR 19, pt. 1, 311, 971, 1010; Andrew J. Grigsby to Ezra A. Carman, May 7, 1895, Statement of John A. Walters to Ezra A. Carman, May 23, 1895, Charles I. Raine to Stapleton Crutchfield, Oct. 31, 1862, John H. O'Connor to Ezra A. Carman, June 14, 1899, and John T. Block to Ezra A. Carman, May 30, 1899, all in NARA Antietam Studies, reel 2, frames 667–68, 665, 660, 945–47, and 948–52, respectively. Gorman's report provides the best description of the withdrawal of Grigsby's and Stafford's command.

15. OR 19, pt. 1, 971; Early, *Narrative*, 147.

16. OR 19, pt. 1, 30; 51, pt. 1, 839; Marion V. Armstrong, *Unfurl Those Colors!: McClellan, Sumner, and the Second Army Corps in the Antietam Campaign* (Tuscaloosa: University of Alabama Press, 2008), 158.

17. *Joint Committee on the Conduct of the War*, pt. 1, 581–82; War Department, Albert V. Colburn to Edwin V. Sumner, Sept. 17, 1862; Telegrams Received, 1862–1865, *Records of U.S. Army Continental Commands*, entry 45, pt. 2, Record Group (RG) 393, National Archives and Records Administration; and Armstrong, *Unfurl Those Colors*, 165–67, 171–72.

18. Armstrong, *Unfurl Those Colors*, 173–76.

19. John H. O'Connor to Ezra A. Carman, June 14, 1899, Statement of Walters to Carman, May 23, 1895, Raine to Crutchfield, Oct. 31, 1862, and Edward A. Moore to Ezra A. Carman, Oct. 12, 1899, all in NARA Antietam Studies, reel 2, frames 945-47, 665, 660, and 649, respectively.

20. OR 19, pt. 1, 971.

21. Ibid., 909.

22. Ibid.; W. H. Andrews to Ezra A. Carman, Feb. 6, 1899, NARA Antietam Studies, reel 2, frames 16–19.

23. OR 19, pt. 1, 858, 865, 871; D. Augustus Dickert, *History of Kershaw's Brigade, with Complete Roll of Companies, Biographical Sketches, Incidents, Anecdotes, etc.* (Newberry, SC: Elbert H. Aull Co., 1899), 155; and LaFayette McLaws to Antietam Battlefield Board, Dec. 13, 1894, NARA Antietam Studies, reel 1, frames 974-80. MacRae's report states that Cobb's brigade was in the lead. Dickert places Barksdale's brigade in the lead, while Kershaw's report says that he was in the rear of the Georgia Brigade (Cobb) and Mississippi Brigade (Barksdale) without specifying their order.

24. OR 19, pt. 1, 865, 909; W. H. Andrews, "Battle of Antietam Md.," and to Ezra A. Carman, Feb. 6, 1893, both in NARA Antietam Studies, reel 2, frames 7–14 and 16–19, respectively; and C. A. C. Waller to Ezra A. Carman, June 7, 1901, reel 1, frames 920–22.

25. OR 19, pt. 1, 871; McLaws to Antietam Battlefield Board, Dec. 13, 1894, NARA Antietam Studies, reel 1, frames 974-80.

26. OR 19, pt. 1, 883; James Dinkins, "The Griffith-Barksdale-Humphrey Mississippi Brigade, and its Campaigns," *Southern Historical Society Papers* 32 (1904): 261. Hereafter cited as *SHSP*.

27. OR 19, pt. 1, 883.

28. Ibid., 858; 865, 868; Andrews, "Battle of Antietam Md.," NARA Antietam Studies, reel 2, frames 7-14.

29. OR 19, pt. 1, 874, 879; Ezra A. Carman, *The Maryland Campaign of September 1862*, ed. Thomas G. Clemens (El Dorado Hills, CA: Savas Beatie, 2012), 2:199; and D. S. McCarthy to Ezra A. Carman, Feb. 5, 1895, NARA Antietam Studies, reel 1, frames 969–70.

30. OR 19, pt. 1, 874; John T. Parham to Ezra Carman, Oct. 5, 1899, and McCarthy to Carman, Feb. 5, 1895, NARA Antietam Studies, reel 1, frames 868–70 and 969–70, respectively; and Carman, *Maryland Campaign*, 2:199.

31. C. A. C. Waller to Ezra A. Carman, June 13, 1901, NARA Antietam Studies, reel 1, frames 923–25.

32. OR 19, pt. 1, 492; John T. Parham, "Thirty-second at Sharpsburg," *SHSP* 34 (1906): 252.

33. OR 19, pt. 1, 320.

34. Carman, *Maryland Campaign*, 2:199, 201.

35. OR 19, pt. 1, 909; Andrews, "Battle of Antietam Md.," NARA Antietam Studies, reel 2, frames 7-14; and Carman, *Maryland Campaign*, 2:201.

36. OR 19, pt. 1, 909; Andrews, "Battle of Antietam, Md.," NARA Antietam Studies, reel 2, frames 7-14; and Carman, *Maryland Campaign*, 2:201.

37. OR 19, pt. 1, 316; Carman, *Maryland Campaign*, 2:201. Carman's account of the fighting in the vicinity of the Dunker Church at this point includes the 72nd Pennsylvania being on the Hagerstown Pike in front of the church and also being driven off by the 2nd South Carolina and Anderson's brigade. In reviewing the reports and letters available to Carman, this author concludes that while the 72nd was on the Hagerstown Pike at the time, it was some two hundred yards north of the church near the point where the woods cut back to the west, what is today Philadelphia Brigade Park. Accordingly, the interpretation in this work will be that the 72nd was driven off by Barksdale's brigade as it continued its attack to the north.

38. OR 19, pt. 1, 320, 868.

39. Ibid., 311; Parham, "Thirty-second at Sharpsburg," *SHSP* (1906): 253.

40. OR 19, pt. 1, 311, 313, 874.

41. Carman, *Maryland Campaign*, 2:212, 217; OR 19, pt. 1, 314.

42. OR 19, pt. 1, 1010; William T. Poague to Harry Heth, May 18, 1893, and to Ezra A. Carman, April 18, 1895; Edward A. Moore to Ezra A. Carman, Oct. 12, 1899, all in NARA Antietam Studies, reel 2, frames 608–10, 611–12 and 649–50, respectively; Edward A. Moore, *The Story of a Cannoneer under Stonewall Jackson* (New York: Neale Publishing Co., 1907), 151; and Carman, *Maryland Campaign*, 2:217–19.

43. OR 19, pt. 1, 875, 878. Semmes reported thirty-six prisoners were captured at the Miller farm, including a lieutenant colonel and first lieutenant.

44. William J. Stores to Ezra A. Carman, Dec. 30, 1899, NARA Antietam Studies, reel 1, frames 875–78.

45. OR 19, pt. 1, 875, 878, 879, 882.

46. Early, *Narrative*, 148; Cyrus B. Coiner to Ezra A. Carman, Nov. 27 and Dec. 5, 1899, NARA Antietam Studies, reel 2, frames 331–33 and 334–36; and Carman, *Maryland Campaign*, 2:224–26.

47. OR 19, pt. 1, 307, 318, 883.

48. Ibid., 868–69; Armstrong, *Unfurl Those Colors*, 194.

49. OR 19, pt. 1, 883; Carman, *Maryland Campaign*, 2:206.

50. OR 19, pt. 1, 914.

51. Ibid., 915, 920.

52. Ibid.; Carman, *Maryland Campaign*, 2:229–30.

53. OR 19, pt. 1, 495, 920.

54. Ibid., 909–10; Andrews, "Battle of Antietam Md.," NARA Antietam Studies, reel 2, frames 7-14.

55. Carman, *Maryland Campaign*, 2:234–35; C. A. C. Waller to Ezra A. Carman, Dec. 14, 1899, and June 7, 1901, NARA Antietam Studies, reel 1, frames 917–19 and 920–22, respectively; and OR 19, pt. 1, 506, 507, 508.

56. Henry H. Carlton to Ezra A. Carman, June 14, 1893, and Lafayette McLaws to Harry Heth, Dec. 13, 1894, NARA Antietam Studies, reel 1, frames 993–94 and 974–80, respectively.

57. Harry H. Carlton to Henry Heth, May 20 and June 14, 1893, and to Ezra A. Carman, Dec. 2, 1899, NARA Antietam Studies, reel 1, frames 981–82, 993–94, and 971–73, respectively. Carlton's recollection was that "when I took position I had no support whatever, I remained in position until Genl. Kershaw['s] S.C. Brigade came up." Carlton was apparently unaware that the 2nd South Carolina and G. B. Anderson's brigade had already driven the 125th Pennsylvania and 34th New York out of the woods, and that the 2nd South Carolina was still in position near the church.

58. OR 19, pt. 1, 865; Curt Johnson and Richard C. Anderson, *Artillery Hell: The Employment of Artillery at Antietam* (College Station: Texas A&M University Press, 1995), 86; and Waller to Carman, Dec. 14, 1899, and June 7, 1901, NARA Antietam Studies, reel 1, frames 917–19 and 920–22, respectively.

59. OR 19, pt. 1, 869. Although most current maps do not show it, some maps of the Antietam Battlefield Board and some regimental histories describe the lower end of the pasture south of Miller's cornfield as being plowed. See Regimental Committee, *History of the One Hundred and Twenty fifth Regiment Pennsylvania Volunteers, 1862–1863* (Philadelphia: J. B. Lippincott Co., 1906), 68.

60. OR 19, pt. 1, 310.

61. Ibid., 865; H. W. Addison to Ezra A. Carman, Nov. 3, 1898, NARA Antietam Studies, reel 1, frames 912–13; Duncan McIntyre to Ezra A. Carman, Feb. 19, 1895, NARA Antietam Studies, reel 1, frames 906–10; and Waller to Carman, June 7, 1901, NARA Antietam Studies, reel 1, frames 920-2.

62. OR 19, pt. 1, 865; H. W. Addison to Ezra Carman, July 4 and Nov. 3, 1898, NARA Antietam Studies, reel 1, frames 915–16 and 912–13, respectively.

63. OR 19, pt. 1, 506.

64. Ibid., 308, 865; Theodore Reichardt, *Diary of Battery A, First Regiment, Rhode Island Light Artillery* (Providence, RI: N. Bangs Williams Publishing, 1865), 65.

65. OR 19, pt. 1, 915.

66. Y. J. Pope to Ezra A. Carman, March 20, 1895, NARA Antietam Studies, reel 1, frames 984–89; OR 19, pt. 1, 865, 918. The breastwork of rails is mentioned by J. S. Johnston, a courier on Law's staff, Hood's division, as having been built the night before. See J. S. Johnston, "A Reminiscence of Sharpsburg," *SHSP* 8 (1880): 528.

67. Robert Knox to Ezra Carman, n.d., and Dec. 10, 1899, NARA Antietam Studies, reel 2, frames 212–15 and 205–8, respectively.

68. OR 19, pt. 1, 918.

69. Ibid., 308, 858; Henry H. Carlton to Ezra A. Carman, Dec. 2, 1899, and to Harry Heth, May 20 and June 14, 1893, NARA Antietam Studies, reel 1, frames 971–73, 981–82 and 993–94, respectively.

70. McIntyre to Carman, Feb. 19, 1895, NARA Antietam Studies reel 1, frames 906-9; OR 19, pt. 1, 869.

71. McIntyre to Carman, Feb. 19, 1895, and Waller to Carman, Dec. 14, 1899, NARA Antietam Studies reel 1, frames 906-9 and 917-9, respectively; OR 19, pt. 1, 965.

72. OR 19, pt. 1, 869; Y. J. Pope to Ezra A. Carman, March 20, 1895, NARA Antietam Studies, reel 1, frames 984–89. Emphasis is in the original.

73. OR 19, pt. 1, 918; Robert Knox to Ezra A. Carman, Nov. 10, 1897, Dec. 10, 1899, and n.d., NARA Antietam Studies, reel 2, frames 225–28, 205–8 and 212–15, respectively.

74. Knox to Carman, Nov. 10, 1897, Dec. 10, 1899, and n.d., NARA Antietam Studies, reel 2, frames 225-8 and 212-5, respectively.

75. OR 19, pt. 1, 918.

76. Ibid.

77. Ibid., 505, 507, 511.

78. Harsh, *Taken at the Flood*, 402.

Chapter 3

1. Carman, *Maryland Campaign*, 1:387–88; OR 19, pt. 1, 1032, 1036.

2. OR 19, pt. 1, 844, 1036; Stephen D. Lee to Harry Heth, Nov. 28, 1893, and to Ezra Carman, Jan. 16, 1895, both in NARA Antietam Studies, RG 94, box 2.

3. OR 19, pt. 1, 844, 922–23; 927; Harsh, *Taken at the Flood*, 325.

4. OR 19, pt. 1, 1022, 1032; Carman, *Maryland Campaign*, 2:27–33; and Harsh, *Taken at the Flood*, 358.

5. Harsh, *Taken at the Flood*, 356–58; Carman, *Maryland Campaign*, 2:33–36.

6. Harsh, *Taken at the Flood*, 362–63; Carman, *Maryland Campaign*, 2:42; OR 19, pt. 1, 976, 1032; and Janet B. Hewett, Noah A. Trudeau, and Bryce A. Suderow, eds., *Supplement to the Official Records of the Union and Confederate Armies* (Wilmington, NC: Broadfoot Publishing Co., 1994), vol. 3, pt. 1, 586. Hereafter cited as SOR.

7. OR 19, pt. 1, 1033; William L. DeRosset, "Third North Carolina," *Wilmington (N.C.) Messenger*, Sept. 8, 1895, NARA Antietam Studies, reel 2, frames 735-39.

8. OR 19, pt. 1, 1033; SOR 3, pt. 1, 586; Thomas D. Boone to Ezra A. Carman, Sept. 27, 1897, Stephen D. Thruston to Carman, Nov. 27, 1896, William L. DeRosset to John M. Gould, June 11, 1895, and Nov. 29, 1890, all in NARA Antietam Studies, reel 2, frames 731-33, 797–98, 822–25, and 815–16, respectively.

9. OR 19, pt. 1, 1033; William L. DeRosset, "The Third North Carolina Infantry at Sharpsburg," *Wilmington (N.C.) Messenger*, April 27, 1890, NARA Antietam Studies, reel 2, frames 742-47; and Carman, *Maryland Campaign*, 2:118–20.

10. Carman, *Maryland Campaign*, 2:120; DeRosset, "Third North Carolina," NARA Antietam Studies, reel 2, frames 735-39; and William L. DeRosset to Harry Heth, Feb. 22, 1894, John C. Key to Ezra A. Carman, Sept. 29, 1897; and Stephen D. Thruston to Carman, July 27 and 28, 1886, and Sept. 3, 1898, all in NARA Antietam Studies, reel 2, frames 819–21, 719–23, 770–74, 775–83, and 805–7, respectively. The battery of six howitzers that Thruston claimed the 3rd North Carolina silenced was likely Battery C, Pennsylvania Light Artillery, commanded by Captain James Thompson. This battery, which consisted of four 3-inch Ordnance rifles, had been driven from an advanced position in the cornfield to the pasture during Hood's counterattack. In attempting to take position in the pasture, the battery lost so many men and horses that Thompson was forced to abandon the guns until he could find enough horses to return and withdraw them farther to the rear. See Thompson's official report, OR 51, pt. 1, 139.

11. DeRosset to Heth, Feb. 22, 1894, and to D. H. Hill, June 1, 1886, Stephen D. Thruston to DeRosset, July 28, 1886, all in NARA Antietam Studies, reel 2, frames 819–21, 735–38, and 775–83, respectively; DeRosset, "The Third North Carolina Infantry at Sharpsburg," NARA Antietam Studies, reel 2, frames 742-47; and Carman, *Maryland Campaign*, 2:122–23.

12. William L. DeRosset to Stephen D. Thruston, June 22, 1885, Thruston to DeRosset, July 27 and 28, 1886, Thruston to Carman, Sept. 3, 1898, NARA Antietam Studies, reel 2, frames 735–38, 770–74, 775–83, and 805–7, respectively; Carman, *Maryland Campaign*, 2:123. Carman in his narrative wrote that only a "strong line of brigade skirmishers" pursued the Pennsylvanians, but Map 6 of the Antietam Battlefield Board Maps supports DeRosset's and Thruston's recollections. That the 3rd North Carolina "passed beyond the battery" in its charge through and beyond the cornfield is supported by Thompson's report, which stated that when he came back to retrieve his guns he found the harness "cut and destroyed." See Thompson's official report, OR 51, pt. 1, 139.

13. Carman, *Maryland Campaign*, 2:128; OR 19, pt. 1, 1036, 1054.

14. OR 19, pt. 1, 1054; Carman, *Maryland Campaign*, 2:128–30, 138, 146; and H. A. Brown to Ezra A. Carman, Aug. 27, 1897, NARA Antietam Studies, reel 2, frames 711–15.

15. OR 19, pt. 1, 1054; Carman, *Maryland Campaign*, 2:131–32; and Thruston to DeRosset, July 28, 1886, NARA Antietam Studies, reel 2, frames 775–83.

16. OR 19, pt. 1, 1043, 1044; Duncan K. McRae to John M. Gould, Dec. 27, 1870, and Jan. 22, 1871, both in NARA Antietam Studies, reel 2, frames 858–61 and 864–69, respectively.

17. OR 19, pt. 1, 1043, 1044; McRae to Gould, Dec. 27, 1870, NARA Antietam Studies, reel 2, frames 858-61.

18. OR 19, pt. 1, 1044.

19. Ibid., 1043; McRae to Gould, Dec. 27, 1870, NARA Antietam Studies, reel 2, frames 858-61.

20. OR 19, pt. 1, 1054; Carman, *Maryland Campaign*, 2:143.

21. Key to Carman, Sept. 29, 1897, Brown to Carman, Aug. 27, 1897,both in NARA Antietam Studies, reel 2, frames 719-23 and 711-15, respectively; and Carman, *Maryland Campaign*, 2:138–39.

22. Key to Carman, Jan. 1, 1900, Thruston to Carman, Jan. 25, 1897, both in NARA Antietam Studies, reel 2, frames 725-6 and 808-10, respectively.

23. OR 19, pt. 1, 1022–23.

24. Ibid., 1023; McRae to Gould, Dec. 27, 1870, reel 2, frames 858-61. Lieutenant Colonel Robert D. Johnston of the 23rd North Carolina, mentioned by Hill, rose to the rank of brigadier general.

25. Carman, *Maryland Campaign*, 2:146, 183, 241; Stephen D. Lee, "New Lights on Sharpsburg," *Richmond Dispatch*, Dec. 20, 1896; and OR 19, pt. 1, 845, 1023. Carman noted that Lee's battalion lost more than 75 men.

26. OR 19, pt. 1, 1023.

27. Ibid., 1037.

28. Ibid., 1049, 1050; Carman, *Maryland Campaign*, 2:241–43; R. T. Bennett to John M. Gould, Dec. 26, 1892,John M. Gould Papers, Dartmouth College Library, Hanover, NH; and John C. Gorman, "From Our Army," *The North Carolina Standard* (Raleigh), Oct. 1, 1862.

29. Lee, "New Lights on Sharpsburg"; Carman, *Maryland Campaign*, 2:182–83; and Harsh, *Taken at the Flood*, 383–84.

30. Harsh, *Taken at the Flood*, 384–85; F. A. D., "In Memoriam," *Selma Morning Reporter*, Dec. 18, 1862; and John B. Gordon, "Antietam and Chancellorsville," *Scribner's Magazine* 33, no. 6 (June 1903): 688.

31. Gordon, "Antietam and Chancellorsville," 688; Bennett to Gould, Dec. 7, 1892, John M. Gould Papers; and John C. Gorman, "From Our Army," *The North Carolina Standard* (Raleigh), Oct. 1, 1862.

32. OR 19, pt. 1, 1037; Gordon, "Antietam and Chancellorsville," 688. The "little stream" that Gordon referred to was the stream running between the Mumma and Roulette farmsteads, and not the Antietam as indicated in the original article.

33. OR 19, pt. 1, 1037; John W. Tullis to Ezra A. Carman, April 3, 1896, March 19, 1900, and April 6, 1900, all in NARA Antietam Studies, reel 2, frames 705–6, 708, and 709, respectively. Tullis would have withdrawn his battery on the approach of Greene's brigades.

34. Gorman, "From Our Army"; Gordon, "Antietam and Chancellorsville," 688–89.

35. Gordon, "Antietam and Chancellorsville," 689–90.

36. OR 19, pt. 1, 1037; Gordon, "Antietam and Chancellorsville," 690.

37. OR 19, pt. 1, 1047; Gorman, "From Our Army"; and Edwin A. Osborne, "Fourth Regiment," *Histories of the Several Regiments and Battalions from North Carolina in the Great War 1861–'65*, ed. Walter Clark, vol. 1 (Raleigh: State of North Carolina, 1901), 247.

38. Marion V. Armstrong, "Sumner and French at Antietam," *Civil War History* 59, no. 1 (2013): 67–92.

39. War Department, George R. Graham, "The Fifth Maryland at Antietam," Antietam Studies, Antietam National Battlefield Board, *Records of the Adjutant General's Office, 1780's to 1917*, RG 94, National Archives and Records Administration.

40. Gordon, "Antietam and Chancellorsville," 690–91; Gorman, "From Our Army"; OR 19, pt. 1, 1037, 1047–48; and Osborne, "Fourth Regiment," 247.

41. Osborne, "Fourth Regiment," 247; OR 19, pt. 1, 1037; and Gorman, "From Our Army."

42. Gordon, "Antietam and Chancellorsville," 691.

43. James Simons to Ezra A. Carman, Dec. 22, 1899, NARA Antietam Studies, reel 2, frames 281–85; OR 19, pt. 1, 925.

44. OR 19, pt. 1, 943, 1023.

45. Ibid., 1037.

46. Ibid., 871–72; Carman, *Maryland Campaign*, 2:251.

47. Carman, *Maryland Campaign*, 2:250; OR 19, pt. 1, 943.

48. Samuel S. Sumner, "The Antietam Campaign," in *Civil War and Miscellaneous Papers*, vol. 14, *Papers of the Historical Society of Massachusetts* (Boston: Military Historical Society of Massachusetts, 1918; reprint, Wilmington, NC: Broadfoot Publishing Co., 1990), 11; and OR 19, pt. 1, 324, 327.

49. OR 19, pt. 1, 849–50; Carman, *Maryland Campaign*, 2:276. Carman says that Miller "immediately opened fire on Richardson's advance" but clearly Richardson's division was not yet on the field.

50. Carman, *Maryland Campaign*, 2:241; Harsh, *Taken at the Flood*, 367, 384.

51. OR 19, pt. 1, 1023.

52. Carman, *Maryland Campaign*, 2:256–57.

53. Ibid., 2:257; Eugene H. Levy to Ezra A. Carman, April 21, 1900, Carman Collection, Library of Congress.

54. Carman, *Maryland Campaign*, 2:257; Levy to Carman, April 21, 1900, Carman Collection, Library of Congress.

55. John H. Thompson to Ezra A. Carman, April 9, 1896, R. D. Parker Papers, Chicago Public Library; John H. Thompson, "Historical Address of the Former Commander of Grimes Battery," *SHSP* 34 (1906): 152; John S. Saunders to Harry Heth, June 8, 1893, NARA Antietam Studies, reel 1, frames 1019–20; Eugene H. Levy to Carman, March 14, 1900, Carman Collection, Library of Congress; and Carman, *Maryland Campaign*, 2:257.

56. Carman, *Maryland Campaign*, 2:259; Statement by Ezra Carman on Pryor's brigade, copy at Antietam National Battlefield.

57. Carman, *Maryland Campaign*, 2:259; Hilary A. Herbert to Ezra A. Carman, Jan. 15, 1902, Ezra A. Carman Papers, New York Public Library, box 3, folder 2.

58. Carman, *Maryland Campaign*, 2:260; John F. Jones to Ezra A. Carman, n.d., copy at Antietam National Battlefield.

59. Carman, *Maryland Campaign*, 2:260; SOR 3, pt. 1, 569; and Jones to Carman, n.d., copy at Antietam National Battlefield.

60. Carman, *Maryland Campaign*, 2:260–62; SOR 3, pt. 1, 569; and Jones to Carman, n.d., copy at Antietam National Battlefield.

61. Carman, *Maryland Campaign*, 2:260–62; SOR 3, pt. 1, 569; Jones to Carman, n.d., copy at Antietam National Battlefield; and OR 19, pt. 1, 327.

62. OR 19, pt. 1, 1048, 1051; James W. Shinn, "Diary," typewritten manuscript (photocopy), p. 139, Edwin Augustus Osborne Papers, Wilson Library, University of North Carolina, Chapel Hill.

63. OR 19, pt. 1, 1048.

64. Ibid., 1037; Carman, *Maryland Campaign*, 2:269–70.

65. Carman, *Maryland Campaign*, 2:270; map and notes by Carman on 8th Florida, Carman Papers, Library of Congress.

66. Carman, *Maryland Campaign*, 2:271; Shinn, "Diary," p. 139.

67. Carman, *Maryland Campaign*, 2:281; Alexander C. Chisholm to John M. Gould, Sept. 5 and 24, 1891, John M. Gould Papers.

68. Note from Sawler Darby to Ezra A. Carman, n.d., Carman Papers, Library of Congress; Chisholm to Gould, Sept. 5 and 24, 1891, and Nov. 22, 1892, John M. Gould Papers.

69. OR 19, pt. 1, 1037–38.

70. Ibid., 1038; "In Memoriam," *Selma Morning Reporter*, Dec. 18, 1862.

71. OR 19, pt. 1, 872.

72. Carman, *Maryland Campaign*, 2:270.

73. John Finn to Ella Tew Lindsay, Dec. 10, 1885, copy at Antietam National Battlefield.

74. OR 19, pt. 1, 1048.

75. Osborne, *The History of the Twenty-Ninth Regiment of Massachusetts Volunteer Infantry in the Late War of the Rebellion* (Boston: Albert J. Wright, Printer, 1877), 186–87; Armstrong, *Unfurl Those Colors*, 224–29.

76. OR 19, pt. 1, 289; Fuller, *Personal Recollections*, 59; and Osborne, *History of the Twenty-Ninth Regiment of Massachusetts Volunteer Infantry*, 187.

77. Chisholm to Gould, Sept. 5, 1891, John M. Gould Papers; Herbert to Carman, Jan. 15, 1902, Carman Papers, New York Public Library, box 3, folder 2.

78. SOR 3, pt. 1, 569; Carman, *Maryland Campaign*, 2:2808–1; OR 19, pt. 1, 1048; Shinn, "Diary," p. 139; and Osborne, "Fourth Regiment," 248–49.

79. OR 19, pt. 1, 289, 1048; William A. Smith, *The Anson Guards: Company C, Fourteenth Regiment, North Carolina Volunteers, 1861–1865* (Charlotte, NC: Stone Publishing Co., 1914), 157; and Gorman, "From Our Army."

80. Jenkins, "Recollections"; OR 19, pt. 1, 289.

81. Thompson to Carman, April 9, 1896, R. D. Parker Papers; Thompson, "Historical Address," 152–53; John S. Saunders to Harry Heth, June 8, 1893, NARA Antietam Studies, reel 1, frames 1019–20; Levy to Carman, March 14, 1900, Carman Collection, Library of Congress; and Carman, *Maryland Campaign*, 2:257.

82. Simons to Carman, Dec. 22, 1899, NARA Antietam Studies, reel 2, frames 281-5.

83. Alexander C. Chisholm to John M. Gould, Sept. 5, 1891, and Nov. 22, 1892, John M. Gould Papers; Gorman, "From Our Army"; Thomas Livermore, *Days and Events, 1860–1866* (Boston: Houghton, Mifflin Co., 1920), 137; and OR 19, pt. 1, 285.

84. OR 19, pt. 1, 849, 943, 1024.

85. Chisholm to Gould, Sept. 5 and 24, 1891, John M. Gould Papers; "Fourth North Carolina," *Daily Charlotte Observer*, March 8, 1895; and Carman, *Maryland Campaign*, 2:281.

86. OR 19, pt. 1, 288; Carman, *Maryland Campaign*, 2:289–90.

87. OR 91, pt. 1, 292; Carman, *Maryland Campaign*, 2:289–90.

88. Armstrong, *Unfurl Those Colors*, 235–36.

89. Alexander C. Chisholm to Gould, Sept. 5 1891 and Nov. 22, 1892, John M. Gould Papers.

90. Carman, *Maryland Campaign*, 2:284, 288.

91. OR 19, pt. 1, 482, 915; James A. Graham, "Twenty-Seventh Regiment," *History of the Several Regiments and Battalions From North Carolina in the Great War 1861-'65*, ed. Walter Clark, vol. 2 (Raleigh: State of North Carolina, 1901), 434; and James D. McGill to P. B. Shriver, Nov. 4, 1897, Ezra A. Carman Papers, U.S. Antietam Battlefield Board, 1863–1904, New York Public Library (P1A R14), item #13.

92. Graham, "Twenty-Seventh Regiment," 435, 436; Carman, *Maryland Campaign*, 2:319.

93. OR 19, pt. 1, 511, 513.

94. Carman, *Maryland Campaign*, 2:315–16; Dixon quote is found on 316, note 27.

95. Ibid., 2:315–18; OR 19, pt. 1, 505, 515; and McGill to Shriver, Nov. 4, 1897, Ezra A. Carman Papers, U.S. Antietam Battlefield Board, 1863–1904, New York Public Library (P1A R14), item #13.

96. McGill to Shriver, Nov. 4, 1897, Ezra A. Carman Papers, U.S. Antietam Battlefield Board, 1863–1904 New York Public Library (P1A R14), item #13; Walter Clark, "Sharpsburg; Reminiscences of Justice Walter Clark," and to Ezra A. Carman, April 24, 1899, NARA Antietam Studies, reel 2, frames 185–98 and 199–200, respectively; and Carman, *Maryland Campaign*, 2:317–18.

97. Graham, "Twenty-Seventh Regiment," 435, 436; R. D. Patterson to Ezra A. Carman, June 16, 1896, Antietam Studies, National Archives and Records Administration, RG 94, box 2.

98. OR 19, pt. 1, 326, 512.

99. Graham, "Twenty-Seventh Regiment," 435; Carman, *Maryland Campaign*, 2:319.

100. Graham, "Twenty-Seventh Regiment," 435; OR 19, pt. 1, 327, 329, 330, 336.

101. OR 19, pt. 1, 284, 343; Graham, "Twenty-Seventh Regiment," 435; and Carman, *Maryland Campaign*, 2:286–87, 320–22.

102. Graham, "Twenty-Seventh Regiment," 435–36; Patterson to Carman, June 16, 1896.

103. Graham, "Twenty-Seventh Regiment," 436; OR 19, pt. 1, 872.

104. OR 19, pt. 1, 872; Carman, *Maryland Campaign*, 2:287.

105. OR 19, pt. 1, 409, 414, 415.

106. James Longstreet, *From Manassas to Appomattox* (Philadelphia: J. B. Lippincott Co., 1896; reprint, Secaucus, NJ: Blue and Grey Press, 1984), 250; and OR 19, pt. 1, 943.

107. G. Moxley Sorrel, *Recollections of a Confederate Staff Officer*, ed. Bell I. Wiley (Wilmington, NC: Broadfoot Publishing Co., 1987), 105–6; OR 19, pt. 1, 850.

108. OR 19, pt. 1, 290, 291.

109. Ibid., 1024, 1038.

110. Chisholm to Gould, Sept. 5 and 24, 1891, John M. Gould Papers.

111. OR 19, pt. 1, 1024; Henry Gerrish, "7th New York Infantry Regiment Memoirs," typewritten manuscript (photocopy), p. 28, Civil War Times Illustrated Collection, Military History Institute, Carlisle Barracks, PA.

112. Gerrish, "7th New York Infantry Regiment Memoirs," 28; OR 19, pt. 1, 910, 924; and Carman, *Maryland Campaign*, 2:292, 374.

113. John Purifoy to Carman, April 28 and 29, 1896, July 15, 1899, and April 23, 1900, all in NARA Antietam Studies, reel 2, frames 687–90, 693–94, 695, and 696–98, respectively; Johnson and Anderson, *Artillery Hell*, 96–97.

114. OR 19, pt. 1, 947. In a letter to Carman on Jan. 13, 1900, Wallace again recalled moving his regiment in support of a battery being attacked by infantry, but remembered it as being Boyce's battery. This could not have been the case at this point in time, because, as discussed above and as Carman points out, at noon Boyce's battery was "farther to the left with D.H. Hill." Later in the afternoon, the 18th South Carolina was in direct support of Boyce's battery just south of the Piper farm. See William H. Wallace to Carman, Jan. 13, 1900, in NARA Antietam Studies, reel 2, frames 379–83; Carman, *Maryland Campaign*, 2:373; and Map 14, Antietam Battlefield Board Maps, 1908. Several accounts of the fighting around the Piper farm make reference to cornfields. But no contempory maps or the Antietam Battlefield Board Maps show any cornfields close to the farmstead.

115. OR 19, pt. 1, 910; Carman, *Maryland Campaign*, 2:293–94; and Gerrish, "7th New York Infantry Regiment Memoirs," 28. Also see "The Sharpsburg Memorial," *Confederate Veteran* 26, no. 2 (February 1918): 73–74.

116. Carman, *Maryland Campaign*, 2:297; Levy to Carman, March 14, 1900; and OR 19, pt. 1, 840.

117. John W. Tullis to Ezra A. Carman, April 6, 1900, NARA Antietam Studies, reel 2, frame 709.

118. OR 19, pt. 1, 1031; Thomas H. Carter to Ezra A. Carman, April 30, 1896, NARA Antietam Studies, reel 2, frame 700; Thomas H. Carter, *A Gunner in Lee's Army, The Civil War Letters of Thomas Henry Carter*, ed. Graham T. Dozier (Chapel Hill: University of North Carolina Press, 2014), 141; and William L. Westwood to Carman, Oct. 5, 1899, NARA Antietam Studies, reel 2, frame 704; Levy to Carman, March 14, 1900.

119. OR 19, pt. 1, 943.

120. Carman, *Maryland Campaign*, 2:294, 296–97; OR 19, pt. 1, 850, 1024; and Longstreet, *From Manassas to Appomattox*, 252.

Chapter 4

1. OR 19, pt. 1, 1048, 1050; Chisholm to Gould, Sept. 5, 1891, John C. Gould Papers.

2. OR 19, pt. 1, 840, 910.

3. Johnston, "A Reminiscence of Sharpsburg," *SHSP* (1880): 528; Harsh, *Taken at the Flood*, 408–9. Harsh scaled down Johnston's claim of 5,000 stragglers to "several thousand." See note 67, p. 573. Carman says that Hood's division on returning to the West Woods had only 800 men. See Carman, *Maryland Campaign*, 2:339.

4. OR 19, pt. 1, 923; Johnston, "A Reminiscence of Sharpsburg," *SHSP* (1880): 528–29.

5. OR 19, pt. 1, 978–9; John Hudgins to Ezra A. Carman, n.d., NARA Antietam Studies, reel 2, frames 216–19.

6. OR 19, pt. 1, 918–19.

7. Early, *Narrative*, 148, 150; OR 19, pt. 1, 971.

8. Carman, *Maryland Campaign*, 2:312–13; Walter Clark to Ezra A. Carman, Jan. 3, 1900, NARA Antietam Studies, reel 2, frames 223–24; and OR 19, pt. 1, 971. Clark actually gave two different accounts of Armistead's wounding. In the other it was by means of a bursting shell.

9. OR 19, pt. 1, 883.

10. Carman, *Maryland Campaign*, 2:36–37.

11. John C. Key to Ezra A. Carman, Jan. 1, 1900, Stephen D. Thruston to Carman, Jan. 25, 1897, both in NARA Antietam Studies, reel 2, frames 725–26 and 808–10, respectively; and OR 19, pt. 1, 972, 977.

12. OR 19, pt. 1, 865, 875.

13. Ibid., 858; Hunter McGuire, "General T.J. ('Stonewall') Jackson, Confederate States Army: His Career and Character," *SHSP* 25 (1897): 95; and Harsh, *Taken at the Flood*, 407.

14. Harsh, *Taken at the Flood*, 407–8; Carman, *Maryland Campaign*, 2:331.

15. OR 19, pt. 1, 151, 820, 859, 956. Stuart is mistaken when he says that the movement to turn the enemy's right was "on the next day."

16. Harsh, *Taken at the Flood*, 408. The interpretation of Lee's purpose and strategy given here was developed by Harsh in his book.

17. Carman, *Maryland Campaign*, 2:337.

18. Walker, "Sharpsburg," 679.

19. Longstreet, *From Manassas to Appomattox*, 256–57.

20. Walter Clark, "Sharpsburg; Reminiscences of Justice Walter Clark," NARA Antietam Studies, reel 2, frames 185–98; Carman, *Maryland Campaign*, 2:333–34. The story of Jackson's visit to Ransom's line, with some variation, is also in William H. S. Burgwyn, "Thirty-fifth Regiment," *Histories of the Several Regiments and Battalions from North Carolina in the Great War 1861–'65,* ed. Walter Clark, vol. 2 (Raleigh: State of North Carolina, 1901), 603–5.

21. Walker, "Sharpsburg," 680; OR 19, pt. 1, 916. Walker tells essentially this same story in both his official report and in his later article. There are some slight variations, especially as to the time of the events.

22. Carman, *Maryland Campaign*, 2:337–38; William T. Poague to Harry Heth, May 18, 1893, and Charles I. Raine to Stapleton Crutchfield, Oct. 31, 1862, both in NARA Antietam Studies, reel 2, frames 608–10 and 660 to 663, respectively; and OR 19, pt. 1, 1010. For an analysis of the complete force with Stuart, see Carman, *Maryland Campaign*, vol. 2, 337, note 61.

23. OR 19, pt. 1, 226.

24. Ibid., 820; Harsh, *Taken at the Flood*, 412.

25. William Thomas Poague, *Gunner with Stonewall; Reminiscences of William Thomas Poague, Lieutenant, Captain, Major, and Lieutenant Colonel of Artillery, Army of Northern Virginia, CSA, 1861–65* (Wilmington, NC: Broadfoot Publishing Co., 1987), 47–48; Harsh, *Taken at the Flood*, 410–12.

26. Walker, "Sharpsburg," 680; OR 19, pt. 1, 916.

27. OR 19, pt. 1, 859, 883, 971–72.

28. Ibid., 1033; Key to Carman, Jan. 1, 1900, and James A. Graham to Ezra A. Carman, Dec. 16, 1899, both in NARA Antietam Studies, reel 2, frames 725–26 and 231–32, respectively.

29. OR 19, pt. 1, 910, 942, 1024. Hill says that the time was 4:00 P.M., but G. T. Anderson and other sources put it at this earlier time. See Carman, *Maryland Campaign*, vol. 2, 376, note 32.

30. Ibid., 939.

31. Ibid., 1044.

32. Ibid., 845–46, 848–49, 926; Carman, *Maryland Campaign*, 2:376–77. Although Lee says he brought up twelve guns, his report accounts for only ten. Rhett's battery, sometimes referred to as Brooks's, was commanded at Antietam by Elliott.

33. OR 19, pt. 1, 351, 355, 357.

34. Ibid., 357.

35. Ibid., 939–40, 944, 948, 949, 1024, 1044–45; Carman, *Maryland Campaign*, 2:380–83. Evans in his official report continually confuses left with right as evidenced by the bracketed corrections made by the OR editors.

36. OR 19, pt. 1, 846, 896; S. D. Lee to Ezra A. Carman, March 19, 1900, National Archives and Records Administration, Antietam Studies, RG 94, Records of the Adjutant General's Office, box 2; and Carman, *Maryland Campaign*, 2:383.

37. William H. Powell, "More Light on 'The Reserve at Antietam,'" *The Century Magzine* 33, no. 5 (March 1887): 804; OR 19, pt. 1, 357.

38. OR 19, pt. 1, 940, 942, 944; Carman, *Maryland Campaign*, 2:389–91.

39. OR 19, pt. 1, 910.

40. Herbert to Carman, Jan. 15, 1902, Carman Papers, New York Public Library, box 3, folder 2; OR 19, pt. 1, 412–3; and Alexander C. Chisholm to John C. Gould, Nov. 22, 1892, John C. Gould Papers.

41. OR 19, pt. 1, 413, 910.

42. Ibid., 923.

43. Edward Porter Alexander, *Fighting for the Confederacy: The Personal Recollections*

of General Edward Porter Alexander, ed. Gary W. Gallagher (Chapel Hill: University of North Carolina Press, 1989), 92.

44. Harsh, *Taken at the Flood*, 424–26.

45. Ibid., 441–43; Harsh, *Sounding the Shallows*, 214–15; and Lee, "New Lights on Sharpsburg."

46. Harsh, *Taken at the Flood*, 444–45, and Harsh, *Sounding the Shallows*, 215–16.

47. OR19, pt. 1, 820; Harsh, *Taken at the Flood*, 457–58.

48. OR19, pt. 1, 833; Harsh, *Taken at the Flood*, 460.

49. OR19, pt. 1, 152; Harsh, *Taken at the Flood*, 466–67.

Selected Bibliography

Primary Sources

Alexander, Edward Porter. *Fighting for the Confederacy: The Personal Recollections of General Edward Porter Alexander*. Edited by Gary W. Gallagher. Chapel Hill: University of North Carolina Press, 1989.

Antietam National Battlefield. National Park Service, Sharpsburg, MD.

Borcke, Heros Von. *Memoirs of the Confederate War for Independence*. 2 vols. Edinburgh: William Blackwood & Sons, 1866. Reprint, Dayton, OH: Morningside, 1985.

Carman, Ezra A. *The Maryland Campaign of September 1862*. Edited by Thomas G. Clemens. 2 vols. El Dorado Hills, CA: Savas Beatie, 2012.

———. "U.S. Antietam Battlefield Board Papers, 1863–1904." Ezra A. Carman Papers, New York Public Library, New York, NY.

Carter, Thomas H. *A Gunner in Lee's Army: The Civil War Letters of Thomas Henry Carter*. Edited by Graham T. Dozier. Chapel Hill: University of North Carolina Press, 2014.

Clark, Walter, ed. *Histories of the Several Regiments and Battalions from North Carolina in the Great War 1861-'65*. 5 vols. Raleigh: State of North Carolina, 1901.

DeRosset, William L. "Third North Carolina." *Wilmington (N.C.) Messenger*, September 8, 1895.

———. "The Third North Carolina Infantry at Sharpsburg." *Wilmington (N.C.) Messenger*, April 27, 1890.

Early, Jubal A. *Narrative of the War between the States*. New York: Da Capo Press, 1989.

F. A. D. "In Memoriam," *Selma Morning Reporter*. December 18, 1862.

"Fourth North Carolina," *Daily Charlotte Observer*, March 8, 1895.

Fuller, Charles A. *Personal Recollections of the War of 1861*. Sherburne, NY: News Job Printing House, 1906.

Gerrish, Henry. "7th New York Infantry Regiment Memoirs." Typewritten manuscript (photocopy). Civil War Times Illustrated Collection, Military History Institute, Carlisle Barracks, PA.

Gordon, John B. "Antietam and Chancellorsville." *Scribner's Magazine* 33, no. 6, June 1903.

Gorman, John C. "From Our Army." *The North Carolina Standard* (Raleigh), October 1, 1862.

Gould, John M. Papers. Antietam Collection. Dartmouth College Library, Hanover, NH.

Hewett, Janet B., Noah A. Trudeau, and Bryce A. Suderow, eds. *Supplement to the Official Records of the Union and Condederate Armies.* 100 vols. Wilmington, NC: Broadfoot Publishing Co., 1994.

Hood, John Bell. *Advance and Retreat: Personal Experiences in the United States and Confederate States Armies.* Edited by Richard N. Current. Bloomington: Indiana University Press, 1959.

Jenkins, Newsom E. "Recollections of Sergeant-Major Newsom Edward Jenkins, Co. A, 14th North Carolina to His Daughters." September 18, 1895. Raleigh: North Carolina Archives. Copy at Antietam National Battlefield.

Johnson, Robert U., and Clarence C. Buel, eds. *Battles and Leaders of the Civil War.* 4 vols. New York: Century, 1887–88. Reprint, New York: Castle Books, 1956.

Lee, Stephen D. "New Lights on Sharpsburg," *Richmond Dispatch,* December 20, 1896.

Livermore, Thomas. *Days and Events, 1860–1866.* Boston: Houghton, Mifflin Co., 1920.

Longstreet, James. *From Manassas to Appomattox.* Philadelphia: J. B. Lippincott Co., 1896. Reprint, Secaucus, NJ: The Blue and Grey Press, 1984.

Moore, Edward A. *The Story of a Cannoneer under Stonewall Jackson.* New York: Neale Publishing Co., 1907.

Palfrey, Francis Winthrop. *The Antietam and Fredericksburg.* Vol. 5, *Campaigns of the Civil War.* New York: Charles Scribner's Sons, 1882.

Parker, R. D. Papers. Special Collections, Chicago Public Library.

Osborne, William H. *The History of the Twenty-Ninth Regiment of Massachusetts Volunteer Infantry in the Late War of the Rebellion.* Boston: Albert J. Wright, Printer, 1877.

Poague, William Thomas. *Gunner with Stonewall; Reminiscences of William Thomas Poague, Lieutenant, Captain, Major, and Lieutenant Colonel of Artillery, Army of Northern Virginia, CSA, 1861–65.* Wilmington, NC: Broadfoot Publishing Co., 1987.

Powell, William H. "More Light on 'The Reserve at Antietam,'" *The Century* 33, no. 5 (March 1887): 804.

Regimental Committee. *History of the One Hundred and Twenty-Fifth Regiment Pennsylvania Volunteers, 1862–1863.* Philadelphia: J. B. Lippincott Co., 1906.

Reichardt, Theodore. *Diary of Battery A, First Regiment, Rhode Island Light Artillery.* Providence, RI: N. Bangs Williams Publishing, 1865.

Shinn, James W. "Diary," Typewritten manuscript (photocopy). Edwin Augustus Osborne Papers, Wilson Library, University of North Carolina, Chapel Hill.

Smith, William A. *The Anson Guards; Company C, Fourteenth Regiment, North Carolina Volunteers, 1861–1865.* Charlotte, NC: Stone Publishing Co., 1914.

Sorrel, G. Moxley. *Recollections of a Confederate Staff Officer.* Edited by Bell I. Wiley. Wilmington, NC: Broadfoot Publishing Co., 1987.

Sumner, Samuel S. "The Antietam Campaign." *Papers of the Military Historical Society of Massachusetts.* Vol. 14, *Civil War and Miscellaneous Papers.* Boston: Military Historical Society of Massachusetts, 1918. Reprint, Wilmington, NC: Broadfoot Publishing Co., 1990.

U.S. Congress. Senate. *Report of the Joint Committee on the Conduct of the War.* 3 pts. 37th Cong., 3rd sess., 1863. Rep. Com. 108.

U.S. National Archives and Records Administration (NARA). Antietam Studies [Microfilm], Record Group 94, Records of the Adjutant General's Office.

U.S. War Department. *Records of the Adjutant General's Office, 1780's-1917.* Record Group 94. Washington: National Archives and Records Administration.

———. *Records of U.S. Army Continental Commands.* Record Group 393. Washington: National Archives and Records Administration.

———. *The War of the Rebellion: A Compilation of the Official Records of the Union and Confederate Armies.* 71 vols. Washington: Government Printing Office, 1881–1901.

Secondary Sources

Armstrong, Marion V. *Unfurl Those Colors!: McClellan, Sumner, and the Second Army Corps in the Antietam Campaign.* Tuscaloosa: University of Alabama Press, 2008.

———. "Sumner and French at Antietam," *Civil War History* 59, no. 1 (2013): 67–92.

Dabney, Robert L. *Life and Campaigns of Lieutenant General Thomas J. Jackson.* New York: Blelock & Co., 1866. Reprint, Harrisonburg, VA: Sprinkle Publications, 1977.

Dickert, D. Augustus. *History of Kershaw's Brigade, with Complete Roll of Companies, Biographical Sketches, Incidents, Anecdotes, etc.* Newberry, SC: Elbert H. Aull Co., 1899.

Fox, William. *Regimental Losses in the American Civil War, 1861–1865.* Albany, NY: Brandow Printing Co., 1898. Reprint, Dayton, OH: Morningside House, 1985.

Harsh, Joseph L. *Sounding the Shallows: A Confederate Companion for the Maryland Campaign of 1862.* Kent, OH: Kent State University Press, 2000.

———. *Taken at the Flood: Robert E. Lee and Confederate Strategy in the Maryland Campaign of 1862.* Kent, OH: Kent State University Press, 1999.

Johnson, Curt, and Richard C. Anderson. *Artillery Hell: The Employment of Artillery at Antietam.* College Station: Texas A&M University Press, 1995.

Murfin, James V. *The Gleam of Bayonets: The Battle of Antietam and the Maryland Campaign of 1862.* New York: Bonanza Books, 1965.

Sears, Stephen W. *Landscape Turned Red: The Battle of Antietam.* New York: Ticknor & Fields, 1983.

Southern Historical Society Papers. Richmond: The Southern Historical Society, 1876–1959. Reprint, Dayton: Morningside, 1992.

Warner, Ezra J. *Generals in Gray, Lives of the Confederate Commanders.* Baton Rouge: Louisiana State University Press, 1959.

Index

Hall, Captain William C., 147

Hall, Colonel Edward D., 59, 61, 64–65, 145

Halsay, Captain D. P., 83

Hampton, Brigadier General Wade, 147, 150

Haney, Sargeant, 61

Hardaway, Captain Robert A., Alabama Battery, 90, 140

Harpers Ferry, capture of Federal garrison by Army of Northern Virginia, 1, 2, 4

Harsh, Joseph, *Taken at the Flood, 3,* 179n16

Hately, Colonel John C., 108, 109

Hauser's farmstead, 54, 64, 146

Hauser's Ridge, Confederate artillery battalions on, 27, 31, 37, 46, 47, 67

Hays, Brigadier General Harry T., 10, 72, 144–45

Herbert, Major Hilary A., 103, 115, 161

Hero, Lieutenant Andrew, 119

Higgins, Colonel Jacob, 40

Hill, Colonel Robert C., 151

Hill, D. H., 158, 161

Hill, Major General Ambrose Powell, 149; countering of advance of Ninth Army Corps, 162, 163; at Harper's Ferry, 11–12

Hill, Major General Daniel Harvey, 6, 10, 11, 32, 69, 71; arrival at Middle Bridge on 15th, 68; attempt to position batteries to support infantry in Sunken Road, 96; attempt to rally regiments that had abandoned Sunken Road, 132–38; attempt to rally remnants of Hill's and Anderson's divisions at Piper farm, 139, 142, *143;* Cornfield quadrangle engagement, 16, 17, 29–30, 84–85; fire on brigades from Federal batteries on 15th and 16th, 70; positioning of batteries along Reel Ridge, 140–43; positioning of Rodes's and Anderson's brigades, 87, 93, 156;

pushing of skirmish line north through Piper's orchard and cornfields, 141; responsibility for center of Confederate line east of Hagerstown Pike, 86; Sunken Road engagement, 18, 19, 30, 67, 113, 131; withdrawal from West Woods, 33

Hilton, Major M., 158–59

Hobson, Major E. Lafayette, 111, 112, 133

Hodges, Colonel James G., 146–47, 164

Holcombe Legion, 97

Hood, Brigadier General John B.: Cornfield quadrangle engagement, 14–15, 72; position near Dunker Church, 9, 13; request for relief, 71; Texas Brigade, 70; West Woods engagement, 6, 33, 69–70, 74, 144, 145, 179n3

Hooker, Major General Joseph: Cornfield quadrangle engagement, 72; crossing of Antietam Creek at Upper Bridge, 8, 9, 70, 163; estimation of Lee's strength, 6; ten brigades, 13

Hopkins, Major Charles A., 126

Houston, Major David C., 8

Howard, Brigadier General Oliver O., 31, 49

Howe, Lieutenant Church, 43

Hudgins, Captain John, 145

Huger, Captain Frank, 102

Hyde, Major Thomas W., 161–62

Irwin, Colonel William H., 129, 131

Irwin (Georgia) Artillery (Lane), 70, 148

Iverson, Colonel Alfred, 135, 141, 156–58

Jackson, Major General Thomas J. (Stonewall): arrival of divisions from Harpers Ferry, 7, 70; artillery batteries on Hauser's Ridge, 27, 31, 37, 45, 46, 67; call for reinforcements, 19, 33; command of left, 8, 11, 12, 71; Corn-